Author in Chief

Author in Chief
The Presidents as Writers from Washington to Trump

Michael B. Costanzo

McFarland & Company, Inc., Publishers
Jefferson, North Carolina

LIBRARY OF CONGRESS AND BRITISH LIBRARY
CATALOGUING DATA ARE AVAILABLE

ISBN (print) 978-1-4766-7570-1
ISBN (ebook) 978-1-4766-3539-2

© 2019 Michael B. Costanzo. All rights reserved

No part of this book may be reproduced or transmitted in any form or by any means, electronic or mechanical, including photocopying or recording, or by any information storage and retrieval system, without permission in writing from the publisher.

Front cover image: President Lyndon B. Johnson, with a copy of his newly-published book, *The Vantage Point*, October 14, 1971, photograph by Frank Wolfe (Lyndon B. Johnson Presidential Library)

Printed in the United States of America

McFarland & Company, Inc., Publishers
Box 611, Jefferson, North Carolina 28640
www.mcfarlandpub.com

For all the presidents,
great or mediocre,
who expressed the need to write.

"Writing is almost the only dignified occupation a President can follow after leaving office."
—John S.D. Eisenhower

Table of Contents

Acknowledgments ix
Preface 1
Diaries and Letters 3

George Washington	5	Grover Cleveland	66
John Adams	11	William McKinley	69
Thomas Jefferson	14	Theodore Roosevelt	69
James Madison	20	William Howard Taft	82
James Monroe	22	Woodrow Wilson	84
John Quincy Adams	25	Warren G. Harding	90
Three Generals: Andrew Jackson, William Henry Harrison and Zachary Taylor	32	Calvin Coolidge	91
		Herbert Hoover	92
		Franklin D. Roosevelt	100
Martin Van Buren	34	Harry S. Truman	101
Two Accidentals: John Tyler and Millard Fillmore	37	Dwight D. Eisenhower	107
		John F. Kennedy	110
James K. Polk	38	Lyndon B. Johnson	118
Franklin Pierce	41	Richard M. Nixon	124
James Buchanan	42	Gerald R. Ford	131
Abraham Lincoln	44	Jimmy Carter	137
Andrew Johnson	48	Ronald Reagan	150
Ulysses S. Grant	50	George H.W. Bush	154
Rutherford B. Hayes	63	Bill Clinton	158
James A. Garfield and Chester A. Arthur	65	George W. Bush	164
		Barack Obama	168
Benjamin Harrison	65	Donald J. Trump	174

*A Brief History of Publishing the Presidents: Booksellers,
    Copyrights, Royalties, Ghostwriters and Literary Agents*   183
First Editions, Limited Editions and Other Collectibles   190
Chronological List of Publications Authored by Presidents   197
Notes   207
Bibliography   219
Index   229

Acknowledgments

Thanks are given to the Nashville Public Library, the Library of Davidson County, particularly its circulating collection, periodicals, as well as the Grantham Collection. Thanks are also given to the John Finnery Library of Columbia State Community College of Columbia, Tennessee.

Photographs and images, as well as additional information, were obtained courtesy the Library of Congress, the White House, and the Presidential Libraries and Museums of Harry S. Truman, John F. Kennedy, and Lyndon B. Johnson.

Thanks also to the presidents themselves, who count among the published authors whose works were consulted for this book. Also to the numerous biographers and historians, noted in the bibliography, who helped fuel the fire.

Thanks are also given to Apple Incorporated and Microsoft Word Office 365. While working on this manuscript I envisioned Thomas Jefferson toiling over the manuscript for *Notes on the State of Virginia* with a quill pen, on a rough sheet of paper by candlelight. Technology has come a long way since my wife surprised me with a Smith Corona Spell Right Electric Typewriter for my birthday back in the 1980s. And while the act of writing hasn't gotten any easier, putting it down on paper certainly has.

In 1899, my mother's ancestors began publishing a small independent newspaper out of New Egypt, New Jersey (*The New Egypt Press*). This sparked an interest in the study of graphic arts as a student in junior and high school, where I got printer ink under my nails and became enamored with the printed word. Because of this I have always believed the association of words and ink were almost a birthright. Mom's family also always wrote things down, saved the old photographs, and kept up a family tree that reached back to pre-colonial days. As for my father's side, little survives except his verbal flair of family history and colorful storytelling. I have always believed that both of their contributions are responsible for my becoming a writer with a particular love of history, and in a way responsible for this book.

Preface

The purpose of this book is to present a history of published works authored by those who have at one time served as President of the United States of America. These works include books published prior to, during, or after serving as president. Autobiographies, diaries, memoirs, political manifestos, speeches, and even works that are not even remotely associated with the nature of the office itself, make an appearance here.

When he wrote his highly successful *Memoirs*, which were published shortly before his death, former president Ulysses S. Grant established what has today become known as the presidential memoir. Several presidents before Grant authored books but shied away from a lengthy memoir. Surprisingly, Grant's memoir did not cover his presidency. Early presidents who had written unfinished autobiographies include Jefferson, Madison, and Monroe. Martin Van Buren completed an autobiography, but it was only published long after his death.

Since Benjamin Harrison in 1901, every president since has authored some sort of memoir, and except for those who have died in office, the appearance of such memoirs have become routine and even expected. Major publishing houses are often eager to bid on the right to publish such works, and frequently offer advances numbering in the millions. These books typically give a former president the opportunity to tell his side of the history which occurred under his watch, as well as to explain the popular, as well as unpopular, decisions he may have made.

In these times of high-profile literary agents, carefully placed reviews, media publicity, and multi-city book tours, such a release will often make national news. Because of this, one can confidently expect to find a presidential memoir on the best seller list shortly after its publication.

Many presidents also authored books before serving, sometimes during their candidacy. Often, these publications served as a political springboard, outlining their proposed agenda and providing a controlled forum to express their opinions and beliefs. Since the twentieth century the appearance of such books has become routine.

Still other books written by future or former office holders do not cater to either format. These include books covering American history in general, such as Washington's *Journal of Major George Washington*, Jefferson's *Notes on the State of Virginia*, Theodore Roosevelt's books on the American West as well as naval history, and Kennedy's *Profiles in Courage*. Roosevelt also authored (and co-authored) several books on hunting and outdoor life, just as presidents Cleveland, Hoover, and Carter authored books on fishing. Carter even successfully placed a fiction novel, and remains the only office holder to do so.

A few presidents never authored anything, which would constitute something in *book* format, during their lifetime. This includes Andrew Jackson, who desired someone else to write his remembrances. Most of the "lesser" presidents of the 1841 to 1856 era, with the exception of Polk, also did not leave behind any published works. Any known histories involving why these presidents averted the field of authorship, are included here as well.

The works presented here attempt to tell the stories behind the books, and include reminiscences from the presidents themselves, notable historians, as well as from publishers and agents.

Diaries and Letters

The appearance of personal diaries throughout this book varies from president to president. Early in the history of our Republic, the keeping of a diary was common practice. The contents of these diaries, however, sometimes contained information considered to be insignificant by later historians. From 1750 to 1825, many diaries were considered personal, and not to be shared with others. Some resemble financial account ledgers, or record daily travels more often than hinting at any musings the writer might have difficulty suppressing in public. Others simply read as an exercise to keep one's grammar in practice. In his introduction to the diary of John Adams, historian L.H. Butterfield noted "the text of the Diary is almost wholly free of indications that the writer supposed anyone, including himself, would read it later."[1] Butterfield continues to imply that Adams seems to have cared little for his numerous diaries, as well as their contents after he had confided in them, and notes that "both the physical nature of the manuscripts and the text itself provide abundant proof that the Diary was intended as a wholly private record.... The booklets are too fragile ever to have been supposed a permanent record, and only by continuous good luck have they survived as all, worn and tattered as they are."[2]

Butterfield also voices the shared frustration of fellow scholars and historians regarding the diaries of George Washington:

> George Washington as an active young man fortunately kept diaries, but being the least introspective of men he recorded only what he thought might prove to be useful information—the weather, state of crops, distances, prices, "Where, how, or with whom my time is Spent." One will look in vain for opinions on issues or persons. Washington was present as a member of the Virginia Convention of March 1775 the day Patrick Henry made his speech ending "Give me liberty or give me death," but his diary entry for that day reads: "Dined at Mr. Patrick Coote's and lodgd where I had done the Night before."[3]

Because of their failure to yield any significant historical information, as well as personal reasons, many diaries written by the presidents were often published long after the passing of their authors, and often constitute the "last scraps" of their unpublished writings. Once published, they were often subjected to heavy editing, with punctuation being corrected to modern day standards in an attempt to make it more accessible to the contemporary reader.

Notable posthumously published diaries that are included here involve the diaries of John Quincy Adams, James K. Polk, and Rutherford B. Hayes. The reasons these diaries are significant are because these were the first presidents to keep diaries while in the White House. In the mid–20th century, keeping a White House diary became a common practice, but few former presidents, with the exception of Jimmy Carter, ever published them in their own lifetime.

Carter published his nearly thirty years after leaving office. His diary is frank at times, and includes a preface emphasizing that at the time it was written the diary was never meant to become public.

Volumes containing select letters written by the presidents are included as well. These include books attributed to Theodore Roosevelt and Ronald Reagan. While George H.W. Bush declined to author an actual memoir, he published a volume of personal correspondence, as well as an informal diary while serving as ambassador to China.

George Washington

> Light reading (by this, I mean books of little importance) may amuse for the moment, but leaves nothing solid behind.[1]
> —George Washington

It has long bothered historians that our first president was, at his most inner core, an extremely private man. Because of this lifelong trait, which increased with his fame, George Washington produced very little as an author.

Perhaps the basis of this was the fact that as a youth, Washington had not been schooled as well as he could have been. Author Ron Chernow mused how "one can't help but surmise that Washington's life would have been vastly different had he attended college. He lacked the liberal education that then distinguished gentlemen, setting him apart from such illustrious peers as Jefferson, Hamilton, Adams, and Madison."[2] Contemporary John Adams, who claimed Washington was "too illiterate, unlearned, unread for his station and reputation," noted this observation.[3] Washington himself would later regret the absence of an academic education, and emphasized others not to forgo one. As a result, Washington was hardly a "bookish" young man. Although he attempted to expand his reading in areas such as fiction and philosophy, Washington would become "especially drawn to military history," thus laying the groundwork for later life.[4]

Washington's first real flirtation as a writer came in the autumn of 1747, when he was invited to accompany a party of experienced surveyors for a month-long journey into western Virginia. For the fifteen-year-old George, now fatherless, the trip promised to be a memorable experience. In anticipation of this, Washington purchased a small notebook, which he titled "A Journal of my Journey over the Mountains." He filled it with descriptions of the land's natural beauty, the joy of sleeping outdoors, and his first encounter with Indians.

At the age of twenty-one, George Washington had absorbed much of the military history he was fond of reading, and found himself a major in the Virginia Regiment. It was during this time that he became a published author.

Between October 31, 1753, and January 16, 1754, Major Washington headed an expedition from Virginia into Ohio. Having been commissioned and appointed by Virginia governor Robert Dinwiddie, the purpose of Washington's journey was to locate the superior French military officer and deliver an ultimatum, in the form of a letter, demanding the French forces vacate existing fortifications in the Ohio Valley. Having finally located Captain Jacques Legardeur de St. Pierre, Washington received a courteous refusal, and swiftly returned to Williamsburg where he delivered his report to Governor Dinwiddie.[5]

Dinwiddie ordered the report to be printed at once. This was done in 1754, at Williamsburg. Thomas Jefferys reprinted a copy sent to London months later. Washington's report "served as propaganda to arouse both the colonist and the English to the danger of the French invasion of the Ohio Valley."[6]

The report's full title was known as *The Journal of Major George Washington, sent by the Hon. Robert Dinwiddie, Esq.; His Majesty's Lieutenant-Governor, and Commander in Chief of Virginia, to the Commandant of the French Forces On Ohio. To which are added, the Governor's Letter: and a Translation of the French Officer's Answer, with A New Map of the Country as far as the Mississippi*.

The Journal consisted of thirty-two pages, twenty-seven of which were written by Washington, and the remainder consisting of Governor Dinwiddie's letter and the French officer's refusal. In his preface, listed in the Journal as "Advertisement," Washington apologizes for its rough nature and his surprise at which the Journal was taken to press.

> As it was thought advisable by his Honour the Governor to have the following Account of my proceedings to and from the French on Ohio, committed to print; I think I can do no less than apologize, in some Measure for the numberless imperfections of it.
>
> There intervened but one Day between my Arrival in Williamsburg, and the Time for the Council's Meeting, from the rough Minutes I had taken in my Travels, this Journal; the writing of which only was sufficient to employ me closely the whole Time, consequently admitted of no Leisure to consult of a new and proper Form to offer it in, or to correct or amend the Diction of the old: Neither was I apprised, not did in

The Journal of Major George Washington as published in 1754. The journal was never intended for publication and brought Washington little fame and even less fortune (author's collection).

the least conceive, when I wrote this for his Honour's Perusal, that it ever would be published, or even have more than a cursory Reading; till I was informed, at the Meeting of the general Assembly, that it was already in the Press.[7]

Historian Ron Chernow noted that Washington's lengthy and apologetic preface to his first published piece of writing was "an early example of Washington being nagged by his sense of an inadequate education."[8] Aside from its swift Williamsburg publication, Washington's *Journal* appeared in several newspapers of the American colonies as well. As for the London printing by Thomas Jefferys, its origins also arose courtesy of Governor Dinwiddie. The Governor had included a copy of the *Journal* sent to the British Board of Trade in London to emphasis the mounting French situation. Once in London, Washington's *Journal* was quickly reprinted in pamphlet form, thus "giving the obscure young man instant renown in the British Empire."[9]

Though Washington's name and *Journal* were now known on both sides of the Atlantic, the young major profited little from it. It was said that Washington "had expected money as well as fame for his trouble," and was not happy when the Virginia Assembly thanked him with a "measly fifty-pound reward."[10] And while his *Journal* became a springboard for what became known as the French and Indian War, Washington's first encounter in politics, as well as his introduction into the world of publishing, had become a bitter experience.

The Journal of Major George Washington would soon appear in a French translation as well. While in Philadelphia in early 1757, Washington came upon a recent edition of the *Pennsylvania Gazette*. In it, Washington found "an unusual advertisement of a forthcoming book."[11] After boarding a French vessel captured at sea, British officers found a book that had been published in Paris by royal order. The volume was basically a hastily printed collection of documents designed to show the current war was the fault of Britain, and not France. Most important, its contents listed Washington's *Journal*. With the confiscated edition at hand, publishers in New York and Philadelphia raced to publish a translation of the French volume in a matter of weeks. This concerned Washington, who felt a proper translation of his notes could not be performed in such short time. This proved correct, as Washington found that "what had been put into English was awkward and poorly expressed."[12] In the end, the volume "proved to be a French elaboration," of the *Journal*, whereas "many things that he had jotted down the French editor of his captured notes had eliminated, and some things of which he had not even thought of at the time were attributed to him."[13] Washington, who had received a copy of the translation before it went to press, attempted to correct as much possible, but in the end the Philadelphia printer chose the available text. If Washington was left bitter by this second experience with publishing, he did not show it, for he was said to have subscribed to the edition.[14]

In later years, especially after the war for independence, Washington became a passionate reader. He purchased and consumed such literary works as *The History of the Decline and Fall of the Roman Empire*. He also displayed an appetite for biographies of such worldly figures as Louis XV and Peter the Great. Whether Washington ever toyed with the idea of producing an autobiography, or even an authorized biography, such thoughts were kept to himself. In June of 1785, however, Washington played host to Catharine Macaulay Graham, a well-respected British historian. For ten days Washington entertained Graham at Mount Vernon, and after discovering the two shared the same political ideologies, allowed her access to his military archives. A month earlier, author Noah Webster had been a guest, and offered to cut a deal with Washington. In exchange for his services as a tutor, Webster asked for unrestricted access to Washington's papers, but Washington turned him down.

Although Washington desired to be remembered, he knew the right writer would make all the difference. Yet, he clung to his privacy by refusing others to undertake the burden of choosing his words for him. Although he had not been able to keep a diary during his service as commander in chief, Washington kept careful military records, including correspondence and notes, of his wartime years. Perhaps Washington one day believed he would be permitted the time to write a proper accounting of his military experience, but any such thoughts would have been put to rest with his election, and subsequent re-election, as president.

After retiring from public office, Washington found he hardly had the occasion to sit down to a quiet dinner with Martha, much less entertain thoughts of writing an autobiography or personal rendering of American history. Farming matters took up a large portion of his waking hours, and he once complained that "I have not looked in a book since I came home, nor shall I be able to do it until I have discharged my workmen; probably not before the nights grow longer, when possibly I may be looking in [the] doomsday book."[15]

Although rich in land and slaves, Washington was cash poor. The notion of authoring a memoir, or even possibly several volumes, either never occurred to him or any of the leading publishers of the day. To have produced one would have provided Washington with additional income, but would have been looked upon by him as an unwelcome burden. Because of this, history can only speculate whether it was cheated or spared the very words and thoughts of the great man. Washington's discomfort with attaining a college or academic education most likely played a hand in the absence of any writing endeavors.

It is also possible that his early experience with his *Journal* left him stung and weary of the publishing trade, for he never saw royalties from the widely published account. In the end, he remained the private individual he wished for, with his final years devoted to his wife, Martha, and the other love of his life: Mount Vernon.

Throughout most of his life, George Washington also kept a diary. The diary, however, was often interrupted when situations arose, and pales when compared to the later diaries of John Quincy Adams. Washington began keeping his diary on March 11, 1748, and made his last entry on what would be the eve of his death, December 13, 1799.

Washington's diaries, which would eventually become known as *The Diaries of George Washington* (1748–1799), first appeared in widespread publication in 1861, by the Press of the (Virginia) Historical Society. Because the diaries were written in various ledgers, many of the early publishers did not have access to the complete set of fifty-one volumes, and were only able to publish what they could obtain. As a result, the *Diaries* grew over time. In 1925, for example, Houghton Mifflin published the *Diaries* in four volumes, at the discretion of the Mount Vernon Ladies Association. In the edition's Prefatory Note, the Association's historic and challenging undertaking was duly noted: "Unrelated portions of the diaries of George Washington have been published in the past, at different times and under various editorial plans: some of these publications are not now readily accessible and all of them, added together, comprise hardly one-sixth of the available record. It remained for the Mount Vernon Ladies Association of the Union, with patriotic understanding and generosity to undertake the publication of every available diary in a complete and uniform edition."[16]

The publisher goes on to note that "Certain [volumes] of the diaries were given away by Bushrod Washington, who inherited his uncle's papers; thus, unfortunately, impairing the completeness of the record, but rendering the title of the present owners unassailable; other diaries, however, disappeared in ways decidedly questionable."[17] Each publisher also had to wrestle with editing the diary as they saw fit. As an example, Washington typically kept a record of the weather for each entry made. Over the course of reading the diary as a whole, such observations became mundane, and a distraction. "This weather record he kept as a separate and distinct series of entries from the other daily diary memoranda and its exclusions from this publication has been a matter of long consideration. It was finally decided to omit it, as much because Washington himself considered it a thing apart from his regular diary record, as because it has no practical value to that record."[18] Thus, changes have been made over the course of the *Diaries* publication ever since.

The four volumes of the Mount Vernon Ladies Association's (1925) edition were considered superior at the time. Shortly after the millennium, the Library of Congress made available on-line the complete set of all fifty-one volumes of Washington's diary. The diary, however, continues to fascinate Americans, and remains in print.

Washington left much out. He did not engage in gossip or record private conversation, even if it were considered public knowledge at the time. Because of this, his diary entries can be agonizingly brief, such as these entries covering four days in December of 1769:

> 10. Dined at the Speaker's and Spent the Evening in my own Room.
> 11. Dined at Mr. Wythe's and the Eveng. Spent in my own Room.
> 12. Dined at Mrs. Campbell's and spent the Evening in my own Room.
> 13. Dined at Mrs. Campbell's and went to the Ball at the Capitol.[19]

Because of his involvement in the War for Independence, Washington was unable to attend to the diary during the Revolution. In fact, there are several blank spots, with some lasting years. Washington was rarely able to keep the diary during his presidency, but it is often filled with accounts of formal dinners and levees attended. When Washington did elaborate, it was often written in a formal manner, and almost devoid of any personal feeling or emotion.

Even Washington's final entry, written the day before he died, is almost cryptic, and somewhat obscure:

> Morning Snowing and abt. 3 inches deep. Wind at No. Et., and Mer. at 30. Contg Snowing till 1 O'clock, and abt. 4 it became perfectly clear. Wind in the same place but not hard. Mer. 28 at Night.[20]

Thus, with this minute account of atmospheric weather observations, Washington leaves us in life, and secures his legacy as a political enigma.

The Diaries of George Washington reminds us that not all diaries are worth reading, no matter how illustrious the writer. Even in writing his diaries, Washington tried to hang on to whatever privacy he had left. In the end, he always seemed happiest at Mount Vernon.

In 1999, the University Press of Virginia published *George Washington's Diaries: An Abridgement*. In the introduction to the one-volume condensed edition, Editor Dorothy Twohig noted how "Washington's diaries are not those of a literary diarist in the conventional sense. There are few of the self-revealing passages that we have come to expect in the diaries of [other] famous men.... Washington was an intensely private man; none of his contemporaries would have expected that he would reveal the inner Washington even to his diaries."[21]

Another book, which is often incorrectly attributed to Washington, is *Rules of Civility & Decent Behavior in Company and Conversation*. This book was copied out in Washington's hand when he was sixteen years old and was actually an early exercise in penmanship. The book lists 110 examples of moral issues, manners, and etiquette, which were taken from a manual written by French Jesuits in 1595. Washington's 1747 handwritten copy survived, and was first published in book form in 1888. *Rules of Civility* can still be found in print today, and exists as a curiosity solely because of Washington's name. Students of Washington will find it of interest, but it is by no means an original manuscript.[22]

Yet even another book, titled *George Washington's Expense Account*, was never meant to see publication. Basically an accounting of expenses attributed over the course of the American Revolution, the ledger was kept by Washington, who submitted it to Congress in lieu of payment as Commander of the Army. It was never intended for widespread publication, and reveals little. Perhaps the most notorious allegations stem from oft-repeated claims that Washington padded his expenses and over-charged the federal government. Unlike Jefferson's wonderfully engaging *Memorandum Books* (which are discussed in a later chapter), George Washington's arithmetic was hardly the stuff of legend.

John Adams

> A pen is certainly an excellent Instrument, to fix a man's Attention and to Inflame his Ambition.[1]
> —John Adams

John Adams's first widely published work was a 1776 pamphlet titled *Thoughts on Government*. Originally provided to fellow delegates of the Second Continental Congress, Adams appears to have written *Thoughts* with the intent of having it publicly digested, for when delegate Richard Henry Lee and others pressed for its publication, Adams quickly consented. Philadelphia printer John Dunlap first published it. Only months later, Dunlap would take his place in American history when he became the first to print and distribute broadsides of the freshly proclaimed Declaration of Independence. *Thoughts* was by no means a lengthy discourse, yet it was considered an important work. Biographer David McCullough noted that "Little that Adams ever wrote had such effect" as *Thoughts*.[2] As with other Revolutionary-era writers, Adams would come to regret the rush to publication, and later wished for the opportunity to perfect and correct the manuscript. Once committed to the printed page, biographer Page Smith wrote how "the sight of his *Thoughts on Government* in print aroused mixed emotions in Adams," because he suspected it would not be met with great favor anywhere it was read.[3] This was a fact Adams himself was well aware of throughout his life; that he would never command the leadership characteristics found in Washington, nor the writing style of Jefferson.

Thoughts was written in rebuttal to Thomas Paine's *Common Sense*. Adams initially liked the book, but eventually claimed it had faults. Despite this the two respected one another as writers, and in an unpublished autobiography, Adams recalled a pleasant evening spent with Paine. "His Business was to reprehend me for publishing my Pamphlet. Said he was afraid it would do hurt, and that it was repugnant to the plan he had proposed in his Common Sense. I told him it was true it was repugnant and for that reason, I had written it and consented to the publication of it: for I was as much afraid of his Work [as] he was of mine."[4]

In the end, *Thoughts* was well received. Adams was particularly happy to hear it being earnestly read in Virginia, a colony he knew would be of great importance in the escalating war for independence. *Thoughts* reveals Adams penchant for building rather than pulling down, and in its summary, invites his fellow countrymen to relish the opportunities before them. "You and I, my dear friend, have been sent into life at a time when the greatest lawmakers of antiquity would have wished to live. How few of the human race have ever enjoyed an opportunity of making an election of government, more than of air, soil or climate, for themselves or their children?"[5]

Adams' second book, *A Defence of the Constitutions of Government of the United States of America*, was written eleven years later, during an idle period as Minister to England. Biographer Page Smith wrote of the zeal Adams possessed in composing the manuscript. "He withdrew to his upstairs library, barred the door to anyone but Abigail and, surrounding himself with histories, philosophical treatises, and political texts, plunged into his disquisition on the nature of government. He worked with a sense of urgency—the time was short; affairs in America were approaching a critical stage. He read and wrote from early morning to late at night, until his eyes were too inflamed to read and his arm too stiff and sore to write."[6]

First published in London in early 1787, Adams felt that publishing *A Defence* would surely make him unpopular, just as a doctor when prescribing bitter medicine. In a letter to a friend, Adams noted how one "must run the risk of their [the people's] displeasure sometimes, or he will never do them any good in the long run."[7]

As with *Thoughts on Government*, Adams would later regret rushing *Defence* into publication. McCullough noted that Adams himself "called it a 'strange book,' which in many ways it was, much of it a hodgepodge overloaded with historical references and extended borrowings from other writers usually without benefit of quotation marks."[8] Fellow biographer Smith agreed, calling it "haphazardly organized," and how it was "full of errors and inconsistencies."[9] Yet, in the end, *Defence* was "a curious jumble, a work that would certainly be sneered at as amateurish and inept by more sophisticated English and Continental scholars. But Adams was not writing for scholars, he was writing for people."[10] Smith also notes that "by the standards of its day it was a best seller, appearing in a number of editions, widely read and hotly debated."[11]

After receiving a copy of *Defence*, Thomas Jefferson suggested that Adams follow up with another book on hereditary aristocracy, but Adams begged off any such opportunity, citing the hasty publication of *Defence*.

Two years after publishing *Defence*, John Adams was elected vice president. Eight years later, in 1797, he was elected to a single term as president. Denied a second term in 1801, Adams wondered what to do with the remainder of his life. Son John Quincy noticed how his father devoured books and suggested he write an autobiography. Doctor and friend Benjamin Rush also encouraged Adams to put his life to paper, and Adams agreed stating, "I shall take your advice and write my own worthless life, merely to keep myself out of idleness."[12] Adams quickly found his papers were in a state of disarray to even consider such an undertaking and became fearful of the project before he had even begun, confessing, "I am afraid I have been the most careless and negligent in preserving papers. To rummage trunks, letterbooks, bits of journals and great heaps and bundles of old papers is a dreadful bondage to old age, and an extinguisher of old eyes."[13] Adams also often questioned his own memory, confessing, "I must write many things from memory and oftentimes facts to which there is no other witness left alive."[14]

In 1805, Mercy Otis Warren published her *History of the Rise, Progress, and Termination of the American Revolution*, which many historians believe to be one of the first important histories of the early United States. Warren and Adams were old friends, but her assessment of his place in history stung. Warren criticized his presidency and policies, which prompted a flood of letters from Adams in which he pointed out her mistakes and suggestions for correcting them in future editions. Warren's book, however, had injured Adams enough to extinguish any desire to continue writing. In the 1962 Belknap Press edition of the *Diary & Autobiography of John Adams*, the editors noted how the "feverish effort" [of letters written by Adams to Warren] had "put an end to the Autobiography John Adams had begun in 1802. He apparently never looked back at the abandoned manuscript, though much if not most of what he was to write in his remaining years was autobiographical."[15]

The fact that John Adams seriously began writing an autobiography is remarkable, and stands alone among the founding fathers. Even though his autobiographical manuscript was poorly structured, rambling and chaotic, historian L.H. Butterfield noted how Adams often had difficulty writing anything lengthy. Butterfield, who edited the multivolume *Diary and Autobiography of John Adams*, felt that Adams' "best writing is always in short forms—in diary entries, in letters and dispatches (some of which, however, are brief treasures in themselves), and in comments that sizzle and sparkle in the margins of the books he read or between passages from other writers (or even himself) that stirred him."[16]

Thomas Jefferson

> I cannot live without books.[1]
> —Thomas Jefferson

Throughout his life, Jefferson maintained a love affair with the written word. This was evident in the volume of books he amassed during his lifetime. Even the loss of his library from fire or through its sale to Congress did little to dampen his reading habits.

The first recognition of Jefferson's talents as a writer came in July 1774, with the publication of *A Summary View of the Rights of British America*. As a newly elected delegate to the Virginia delegation of the Continental Congress, Jefferson had drawn up *A Summary View* to act as a guidepost for his fellow Virginia delegates. Before the Congress was scheduled to meet in Philadelphia that September, however, a convention had been called to take place in Williamsburg in August. Jefferson had intended to present the proposals before the convention himself, but became ill en route from Monticello and was forced to return home. Fortunately, Jefferson forwarded two copies of the paper to members of the delegation. Patrick Henry received a copy but never acknowledged it, and was believed to have lost it. The other copy was wisely sent to Peyton Randolph, who resided over the convention. Randolph had the paper read in the presence of the delegates at his home. Though the delegation did not act upon any of the proposals a few members arraigned to have the paper publicly printed.

A Summary View of the Rights of British America was first published in Williamsburg. Jefferson himself had been unaware of its publication until it had materialized in pamphlet form. As with other writings of the time that could be considered treasonous, it appeared as an anonymous work. Jefferson had nothing else to do with the paper after sending it to Randolph, and even its title was the work of someone else. By the end of 1774, it had been reprinted in Philadelphia and had appeared twice in England. Biographer Dumas Malone wrote, "This accidental pamphlet of twenty-three pages gained wider currency than any other writing of his that was published during the Revolution except the Declaration, and it clearly anticipated that more famous and more polished document. It contributed to his contemporary reputation, and until this day it has commanded the deeply respectful attention of historians."[2] Author Joseph Ellis concurs, calling *Summary View* a "preliminary draft of the bill of indictment against George III contained in the Declaration, written a full two years before the more famous document and before Jefferson had even taken his seat in the Continental Congress."[3]

As an author, Thomas Jefferson dabbled in a vast array of subjects. While his *Notes on the State of Virginia* and *Manual of Parliamentary Practice* were noteworthy contributions, historians still pore over his delightful *Memorandum Books* (Library of Congress).

As Major George Washington had experienced with the rapid publication of his *Journal* in 1754, Jefferson was not afforded the time to properly proofread and edit it. After its publication, however, Jefferson realized that its language was too stern to ever have been formally adopted by the Virginia convention, and seemed content with having it appear as it was.

In *American Sphinx*, Joseph Ellis observed that *A Summary View* revealed a great deal of what and whom Jefferson had read and had been exposed to. "The 'once upon a time' character of Jefferson's interpretation, which has also come to be known as the Whig interpretation of history, deserves studied attention as a crucial clue to Jefferson's deepest intellectual instincts."[4]

With *A Summary View*, Jefferson had "foreshadowed his fame," as biographer Malone noted, by appearing "not as a soldier or speaker, but as a writer."[5] His fellow delegates in the Continental Congress would remember Jefferson's expertise as a wordsmith two years later, when they nominated him to serve on the committee to draft the Declaration. Although a single sheet of parchment, the Declaration of Independence remains Jefferson's best-known work. Like his *Summary View*, the Declaration's authorship remained a secret among fellow delegates until it was considered safe to devolve such information. When the Declaration was first publicly read in Philadelphia on July 8, 1776, Malone notes that Jefferson was most likely among those present, but that "nobody announced that he was the author of this paper or led him forward upon the stage to take a bow."[6] In fact, Jefferson probably found the anonymity comforting, as he felt that through editing the Congress had "manhandled his composition and marred its strength."[7] Despite the document's stirring prose, it would be the last time Thomas Jefferson co-wrote anything of any major significance.

In the summer of 1781, Jefferson had injured his wrist in a fall from his horse, and was unable to ride. To pass the hours that kept him confined to Monticello, he had begun to write detailed replies to a series of questions addressed to him by Marquis de Marbois, Secretary of the French Legation at Philadelphia. Marbois's inquiries specifically dealt with the State of Virginia. This included information regarding geography, natural resources, manufacturing, government and laws, history, navigation and other topics. Jefferson soon amassed a collection of "loose memoranda kept in bundles" which he kept at Monticello.[8] This loose collection of facts would become *Notes on the State of Virginia*.

When Jefferson sent Marbois the information he requested in December, he also wrote to Charles Thomson, a fellow member of the American Philosophical Society, to ask his opinion of the work and of possibly contributing it to the society. While Thomson encouraged Jefferson to continue, Jefferson had already made his mind up and decided to expand the ongoing project. On September 6, 1782, Martha Jefferson died. It was a deep loss for Jefferson, and his work on *Notes* stopped, as did everything else at Monticello for several weeks.

In 1784, Jefferson traveled to France as minister plenipotentiary with John Adams and Benjamin Franklin to negotiate treaties. When Jefferson arrived he carried with him his newly revised manuscript of *Notes on the State of Virginia*. Though he complained that it had "swelled nearly to treble [or triple] bulk," Jefferson still desired to have it privately printed.[9] At first, plans were to strike off a few copies for friends by a Philadelphia printer. Shocked at the cost of such a small printing, Jefferson waited until reaching France, where he learned the cost of printing would be one-fourth that in Philadelphia. With this sudden windfall, Jefferson was able to order a printing of two hundred copies. When the printing was delivered from the printers in the spring of 1785, Jefferson began offering copies to a select group of trusted friends. Apparently, Jefferson did not wish his authorship with *Notes* made public. He confided to James Monroe that "My reason is that I fear the terms in which I speak of slavery and of our constitution may produce an irritation which will revolt the minds of our countrymen against the reformation of these two articles, and thus do more harm than good."[10]

Jefferson's desires to remain anonymous were dashed when an owner of a copy died, and his treasured copy fell into the hands of a bookseller. The bookseller soon hired a translator and planned to publish a French translation. Under the threat of a poor translation, Jefferson accepted an offer from a friend and member of the French Academy to properly supervise the translation. As was custom then, once a book was published in France, an English edition was sure to follow. James Madison warned Jefferson that if not properly corrected, any inconsistencies would find their way into the English edition, which would quickly find their way into future American editions. The thought of his own words mangled into the minds of his fellow Americans was too much to bear, and in 1787 Jefferson permitted publisher John Stockdale to publish an authorized edition that bore Jefferson's name as author on the title page.

Despite his reservations, *Notes* was well received. The *Monthly Review* of London found "much to applaud," and leading French periodicals were just as enthusiastic.[11] Such enthusiasm can be easily found in Jefferson's *Notes*, and despite the stoic title, it displays the flashes of writing that can only come from Jefferson's pen. As an example, Jefferson described a visit to Virginia's famous Natural Bridge. "Though the sides of this bridge are provided in some parts with a parapet of fixed rocks, yet few men have resolution to walk to them, and look over into the abyss. You involuntarily fall on your hands and feet, creep to the parapet, and peep over it. Looking down from this height about a minute, gave me a violent headache. It is impossible for the emotions arising from the sublime to be felt beyond what they are here; so beautiful an arch, so elevated, so light, and springing as it were up to heaven!"[12]

Notes on the State of Virginia remains as interesting as when first published by Jefferson in 1785. When the Modern Library published *The Life and Selected Writings of Thomas Jefferson* in 1944, it included *Notes* in its entirety, noting that "it has been praised by reputable twentieth-century historians of science as the most influential scientific book written by an American," and how *Notes* continues "to be of interest for the clarity, vigor, and occasional beauty of Jefferson's prose."[13]

Of all of the various editions of Jefferson's *Notes*, John Stockdale's edition of 1787 is considered the finest. This is primarily because Jefferson authorized the edition, and worked with the publisher concerning existing errors found in previous printings. Jefferson also included a map of the State of Virginia, which he had engraved out of pocket, and offered it to Stockdale for use in his edition. Because of this, Jefferson expected to be paid a royalty of one shilling for every printing of the map Stockdale produced.[14]

In 1797, Jefferson was elected vice president under John Adams. Jefferson had not held a position in legislative government since 1781, and feared he would find himself ignorant of the rules of Parliamentary procedure. Like John Adams, Jefferson expected the office of vice president to be unremarkable, and largely spent residing over the Senate. In anticipation, Jefferson began researching existing rules and ways they could be improved upon. He also discovered rules and customs, though not formally written down, which had become incorporated into everyday practice. These rules were gathered along with existing rules and authored into proper book form by Jefferson as *A Manual of Parliamentary Practice for the Senate of the United States*.

Jefferson had previous knowledge in parliamentary procedure while a student at the College of William and Mary, where he studied extensively. He later served on the committee appointed to establish the rules of order for the Continental Congress, but considered the rules of the old Congress as prototype and antiquated. For his *Manual*, Jefferson relied heavily on previous sources such as those found in his library. He also sought opinions of well-respected mentors such as George Wythe and Edmund Pendleton. Because of this, Jefferson's *Manual* is not considered an original work, such as his *Notes on the State of Virginia*.

A Manual of Parliamentary Practice would be published by Jefferson just days before his term as vice president came to a close in early 1801. It was well received and became incorporated into the rules of not only the Senate, but also the House of Representatives. Further editions appeared in 1812 and 1813. In 1962, biographer Dumas Malone noted that "within half a century after the original publication there would be no fewer than seventeen of these, two being in Spanish. A count beyond that would assuredly run into the hundreds."[15] More than two hundred years later, the *Manual* is still in print. Jefferson himself would later consider it a "mere compilation" of previously published arrangements, along with "a few explanatory observations."[16] In a 1955 review of books for lawyers, the American Bar Association noted that Jefferson's *Manual* "indicates that he had a broad, scholarly and legal grasp of the essential rules of parliamentary procedure. His book is an outstanding work of a great lawyer."[17]

Though *Notes on the State of Virginia* became the only book solely authored by Jefferson and published in his lifetime, he prepared other manuscripts as well. One of these was titled *Anas*, or *Notes*. It was written while serving as secretary of state and is autobiographical in nature. As the title suggests, *Anas* reads like a jumble of loose notes, possibly intended for use at a later date. It was never published in Jefferson's lifetime, and became just another part of the extensive collection of papers he left behind. *Anas* seems compatible with a second would-be manuscript prepared by Jefferson, and known as his *Autobiography*.

Autobiography was begun by Jefferson at the age of seventy-seven, and its opening entry bears the date of January 6, 1821. Jefferson writes, "At the age of 77, I begin to make some memoranda, and state some recollections of dates and facts concerning myself, for my own more ready reference, and for the information of my family."[18] *Anas* and *Autobiography* are compatible in the fact that *Autobiography* covers the time of Jefferson's birth (1743) to the year 1790, while *Anas* begins in the year 1790 and runs until 1809. It has been speculated that Jefferson would have possibly added more to his autobiography, but at the time was busy establishing the University of Virginia.

Jefferson rarely threw anything away, which accounts for the great volume of his writings and papers that survive. Late in his life, an "enterprising publisher" who desired to publish "every last one of these papers" approached Jefferson.[19] Jefferson, however, passed on the rare opportunity, stating that many of them "would be like old newspapers, materials for future historians, but no longer interesting to the readers of the day."[20]

So much written by Jefferson survives, that even Jefferson's *Memorandum Books* were published in two volumes (1997). The two volume set consists of brief notes made by Jefferson, largely to himself, documenting accounts such as traveling experiences, book buying, purchasing furniture, and other seemingly mundane everyday occurrences. It reveals the multifaceted, multitasking genius known as Thomas Jefferson. *Memorandum Books* remain rivaled perhaps only by Samuel Pepys *Diary*. At the National Book Festival in 2017, even historian David McCullough humorously observed how Jefferson, who died in debt, wrote down everything he ever purchased, including the price, but "never added it up."[21]

James Madison

James Madison's notoriety as an author is primarily through his association with *The Federalist*. This seems only fitting, since *The Federalist* was written in defense of the United States Constitution, and Madison has often been referred to as the "Father of the Constitution."[1]

After serving as a delegate for the 1787 Constitutional Convention in Philadelphia, Madison was approached by fellow delegate Alexander Hamilton. Hamilton invited Madison to join him and John Jay in writing a series of essays to be published in New York newspapers. These essays would be written in favor of the Constitution, which had yet to be ratified by the States. As with the Declaration of Independence, Hamilton felt that New York would be a pivotal state in adopting the Constitution, and that the essays would prove beneficial for its passage by the state legislature. To have the essays published in out-of-state newspapers would not prove to be a hindrance either. Apparently sometime before Hamilton ever submitted his first essay, the decision was made to keep the identity of the author(s) anonymous, and all merely signed with the pseudonym "Publius." This proved to be beneficial to Madison, for he was not a New Yorker, but a Virginian, and to have the essays addressed "To the People of the State of New York," would have only instigated an unnecessary distraction.

In all, eighty-five Federalist essays were published between October 27, 1787, and May 28, 1788. The primary New York newspapers that published them were *The Independent Journal, The New-York Packet* and *The Daily Advertiser*. Because of illness, John Jay only authored five of the essays. Either Hamilton or Madison wrote the rest. Madison's published essays are numbers 10, 14, 18 through 20, and numbers 37 through 58, along with 62 and 63. In the end, Hamilton wrote fifty-one, Madison twenty-nine, and Jay five.

J. and A. McLean first published *The Federalist* in book form in 1788. Announced as "The Federalist, A Collection of Essays, written in favour of the New Constitution, *By a Citizen of New York*, Corrected by the Author, with Additions and Alterations," McLean published the collection in two volumes.[2] It is generally accepted that Hamilton did the editing without the assistance of Madison or Jay. A second American edition was published by John Tiebout in 1799, but proved to merely be remainder copies of McLean's edition, with the addition of new title pages. French translations were published as well.

In 1802, publisher George F. Hopkins announced a new edition entitled "The Federalist, on the Constitution, by Publius Written in 1788. To Which is Added, Pacificus, On the Proclamation of Neutrality. Written in 1793. The whole Revised and Corrected. *With new passages and notes*."[3] Hopkins also intended to name the authors of each essay, thus breaking "the poorly kept secret surrounding its authorship."[4] Regarding the revision of the text, Hamilton's involvement is disputed. Some claim that Hamilton supervised the editing, while others state they were made without his authorization or approval.[5] In 1804, Alexander Hamilton was fatally wounded during a duel with Aaron Burr.

Jacob Gideon published a new edition of *The Federalist* in 1818. With Hamilton now dead, Gideon requested information directly from Madison, who graciously complied. Gideon used a McLean first edition that had been Madison's personal copy, which included corrections in his own hand. Because of this Gideon claimed, "The publication of *The Federalist*, therefore, may be considered, in this instance, as perfect; and is confidently presented to the public as a standard reference."[6] Gideon's edition became the norm for publication until sometime after the Civil War when "the apotheosis of Hamilton caused publishers to revert to the 'pre-duel' ascription."[7] On June 27, 1836, Madison died, and the disputes of exactly who wrote what were never satisfactorily accepted by scholars.

During 1830 and 1831, Madison wrote something resembling an autobiography. Actually an outline to aid a friend in the writing a full-scale biography of the former president, Madison's reminiscences of his eight year presidency were brief, totaling only 233 words.

James Madison's only other work of great significance was his notes of the debates in the Constitutional Convention of 1787. Madison had always been opposed to the publication of his own notes during his lifetime, as well as the official record of the convention. Madison eventually agreed to allow his notes to be purchased for publication after his death. This was largely done out of concern for his wife, Dolley, who would have otherwise been left with a failed plantation and other debts.

Finding a ready audience for her husband's notes, Dolley Madison accepted an offer of $30,000 from the United States Congress. Madison's *Notes* were first published in 1840. In 1848, Congress purchased all of Madison's unpublished manuscripts in her possession for an additional $25,000. Thus began the practice of selling as well as publishing the former president's papers, something that only years earlier Madison's predecessor, Thomas Jefferson, frowned upon.

Among Madison's papers was a 122-page notebook complete with a stitched cardboard cover. Its given title was *James Madison His Book of Logick*, and scholars have concluded that while Madison purchased and dated the notebook while at boarding school in 1766, he most likely completed the majority of its entries while attending college.[8] Madison's *Book of Logick* is basically his reference book regarding philosophy, which he studied while at the College of New Jersey (now Princeton University) and includes references to Socrates, Plato, and Euclid. Biographer Irving Brant noted how "the contents clearly represented school work, with no indication of original thinking by Madison."[9]

Madison's *Book of Logick* was never published, but remains an interesting manuscript. It continues to capture the attention of historians when one considers the subject matter that such an adolescent was digesting. Brant best sums up the notebook by pointing out how "the intellectual strength and maturity shown by Madison in his early adult years have been a marvel to later generations."[10] Brant also notes that the notebook was such a curiosity that for many years it "reposed under a glass case in the exhibition hall of the Library of Congress."[11]

James Monroe

In 1793, Monroe was appointed American Minister to France. Prior to Monroe's arrival, France had undergone a bloody revolution, and relations between France and England had deteriorated to the point of war. Despite seeking a position of neutrality between the two, American relations with France were damaged and in 1796 both nations recalled their ambassadors. Once back in America, Monroe quickly found his reputation in the midst of political scandal. Biographer W.P. Cresson noted, "Monroe's doings in France had become a football of party politicians, and now that he had returned, it was inevitable that he became involved in the factional disputes between Federalists and Republicans."[1]

After consulting with friends about how to publicly address the charges against him, Monroe decided to simply publish his documented correspondence with the State Department, along with a defense of his actions as a narrative. This resulted in a pamphlet totaling more than one hundred pages and titled *A View of the Conduct of the Executive, in the Foreign Affairs of the United States, connected with the mission to the French Republic, during the years 1794, 5, & 6*. In summing up the work, Monroe biographer Cresson wrote that through Monroe's interpretation "the reader was left with the impression that both the United States and its minister to France had been betrayed by the federalist administration for the sake of a connection with England."[2] The *View* was widely circulated despite its size and cost of $1.50. John Adams, who was now president, wrote that Monroe's *View* was "a studied insult to the government of my country … by a disgraced minister, recalled in displeasure for misconduct."[3] As for Washington, who had retired to Mount Vernon, the former president kept his comments to himself. He did, however, obtain a copy of the *View*, and filled it with marginal notes critical of Monroe's argument.

In his biography of Monroe, Cresson wrote that it was "a dark period in Monroe's life and one that almost left him permanently warped in mind and spirit."[4] He had resolved never to seek public office again, and instead focus on his law practice. Through his publication of the *View*, however, Monroe regained his political standing and returned to France as a diplomat, where he negotiated the Louisiana Purchase with Napoleon. He then went on to bigger and better things, such as governor of Virginia, secretary of state and war, and eventually president.

After Monroe's conclusion of his second term, he retired to his estate. As with Jefferson and Adams, Monroe enjoyed a well-stocked library at his Oak Hill estate in Virginia, numbering nearly 3,000 volumes. Monroe spent much of his leisure time reading, and his interests included political theory and history. It is not surprising then that Monroe's first attempt at post-presidential writing was a manuscript titled *The People the Sovereigns, Being a Comparison of the Government of the United States with those of the Republics Which have Existed Before, with the Causes of their Decadence and Fall.*

Biographer Harry Ammon described the title as being "cumbersome but descriptive," and that it had been "long-contemplated" by Monroe.[5] From its title, one can easily see the influences of Monroe's service abroad as minister to England and France, as well as secretary of state. Like most well read gentlemen of post–Revolutionary America, much of Monroe's library had been obtained while in Europe, with many titles published in French. Monroe's manuscript progressed slowly, being partially completed with only a first draft to show for his labors. "In short," Ammon wrote, "[Monroe] was attempting to answer the question why a government based on the sovereignty of the people could be expected to function permanently in the United States, whereas previous examples of such governments had ended in disaster."[6] The manuscript compared the governments of Sparta, Athens, Rome and Carthage to the United States, and theories on why they failed. Biographer Ammon concluded that while the manuscript was never fully realized, "it was obvious that [Monroe] believed that the United States had achieved this goal by dividing power between the state and federal governments."[7] Ammon further points out that Monroe's manuscript owed "a considerable debt to Rousseau," and "revealed a familiarity with the Greek historians and Aristotle's *Politics*."[8]

Sometime during 1829 Monroe showed a copy of *The People the Sovereigns* to George Hay. Hay, who had been Monroe's son-in-law since his marriage to daughter Eliza in 1808, also served as Monroe's Virginia campaign manager during the 1816 election. Now with a law degree, President John Quincy Adams appointed Hay to a federal judgeship soon after Monroe had left office, and Hay frequently stayed at Monroe's Oak Hill estate. Monroe obviously valued Hay's opinion, and when Hay pronounced the manuscript as a waste of Monroe's time, Monroe swiftly abandoned it. "I think your time could have been better employed," Hay bluntly informed the former president.[9] "If the framers of our Constitution could have had some work, from a modern standpoint, on the Constitutions of Greece and Rome, it might have been of value to them. I do not think yours is of practical value now."[10] Hay expressed these sentiments to John Quincy Adams as well, claiming that Monroe had written a book "which nobody would read."[11] Even biographer Harlow Giles Unger would later note how "its honest but unimaginative title provoked little interest."[12] Samuel L. Gouverneur finally published *The People the Sovereigns* in 1867. "Not one word had been added to the original text, neither has one been erased from the manuscript copy," he wrote, adding that the manuscript was "the true exposition of the Monroe Doctrine."[13]

In 2001, James P. Lucier published *The Political Writings of James Monroe*. Lucier noted, "Monroe was not a speculative thinker or constructor of abstract systems."[14] As with other historians, Lucier contends that despite his best intentions, Monroe produced a flawed manuscript, and was "fully aware that "the people" did not always possess virtue, [and] intelligence," but "still remains the summing up of Monroe's life work, the most relevant analysis of the principles which guided his years of service."[15] Lucier would also include *The People the Sovereigns* in the same volume.

Perhaps to help reflect the blow from *The People the Sovereigns*, George Hay suggested that Monroe instead write his autobiography which would be of greater interest to his fellow countrymen and more easily digestible. Monroe was smitten with Hay's suggestion, and began work on the autobiography immediately. Monroe died on July 4, 1831, although it is likely that he no longer continued working on the manuscript after November 1830. *Autobiography* remained a manuscript until it was edited by Stuart Gerry Brown in 1959 and published by Syracuse University Press. In the preface, Brown writes that the manuscript consisted of approximately 400 pages, and notes, "The reader should understand that the manuscript is a draft. There are only occasional corrections, suggesting that for the most part Monroe went over it only once."[16]

Brown goes on to muse how "one cannot help wishing that Monroe had either begun to write his autobiography earlier, or had lived long enough to finish it."[17] His feelings echoed other scholars and historians, for Monroe was the last of the founding fathers and the door to the history he had witnessed was drawing to a close. The manuscript was unrevealing, however, mostly from Monroe's habit of writing in the third person.

Biographer Harry Ammon expressed his frustration of Monroe's abundance of reserve when summing up the *Autobiography*. "Age had not modified Monroe's habit of reticence. Still very much bound by the attitudes current in his youth, he composed a work (he only carried it to 1805) which does no more than depict the public events in which he participated. Written in the third person, it offers little that cannot be found in official records. There are few anecdotes, only a handful of references to his private life, no glimpses behind the scenes and no revealing portraits of the great men of his day."[18]

John Quincy Adams

> He is the most exhaustless writer that I ever knew.
> —Thomas Adams[1]

John Quincy Adams's first taste of being a published writer occurred in 1791, at the age of 23. On June 8 of that year, the first of a series of essays written by the son of then vice president Adams appeared in a Boston newspaper. Adams, who preferred to remain anonymous, called his essays *Letters of Publicola*, after a Latin expression translating to "friend of the people." *Publicola* totaled eleven essays in all, and mirrored his father's conservation views. So much in fact, that many readers assumed John Adams had authored them. Adams *Publicola* essays were so successful that they were republished elsewhere, not only in the United States, but also England, France, Ireland and Scotland.

The origins of *Letters of Publicola* can be traced back to Thomas Paine's *The Rights of Man*. Just as father John had earlier detested Paine's writings, John Quincy felt the best rebuttal was to answer Paine through print. As to John Adams's earlier claims that Paine was only good for pulling down but not for building up, John Quincy criticized Paine when he wrote how "Mr. Paine seems to think it is as easy for a nation to change its government, as

John Quincy Adams authored everything from political essays, a travel diary, translations of German literature, and even an official government report on weights and measures. For most of his life Adams also kept a diary, considered by many to be among the best ever kept by a president (Library of Congress).

for a man to change his coat."[2] *Letters of Publicola* would eventually be published in book form, but only after Adams's death. It has been common practice to include Paine's *Rights of Man* in the same volume, as a tool for political debate.

Inspired by the success of the *Publicola* essays, Adams penned others which appeared in Boston area newspapers between 1792 and early 1794. During this time his father had urged him to pursue a career in law, which John Quincy found dull. His success as a writer encouraged him to contemplate what life could hold for him if he worked at it. Biographer Paul Nagel wrote, "He foresaw that perhaps he could achieve literary success if he spent his free time at his writing desk."[3] Whatever plans, literary or otherwise that Adams envisioned, were soon squashed by his father's political maneuvering, which led to President Washington appointing John Quincy Adams as American minister to Holland. Thus began a lifelong political career that often clashed with literary pursuits.

Adams completed his service as minister to Holland in 1797, only to discover that his father, now president, appointed him minister to Prussia. Over the next two years, Adams saw a good deal of Germany before settling in Berlin with his new bride, Louisa. It was while in Berlin in late 1799 that Adams undertook translating Christopher Martin Wieland's *Oberon*, a "poetical treatment of the legendary king of elves or fairies."[4] Biographer Marie B. Hecht noted that while the translation was "started as an amusement, it absorbed him so completely that he hated to stop even for an hour, although he was dissatisfied with the finished product."[5] In early 1801, however, Adams discovered that another English translation of *Oberon* had recently been published, prompting him to lay the manuscript aside. In 1940, editor A.B. Faust finally published Adams' translation "in a handsome volume amid such acclaim as might have convinced even John that his time had not been wasted."[6] Around the time Adams was toiling over *Oberon*, he authored an English version of Friedrich von Gentz' *The Origin and Principles of the American Revolution Compared with the Origin of the French Revolution*. Whereas Jefferson and father John Adams absorbed French literature, John Quincy led the "campaign to place German titles in American libraries."[7]

While on summer holiday in 1800, John Quincy and Louisa Adams toured the providence of Silesia. Originally intending to sketch their travels in his diary, Adams instead wrote a series of letters to his brother, Tom. It was Thomas Adams who took the liberty of forwarding them to Joseph Dennie, the publisher of a Philadelphia literary periodical, *Port Folio*. From the attention received in *Port Folio*, an anonymous London edition appeared in 1804 titled *Letters on Silesia*, and crediting Adams as the author. German and French translations soon followed. Adams was unaware of the foreign editions and doubted his ability as an author, confiding to Louisa, "If I should ever appear voluntarily before the public as a candidate for the reputation as an author, it should be with pretensions of rather more elevation."[8]

In 1809, Adams delivered a farewell address at Harvard University, where he had served as the Boylston Professor of Rhetoric and Oratory since 1806. The address was classical Adams, with John Quincy reminding those in attendance "at no hour of your life will the love of letters ever oppress you as a burden, or fail you as a resource."[9] Adams then resumed his distant State Department travels, but not before giving his collected lectures to his brother "to be published in two volumes, fully expecting them to be harshly handled by critics on both sides of the Atlantic."[10] As he did with *Letters on Silesia*, Adams felt he had once again failed miserably as an author, and bitterly commented, "To live in the memory of mankind by college lectures is not the aim of a very soaring ambition."[11]

It is only natural that his service within the Department of State would lead Adams to the office of secretary under the administration of James Monroe. Adams assumed the office of secretary of state on September 22, 1817. He quickly discovered a Senate resolution, from March of that year, directing the secretary to prepare a report on weights and measures. Up until that time, the United States had no uniform standard, and Congress assumed the secretary would find ample information of how other nations dealt with such matters within the department. Adams had previously studied Europe's standards out of boredom while in St. Petersburg as a youth, which gave him some insight to the task before him. Yet, the bulk of the report fell upon his shoulders, as "there were no research associates or other aides to whom he might have handed the chore."[12]

Begun in earnest in late 1817, Adams soon found himself consumed with the project. He wrote how it "fascinates and absorbs me to the neglect of the most necessary [departmental] business and even to my daily diary."[13] Hours would be spent toiling over mathematical calculations, only to be followed by distractions and other interruptions. By early 1820, Adams had become so guilt stricken that he concluded that if the report were not completed the course of a year, it would not only amount to a personal embarrassment, but an embarrassment for the Monroe administration as well. The secretary then accelerated his pace, even remaining in Washington during the intolerable heat of the summer months, to complete the report. With Louisa and his family now in Maryland, Adams routinely rose at 3 a.m., attempting to fulfill his quota of writing three pages per day in solitude. Adams felt confident enough to share the manuscript with Secretary of War John Calhoun in February 1821. Calhoun cautioned Adams that there would be those in Congress who would look upon the manuscript as "too much of a Book for a mere Report."[14] Calhoun's words probably came as no surprise, as Adams had long known he was presenting Congress with more than they asked for.

When finally published, the *Report of the Secretary of State Upon Weights and Measures* quickly became the finest work available. Originally published at 245 pages, John Calhoun was correct in describing it as a "book." An early advocate of a universal metric system, Adams felt that an international standard would prove a great leap forward for mankind. In *John Quincy Adams: A Public Life, a Private Life*, author Paul Nagel noted that the *Report* was not taken lightly, and continues to astound readers to this day. "Although it had slight impact at the time, Secretary Adams' *Report* became, for the small circle of those genuinely interested, the finest scholarly evaluation of the subject ever written. It has remained so for nearly two centuries. While the work is ponderous and complex beyond belief, and begs for the revision that its author knew was merited but had no time to give, it clearly reveals his love of learning—and possibly his pleasure in flourishing his erudition."[15]

Like Jefferson's *Notes on the State of Virginia*, Adams' *Report* reveals just how consumed an individual can become with a subject. What makes the *Report* remarkable is the fact that it was researched, written, and published while Adams was actively serving as secretary of state. Originally, the *Report* was not a labor of love, but an assignment from Congress. The fact that Adams incorporated his love of history and philosophy into it displays his versatility as a writer, and is hardly what the reader would expect to follow *Letters on Silesia*.

Soon after the publication of his *Report Upon Weights and Measures*, Adams found himself at work on yet another book. In 1814, Adams had served on the U.S. Delegation that negotiated the Treaty of Ghent, thus concluding the hostilities that became known as the War of 1812. In adopting the treaty, issues such as boundaries and fishing rights were left to further negotiation. In 1822, with Adams now secretary of state, the unfinished business of the 1814 treaty became a political issue. At the time, the office of secretary had become a stepping-stone to the presidency, and Adams was grooming himself to succeed Monroe. All hopes for a smooth campaign were dashed when Jonathan Russell, a former member of the 1814 treaty delegation and now a Massachusetts congressman, claimed that Adams had forsaken the interests of the western states while favoring the New England region. When Russell presented documents that included added falsifications, Adams fired back in essays that were published in several newspapers. Not content with his essays, Adams felt the only path to vindication was through a report that would contain an exhaustive review of the facts.

Thus, through the summer and autumn of 1822 Adams wrote what would become *The Duplicate Letters, the Fisheries and the Mississippi, Documents Relating to Transactions at the Negotiations of Ghent*. In the end Adams had written an "enormous "pamphlet" [which] was filled with official papers [and] interspersed with Adams' "remarks."[16] Adams expressed the opinion that Russell was merely trying to "inflame passions between the nation's geographic sections," and hoped the book would "warn of the broader danger in Russell's sin."[17] By this time, Russell's political career was in ruins, and reflected in his failure to win reelection to the House. Because of this, *The Duplicate Letters* have been summed up by one Adams biographer as "a depressing example of time wasted by treading on an already fallen enemy."[18]

The Duplicate Letters stands as an example of Adams' inability to let things pass. This personal nature became more evident after his failure to win a second term as president in 1828. The campaign against Andrew Jackson was bitter, with claims by Federalists that while a senator, Adams had betrayed his own New England constituents by placing national concerns first. Adams had begun drafting a reply to theses changes during the closing months of the 1828 election, and studied old Senate journals as well. After March 4, 1829, Adams was once again a private citizen and soon produced a manuscript in which he claimed to have written "with the boldness of truth."[19] Adams finished the manuscript by the end of April, less than two months after leaving office. He had originally intended to publish it, but the news of his son George's death subdued his spirit and "the huge manuscript was left to posterity."[20] Charles Adams wrote that his father's manuscript "told the truth far too violently to be useful," and also passed on publishing it.[21] Only after grandson Henry Adams had edited the manuscript in 1877, it finally was posthumously published as *Documents Relating to New England Federalism, 1800–1815*.

While other presidents discovered that the best time for writing was after leaving office, Adams found that aside from the brief spurt which would one day become *Documents Relating to New England Federalism*, he faced great difficulty in picking up the pen. He seriously considered writing a biography of father John Adams, while admitting to his diary how easily he wasted time. His father had left extensive notes and letters, which overwhelmed John Quincy whenever he approached the subject. Once his library arrived from Washington, Adams instead poured over the contents of its thirty-eight boxes and six trunks, often losing himself in old classics. He would eventually attempt to write an essay on the Russo-Turkish War, but in the end the manuscript had veered off course and ran much too long. Adams soon came to the conclusion that "drudging through his father's papers lacked thrills," and in late 1831 admitted that he had "suspended the biography of my father."[22] This drew the ire of wife Louisa, who reminded him of the vow he had made to the family. The escape he sought from his writer's block was found in his recent election to Congress, which he began that December.

In late 1830, Adams had also begun tinkering with poetry. That winter Adams composed a long narrative poem that he called *Dermot MacMorrogh*. Adams had written the poem during his daily morning and afternoon walks around Washington. The poem, Adams said, was a "historical tale about events in Ireland about 1172, was written to teach the virtues of marital fidelity, patriotism, and piety."[23] While Adams was unsure of his talent as a published poet, he confidently "assured his publisher that the first edition would sell because of momentary curiosity about the author and the singularity of the subject."[24] Adams was correct with his forecast of sales and quickly considered himself a success in literature.

As a member of Congress, Adams soon found himself in demand as a public speaker and wrote numerous lectures. His dreams of literary fame without a doubt revisited him in 1842, when acclaimed author Charles Dickens visited him at home during a speaking tour. The two shared lunch and talked of books, with the highlight of the visit being when Dickens asked Adams for his autograph. In 1845, Adams felt the need to gather his publications together, and had them bound in five volumes. Plans were made for publishing one hundred sets, calling them "the most complete daguerreotype of my mind for more than a half century that has ever been made, or ever will be made."[25] The project was abandoned after Adams considered them to be of little value to a public that had never embraced him in the same manner as the likes of Daniel Webster.

John Quincy Adams died February 23, 1848, two days after collapsing while on the floor of the House. Within months of his death, two books of his writings appeared, both religious tracts. These books would soon be followed by other posthumous writings of Adams, such as an 1850 biography of Madison and Monroe.

It was the *Diary of John Quincy Adams* that would become his most extensively posthumously published work. Begun in 1779 when Adams was twelve, the *Diary* spans sixty-eight years. John Quincy was encouraged to keep up his diary by his father. John Adams wrote, "One contracts a fondness of writing by use. We learn to write readily, and what is of more importance, we think, and improve our judgments, by committing our thoughts to paper."[26] This was good advice for a young man and budding writer. After Adams' death in 1848, son Charles Francis Adams began permitting extracts of the *Diary* to be published as early as 1850. In the introduction of the Belknap Press edition of the *Diary of John Quincy Adams*, it is noted, "The will of John Quincy Adams makes no allusion to publication of the Diary, nor indeed the Diary itself. In what apparently was the last conversation between father and son on the subject of the Diary, Charles Francis recorded that John Quincy Adams "said that his Diary was closed, he should never write any more of it.

He should place it in my hands to do with it what I might think proper, at the same time, distinctly stating that it had never been written for extended publication and it was not his wish that such publication be made."[27]

Eventually, Charles "came to believe that he had a mandate to publish the diary, but was also committed by his father's wishes."[28] While excerpts from the diary were often used by scholars as an aid in their biographies on Adams, it was never published in its entirety until 1952, when the Adams Manuscript Trust planned to publish an edition on microfilm. On April 4, 1956, the trustees' transferred ownership of the papers, which included the diary manuscripts, to the Massachusetts Historical Society, which published a letterpress edition of the entire diary. What makes the *Diary of John Quincy Adams* unique among his contemporaries are the rich and fluent descriptions of the places he traveled to, and the people he encountered. The reader easily walks in his shoes throughout Europe and America, and witnesses a boy, having grown into a man, finally into an accomplished writer. Historically noteworthy is the fact that Adams kept up the *Diary* while in the White House, the first occupant to do so.

Biographer Paul C. Nagel writes that with his death, John Quincy Adams "knew that he had failed in his yearning to make a contribution to literature, philosophy, or science worthy of the world's admiration and gratitude."[29] Nagel also notes that perhaps Adams' greatest contribution to American literature was how he "awakened" it to "the beauty of German literature."[30]

The writings of John Quincy Adams stand equal among the writings of other early presidents. If Thomas Jefferson had not overshadowed him, Adams' diversity as an author might have been better known. This feat is complicated by the fact that whether it be a study of weights and measures, a travelogue of a German providence, an English translation, or one of his lengthy vindication's of his political character, much of what Adams wrote had never "taken hold of the public mind," a fact he painfully admitted.[31]

Three Generals: Andrew Jackson, William Henry Harrison and Zachary Taylor

If you would not be forgotten, as soon as you are dead and rotten, either write things worth reading, or do things worth writing.[1]

—Benjamin Franklin

In the period spanning 1829 to 1850, the United States elected three presidential candidates with military backgrounds. Like Washington, all three were generals: Andrew Jackson, William Henry Harrison, and Zachary Taylor. As with Washington, none came from an exceptional background, nor were they subject to an academic education. As a result, none of the three authored any books or penned manuscripts worthy of note.

Andrew Jackson, who, with Washington and Jefferson, is rated by historians as one the early "great presidents," received limited education as a youth. Biographer Andrew Burnstein noted, "Like Washington, Jackson received a meager education."[2] Even historians on Jackson's day considered him to be an "unlettered man," and "little versed in books."[3] In *American Lion*, author Jon Meacham wrote of predecessor John Quincy Adams' disdain for Jackson's intellectual flaws:

> Jackson had only a handful of years of formal education—he was the least intellectually schooled president in the short history of the office—and his opponents made much of his lack of schooling. When Harvard University bestowed an honorary degree upon President Jackson in 1833, the man he had beaten for the White House, John Quincy Adams, a Harvard graduate, refused to come, telling the university's president that "as myself an affectionate child of our Alma Mater, I would not be present to witness her disgrace in conferring her highest literary honors upon a barbarian who could not write a sentence of grammar and hardly could spell his own name." Adams's view was common in Jackson's lifetime.[4]

Regarding reading material, Jackson mainly kept to the Bible, although his library included works relating to history, biography and theology. As might be expected, Washington as well as Napoleon heavily influenced him. Meacham further notes that while Jackson "was no scholar … he issued elegant Caesar-like proclamations to his troops," and that "when he put his mind and hand to it … could produce stirring rhetoric."[5]

While Andrew Jackson never wrote his memoirs, he did authorize a close friend, Amos Kendall, to author a biography. Amos Kendall was a graduate of Dartmouth, an editor of one newspaper, and the founder of another. He came into Jackson's orbit during the campaigns of 1828 and 1832, and soon became "a critical figure in Jackson's universe."[6] Although Kendall held no cabinet post, he was acknowledged as being "the moving spring of the whole administration," and "one of the most remarkable men in America."[7] Author Jon Meacham summed up Kendall's career with the observation, "He was what later generations would call a networker."[8]

Kendall began work on his biography of Jackson in 1840. Burnstein wrote, "One would naturally expect Jackson to take a lively interest, but he did more than that; he expended a good deal of his dwindling energy making certain that Kendall got the details right, especially those that glorified the subject for posterity."[9] Kendall's biography of Jackson was eventually published in 1843, two years before the former president's death.

William Henry Harrison and Zachary Taylor were generals as well, and both have the distinction of being the first and second presidents to die in office. Harrison's month-long presidency was unremarkable, except for the trivial fact that it also featured the longest inaugural address ever presented. Harrison went to great lengths to appear as a well-read intellectual, and touched upon ancient and Roman history in the address. Fortunately, Daniel Webster stepped in and edited the text, which still fell on deaf ears.

Zachary Taylor had little regard for politics and never even voted prior to becoming president in 1849. Like Harrison, Taylor's inaugural address was also unmemorable, but much shorter. In his later-published White House diary, predecessor James K. Polk recorded his comments of the general made at Taylor's own inauguration. "After being there a few minutes General Taylor read his inaugural address. He read it in a very low voice and very badly as to his pronunciation and manner.... General Taylor is, I have no doubt, a well-meaning old man. He is, however, uneducated, exceedingly ignorant of public affairs, and, I should judge, of very ordinary capacity."[10]

Had Harrison and Taylor survived their terms of office, it is likely they would have allowed a competent author to compose an authorized biography of themselves, as Jackson did. It is interesting to note that up until now, the great military minds that had occupied the American presidency had little regard for literary pursuits. One must remember that if Washington's *Journal* had not been rushed to publication, our founding father would have also gone down in history without any literary merit.

Surprisingly, it would be the next general-turned-president who would author one of the acclaimed greatest historical memoirs ever published: Ulysses S. Grant.

Martin Van Buren

The first publication loosely associated with Martin Van Buren was entitled *Mr. Van Buren's Opinions*, and appeared during his 1835 campaign for the presidency. While not published in its entirety by Van Buren, it contained letters, essays, and opinions expressed by Van Buren that had been previously published in several newspapers. It marked a unique experience in American politics. Biographer John Niven noted:

> Never before in any campaign had a candidate spoken so often on public issues; never had a presidential candidate, excepting Jefferson and Madison, published his own ideas on government or so highly praised the federal system. Taken all together, published in a pamphlet, and entitled *Mr. Van Buren's Opinions*, the *Globe*, the *Richmond Enquirer*, and the *Argus* printed and broadcast them throughout the country providing partisan editors with political ideas, stump speakers with material for their rural audiences and answers for hecklers in the crowds at militia meetings, festivals and debates.[1]

Opinions had a positive impact on Van Buren's campaign, and by July of 1836 had swelled to "a bulky pamphlet of forty pages of fine type. For those who were willing to wade through the material, and there were many who did, Van Buren had commented fully on all the controversial topics of the day."[2] Van Buren served one term as president, from 1837 to 1841, partly due to being Andrew Jackson's vice president. Van Buren retired from politics after being defeated for reelection, and returned to his estate in Lindenwald, New York. Van Buren left office as a widower, and had ample time on his hands. He spent it reading. He "also occupied a part of his time with a serious work on his history of political parties in the United States. He had long had such a project in mind but something or somebody always seemed to require his attention when he was ready to begin. He was also thinking about an autobiography."[3] During this time, Van Buren also began gathering letters written to friends and associates from years past to help spark his memory. Former Senator Thomas Hart Benton also was in the process of writing his recollections, and asked Van Buren to review his early drafts. This spurred his interest in writing his own memoir, and Van Buren soon enlisted son Martin Jr. as his personal secretary.

Van Buren started what would eventually become his *Autobiography* while traveling in Europe. Biographer Ted Widmer suggested that perhaps "Sorrento's distance from Kinderhook was exactly what opened the floodgates of his memory," adding that "once the words came, they came in a torrent, written hastily in his unreadable handwriting."[4] Van Buren quickly discovered his inability in "marshaling his thoughts, organizing his notes and putting them all together in a cohesive narrative."[5] To assist him, he begged another son, Smith, to arrange and edit his manuscripts. By then, Van Buren had separated his own autobiographical notes from existing biographies and volumes on political philosophy which he intended to use as sources for the autobiography. Van Buren referred to this accumulation of books and notes as the "Inquiry," and it was Smith's task to organize it. Van Buren had originally hoped Smith would move into the sprawling mansion at Lindenwald and be his "literary executor," but Smith had obligations to his own family.[6] Like his father, Smith Van Buren found writing a difficult and unpleasant task, and work progressed slowly. Biographer John Niven wrote how "the drudgery of deciphering Van Buren's sprawling hand and arranging the masses of unorganized material would have strained the patience, if not the skill, of the most devoted offspring."[7]

With the help of his sons, Van Buren eventually separated his accumulation of notes and books into two manuscripts. The first of these Van Buren titled *Inquiry into the Origin and Course of Political Parties in the United States*. Given its title, *Inquiry* is self-explanatory and provides an early history of the fracture of the American political system after the death of Washington. This fracture continued with the deaths of other significant founding fathers such as Jefferson and Adams. Author Ted Widmer described the *Inquiry* as "a learned work, deeply immersed in the rivalry between Jefferson and Hamilton, but less forthright about the struggles of his own generation."[8] *Inquiry* would be published in 1867, five years after Van Buren's death.

When comparing Van Buren's *Inquiry* and *Autobiography*, John Niven added, "Neither work compares favorably with the political essays, letters and partisan tracts Van Buren wrote in the thirties and forties. Still, in substance, the *Inquiry* and the *Autobiography* are valuable sources for political and economic thought of the Jacksonian era. The *Inquiry* stands as the first major effort any American attempted to write as history of the political process in the United States from the founding of the Republic."[9]

Niven also pointed out the manuscript's problems, adding, "The ponderous style, the digressions, the arguments that interrupt the narrative, make it tedious reading. No doubt Martin's illness and death, and Smith's casual attitude toward his father's work, left this valuable manuscript unfinished and poorly edited."[10] Niven goes on to note how the *Autobiography* lacked any substantial information in regards to his administration, as well as his campaigns, though Van Buren "clearly intended to fill in these great gaps."[11] As an example, his service as minister to England is covered in greater detail than his time as secretary of state or vice president. His criticism, however, soon softens, admitting that "here and there the diligent reader, if persistent, will uncover wonderful vignettes of historical episodes," and that "with all its faults, is yet an impressive source, [and] one of the most important legacies Van Buren left to future generations."[12]

Van Buren stopped adding to the *Autobiography* in 1858, after falling under poor health. He died in 1862. In 1920, the Library of Congress published the *Autobiography* in its entirety. In a prefatory note, John C. Fitzpatrick, who was the assistant chief of the Library's Manuscript Division, rendered his opinion of the manuscript:

The Autobiography is written with engaging frankness, and the insight it affords to the mental processes of a master politician is deeply interesting. Van Buren's desire to be scrupulously fair in his estimates is evident, and, if he did not always succeed, his failures are not discreditable.

In analyzing men and measures, Van Buren all unconsciously paints a picture of himself and it is a truthful and worthy portrait. It is impossible to read the Autobiography through without greatly regretting that it was not carried beyond the point it reaches.

As a contribution to the political history of the United States, its presentation of facts is too valuable to be ignored safely by the conscientious investigator.[13]

The Library published the manuscript under the title of *The Autobiography of Martin Van Buren*. It was significant by the fact that it was the earliest presidential autobiography to be published at the time. Only James Monroe's dates earlier, but was not published until 1959. Author Ted Widmer noted that Van Buren's *Autobiography* was "not exactly a book to launch the Jazz Age, but the miracle is perhaps that it made it into print at all."[14]

Van Buren found writing to be slow and difficult and confessed that he neglected working on the manuscript at times. An experienced editor would have surely helped, and could have probably offered more assistance than his son Smith had. Perhaps Van Buren was aware that in the end, no matter how well the manuscript was written, history would ultimately judge him to be a lessor man than Jackson ever was. Van Buren knew this, for in his inaugural address he claimed, "I belong to a later age." Yet the historical separation must have been painful at times. In his 2005 biography of Van Buren, author Ted Widmer suggested that Martin Van Buren only turned to writing in an attempt to "keep his own story from disappearing, and to achieve the peculiar immortality we reserve for the writers of very long books that are never checked out of the library."[15]

Two Accidentals: John Tyler and Millard Fillmore

John Tyler held numerous offices during his long political career, including governor of Virginia, as well as serving in both the U.S. House and Senate. After William Henry Harrison's death Tyler succeeded to the presidency. Tyler came from a wealthy family and attended William and Mary College, where he studied law. While at college his father wrote to criticize his penmanship, telling him, "Writing and cyphering well are absolutely necessary and cannot be dispensed with."[1]

After leaving college Tyler continued to pursue an interest in Greek and Roman history and literature, as well as "the masterpieces of English literature."[2] He established a law practice that led to a career in public service. Despite his interest in classical history and literature, there is no evidence that suggests Tyler ever entertained any thought of writing for publication. After completing the remainder of Harrison's term in 1844, Tyler returned to his Virginia estate.

During the Civil War, Tyler sided with the Confederacy, which ostracized him from what few friends he had in Washington. In 1861, Tyler was elected to a seat in the Provisional Congress of the Confederacy, but died before he could take his seat. Tyler was not working on any political manuscripts or autobiography at the time of his death, and if he had, it is safe to assume they would have been hard pressed to find a willing publisher north of the Mason-Dixon line.

Millard Fillmore, who assumed the presidency upon the death of Zachary Taylor, was well read and a bit of a bibliophile, yet never found the urge to publish any works to add to his overflowing bookshelves. Biographer Robert J. Rayback noted, "Fillmore haunted bookstores wherever he found them. Never was he to return from New York City without a few books under his arm, and he 'was often followed or preceded by a package sent by express.' After many years their library reached 4,000 volumes, and each time it grew beyond its bounds, Abigail [Fillmore] would happily call in a carpenter to extend the bookcases. To collectors of rare books the Fillmore library was undistinguished."[3]

As with Tyler, Fillmore returned home to Buffalo after serving out the remainder of Taylor's term. Within a month his wife had died, and Fillmore found himself alone in retirement. He filled his days "slumped into his library chair to read, or sat at his expansive desk to write," and led "an unhurried life."[4] "He kept looking around for something to do," but did not find the answer through becoming a published author.[5]

James K. Polk

As a youth, Polk received a formal education at the University of North Carolina at Chapel Hill. While there, Polk joined one of the college's literary societies, the Dialectic Society. As a member, Polk was required to participate in debates as well as prepare written compositions. The best essays were then "filed in the society archives," and a total of eight written by Polk were "so honored, and two of them are still extant."[1] Of the two that still survive, their subjects include an argument against "The Admission of Foreigners into office in the United States, and "The Powers of Invention." Polk was well read, and library records show him borrowing volumes such as Edward Gibbon's *Decline and Fall of the Roman Empire.* Polk was elected president of the Dialectic Society during his junior and senior years, and historians claim it was while at Chapel Hill that Polk learned the basics that he later applied to statesmanship.

Like John Quincy Adams, James K. Polk kept a White House diary that was posthumously published. First published in 1910, the diary remained greatly unknown except to historians until Longmans, Green and Company republished it in 1929. The Longmans and Green edition was also edited by Allan Nevins, and in the preface of the 1929 edition, Nevins touched upon the history of the original manuscript.

"This volume is a selection from "The Diary of James K. Polk During His Presidency, 1845 to 1849," edited and annotated by Milo Milton Quaife, and published in four volumes in 1910 by A.C. McClurg & Company of Chicago for the Chicago Historical Society, in whose collections the original manuscript rests. Having been printed in an edition of but five hundred copies, the work is unfortunately but little known to the general public. The editor has attempted to select from the portions most interesting and valuable to ordinary students and readers, and to knit them together by a full body of notes."[2]

As the Longmans edition is condensed into one volume and totals 404 pages, the McClurg & Company edition of four volumes without a doubt remains superior, but unfortunately just as rare. Editor Allan Nevins acknowledged that Polk was "unknown as an orator or thinker," and a "secondary figure in the field of politics."[3] "That such a man, colorless, methodical, plodding, narrow, should become President of the United States was itself remarkable," Nevins continues, adding Polk even defeated Henry Clay.[4] With this comment, Nevins touches upon an observation that has mystified historians for quite some time now: Namely, how men like Harrison, Polk, and even Zachary Taylor wrestled the presidency away from acknowledged statesmen and orators of the day such as Henry Clay and Daniel Webster.

Nevins noted, "No man can keep a full diary week after week, month after month, for four years, without revealing himself in it; and all of Polk's salient traits appear in these pages."[5] Nevins continues to add that Polk's "range of interests also was remarkably limited, and his mind strikes us as rather arid and inelastic. Did he ever read a novel in his life, or attend a nineteenth century play, or read any modern poetry? If so, the evidence is not here."[6] Polk's writing, however, is fluent, and writing appeared to come easily to him. Above all, it is honest but polite, and reflects Polk's inner character. As an example, when Polk was introduced to an acquaintance of a senator, Polk wrote how the visitor "put on a smiling and hypocritical air, and acted as though he had been one of my friends. I of course treated him civilly in my own office, but I felt great contempt for him."[7]

Polk's White House diary begins March 28, 1845. In an entry made exactly one year later, Polk relates the origins of the diary:

> Twelve months ago this day, a very important conversation took place in the Cabinet between myself and Mr. Buchanan on the Oregon question. This conversation was of so important a character, that I deemed it proper on the same evening to reduce the substance of it to writing for the purpose of retaining it more distinctly in my memory. This I did on separate sheets. It was this circumstance, which first suggested to me the idea, if not the necessity, of keeping a journal or diary of events and transactions, which might occur during my Presidency. I resolved to do so and accordingly procured a blank book for that purpose on the next day, in which I have every day since noted whatever occurred that I deemed of interest. Sometimes I have found myself so much engaged with my public duties, as to be able to make only a very condensed and imperfect statement of events and incidents which occurred, and to be forced to omit others altogether which I would have been pleased to have noted.[8]

A predominant impression that the reader of Polk's diary is left with is just how hard Polk worked. As president, he seemed constantly at his desk or in conference with either his cabinet or military advisors. Even on the last full day of his presidency, Polk was left to wrestle whether he was constitutionally empowered to veto a bill should Congress submit it to him. This dilemma occurred because inauguration day had fallen on a Sunday, and President-elect Taylor chose to wait until Monday, March 5, to be sworn in. Only Polk could imply that he was burdened with the technicality of having to deal with the affairs of the office up until the very end of his term, and he most likely did not relish the additional day given to him by Taylor refusing to take the oath until Monday.

Polk's White House diary is easily readable, so much in fact that one wonders whether he wrote it for future historians to peruse, and not just for his eyes only. It provides a good description of the inner workings of the office of the president, and creates a picture of how Washington, D.C., politics operated prior to the Civil War.

Polk died four months after leaving office and was not working on any manuscript at the time of his death.

Franklin Pierce

With his Democratic Party nomination as candidate for president in 1852, Franklin Pierce was given the nickname "Young Hickory of the Granite Hills," in reference to Andrew Jackson. As with Jackson, Pierce delegated someone else to write an authorized campaign biography for him. That someone else was none other than celebrated author Nathaniel Hawthorne.

Pierce and Hawthorne met while both were attending Bowdoin, a cadet academy, in 1821. Pierce biographer Roy Franklin Nichols wrote that their acquaintance "ripened into a friendship ... which resulted in insuring for himself his own greatest monument; for the mutual attachment between him and Nathaniel Hawthorne was life-long and led the latter to record a phrase of Pierce's personality which otherwise might never have survived."[1]

Pierce, who received his party's nomination on the 49th ballot, was not well known, and was aware of the value of a well-written biography. Hawthorne was a successful author by then, and Pierce reached out to him. Hawthorne quickly accepted Pierce's invitation, writing, "it has occurred to me that you might have some thoughts of getting me to write the necessary biography. Whatever service I can do you, I need not say, would be at your command."[2]

Pierce and Hawthorne spent time together during the course of the campaign, but as Roy Nichols noted, "Presumably Pierce never knew what this little volume cost its author. To [Pierce's] unreflecting mind it was all very simple. Hawthorne was an author, authors wrote biographies, and he needed a biography, what else was easier? But to the more sensitive artist it had been difficult. Writing was a matter of brooding and inspiration, of fancy and creation, and the necessary hurry was foreign to his mode of production. He had done it, but never deemed this effort worthy of inclusion with his other works."[3] Once elected, Pierce rewarded Hawthorne with a consulship in England.

Pierce's presidency was unrewarding, he lost the favoritism of his own party and was not nominated for a second term. By the time he left office in 1857 the last of his three children had died, and his wife, who suffered from depression, died in 1863. Hawthorne passed away a year later, leaving no one left to help author any possible memoirs. But by then Pierce had begun drinking heavily, perhaps choosing to forget any glories of the past instead of embracing them in print.

James Buchanan

> I have no regret for any public act of my life, and history will vindicate my memory.[1]
>
> —James Buchanan

James Buchanan's name is often included among the least successful presidencies, mainly because of his mishandling of the events that would quickly escalate into the Civil War. Buchanan, however, is noteworthy because he published the first presidential memoir.

Despite achieving an impressive political career that included the office of secretary of state, Buchanan was ill prepared to handle the growing crisis of the war, and had tired of the presidency by the time the 1860 election arrived. He did not seek the nomination of his party for a second term. Though retired from politics, Buchanan soon found himself the target of "violent, insulting & threatening letters," which were often "stuck under the back door of Wheatland," his Pennsylvania estate, warning that "the house would be set on fire some night."[2] On December 15, 1862, a resolution was even introduced in the Senate seeking censure and condemnation of the former president.

Buchanan refused to accept such charges without a fight. He answered claims of wrongdoing with signed letters in public newspapers, only to discover they inflamed the readership. It soon became apparent that the only way to offer his explanations and to silence his critics, was to author a full-fledged book explaining his actions. Therefore, Buchanan "began collecting documents and letters which he hoped someday to publish in vindication of his presidential policies."[3] In preparation for such an endeavor, Buchanan also "catalogued the charges against him and jotted down the main errors in them."[4]

Buchanan became consumed by vindicating his place in history. "Nobody seems to understand the course pursued by the late administration," he complained.[5] Jeremiah S. Black, a lifelong friend and former secretary of state under Buchanan, shared his feelings and became instrumental in launching a book proposal. "You owe it to friends and to your country to give them a full and clear vindication of your conduct & character. If this not be done, you will continue to be slandered for half a century to come."[6] Black offered to prepare a biography of Buchanan for the sum of $7,000, to which Buchanan agreed. It soon became apparent that Black and Buchanan disagreed on major points of the former president's war policy, and Black bluntly informed

Buchanan that he not only disagreed with these policies, but also could not write a book defending them. Black's biography of Buchanan was abandoned, although they remained friends.

Buchanan then decided to author the book himself. "I presume the biography is all over. I shall now depend on myself, with God's assistance," he wrote to his sister.[7] He threw himself into the task, collecting published documents as well as private correspondence from those who had served in his administration. Many of those who he sought letters from urged him not to attempt to publish the book as long as the war continued, as certain revelations would prove damaging to even then-president Lincoln. Biographer Philip S. Klein wrote, "The witch hunt had frightened everyone, and the last thing Buchanan's friends wanted at this moment was the truth about political events preceding Lincoln's inauguration. The republicans were equally unwilling to have the facts made public; they would crucify anyone who attempted to give a true account."[8] Buchanan finished the manuscript in late 1862 and sent it around to old friends such as Augustus Schell, who was a member of the New York Historical Society, for constructive criticism. In 1866, John Applewood published the manuscript under the title *Mr. Buchanan's Administration on the Eve of the Rebellion*. Buchanan had apparently listened to his friends and delayed the publication until after the war's end, noting in the preface that it was never his intention to embarrass neither Lincoln nor his administration.

In his 1962 biography of Buchanan, Klein noted, "The book, like its author, was dignified, restrained, and rather dull, but it marshalled the evidence in orderly array, documented it from official records, and presented a powerful case for his presidential policy."[9] Klein also wrote that Buchanan produced the book "as a historical document in the hope that in the years after his death, when passions had cooled, an organized record of his efforts to prevent the war might be available."[10]

Buchanan, however, still desired the "anecdotal biography" that Jeremiah Black had begun in 1861.[11] To assist him, Buchanan arranged for author James F. Shunk and his wife to live at Wheatland for the good part of a year and take notes while Buchanan reminisced. The couple returned to New York once they had enough material, but never wrote any book. Hoping that the third time would be the charm, Buchanan employed the literary talents of friend William B. Reed of Philadelphia, to resume where Shunk had left off. Now past the age of seventy-five, Buchanan displayed his sharp mind by paying Reed "an outright fee plus a conditional grant to his wife, for he knew that Reed procrastinated and thought that his wife might keep him at work if she knew she would get $5,000 when the job was done."[12] Reed asked Shunk for his notes but never received them, thus preventing him from completing what would have become the first authorized biography of a president.[13]

Perhaps the reason Buchanan was so persistent in having the biography completed was that it would compliment his *Administration on the Eve of Rebellion*, and add some much needed humility to his character. In the end, however, Buchanan's *Eve of Rebellion* never reached the desired effect its author hoped, and Buchanan's presidency remained firmly locked in the doldrums of American history. In her 2004 biography on Buchanan, historian Jean H. Baker noted how "Only [Richard] Nixon matched his strenuous after-the-fact effort to rehabilitate a failed presidency."[14]

Abraham Lincoln

> Writing—the art of communicating thoughts to the mind, through the eye—is the greatest invention of the world.[1]
> —Abraham Lincoln

Despite the fact that historians have placed Abraham Lincoln among the legions of great American writers, he never authored a complete book in his own lifetime. Except for a slim pamphlet of his literary talents, his 1860 Cooper Union Address, the Lincoln that history has come to know from his writings has largely been culled from letters and speeches. Editor David D. Anderson noted this fact in his introduction to *The Literary Works of Abraham Lincoln*, which was published in 1970:

> Abraham Lincoln was not a conscious literary artist, nor is there any evidence other than a few weak verses and several often-cited but perhaps apocryphal comments to suggest that he had ever held literary ambitions. Nevertheless, he is the only President of the United States—and the list of presidents includes several, particularly Theodore Roosevelt and Woodrow Wilson, who did consider themselves men of letters—whose writings regularly appear in anthologies of American literature. Yet, paradoxically, the writings that are collected in anthologies are not literature in the conventional sense—that is, they are not poems, stories, or essays; they are speeches and letters—but in each Lincoln has come close to laying bare the meaning of human life for his time and the ages.[2]

Anderson notes that Lincoln's attempts at creative writing were "conventional weak exercises, redeemed only by a sharpness of detail."[3] One example of Lincoln's creative writing was an autobiography written in 1860 for newspaper editor John L. Scripps. Lincoln wrote a concise autobiography of his life up until that point, but revealed little except for the fact that he had little formal schooling but enjoyed reading and writing. Lincoln also briefly dabbled with poetry, and an example was published in the August 25, 1838, issue of the *Sangamo Journal*. Although published anonymously, "The Suicide's Soliloquy," revealed Lincoln's dark and moody side, and was written during one of his battles with depression. Later examples of Lincoln's poetry can be found in existing letters, such as two ironically written to future vice president and presidential successor, Andrew Johnson.

From 1847 to 1849, Lincoln served a single term as a congressman from Illinois. Moving to the nation's capital would expose him to a wealth of books and libraries, which was a far cry from the homespun stories of young Lincoln walking miles to borrow a single book. In his book, *Congressman Lincoln*, author Chris DeRose imagined how Lincoln must have been enraptured by the huge collection. "A bibliophile, Lincoln from his earliest days on the frontier had read everything he could get his hands on. [But] Nothing could have possibly prepared him for the Library of Congress."[4] By then the Library had grown to about thirty thousand books, seven thousand of which had once belonged to Thomas Jefferson, and "it is something to imagine Congressman Lincoln, lying with his legs stretched out, reading a book from the personal collection of the third president."[5]

In 1858, Lincoln debated Stephen Douglas for the U.S. Senate. Lincoln would ultimately lose the election, but considered their series of seven debates worthy to be properly published as a whole. Esteemed historian and Lincoln biographer Harold Holzer, who has published more than forty books on Lincoln, noted how Lincoln threw himself into the project.

"Even since his Senate loss the year before, Lincoln had been "desirous of preserving in some permanent form, the late joint discussions between Douglas and myself." In other words, he wanted them published as a book. To facilitate such a project, he personally collected, and pasted into an oversized scrapbook, a complete run of debate transcript, the pro–Republican *Chicago Press and Tribune* reprints of his own remarks, and the pro–Democratic *Chicago Daily Times* reports of Douglas's. "In my own speeches I have corrected only a few small typographical errors," he wrote a prospective publisher. He was perfectly willing to allow Douglas, in turn, 'the right to correct typographical errors in his, if he desired."

As early as Christmas 1858, Lincoln was convinced that "my scrapbook will be reprinted," and by the following March several publishers were indeed expressing interest. But Lincoln was oddly reluctant to let the scrapbook out of his possession, and the proposal stalled. Not until he stumped Ohio for the Republicans in September 1859 was the project reinvigorated—and then, by chance. One day during his campaign tour, he inadvertently left his scrapbook behind in a hotel room. In frantically sending out the word that he wanted its safe return, he alerted local republicans to its existence; they, in turn, took up the idea that it should be reproduced. Before long, the Columbus publishers Follett, Foster & Co. made plans to put out an edition the following spring, and to include Lincoln's Ohio speeches as well.[6]

The Political Debates between Hon. Abraham Lincoln and Hon. Stephen A. Douglas in the celebrated Campaign of 1858 in Illinois was published in April 1860. The Lincoln Financial Foundation Collection describes a copy in their possession as being "Bound in cloth over bookstore wrapper, embossed covers, [with] gold lettering on spine."[7] It is 292 pages in length, and was apparently among one hundred copies that had been allocated to Lincoln as payment. Although Lincoln and Douglas are dually credited as co-authors, and the subject matter was from previously delivered speeches, it marks the first appearance of any significant body of Lincoln's work in book form.

Lincoln's second significant offering was procured from a February 1860 speech delivered at Cooper Union (Institute) in New York City. Known as the Cooper Union Address, it firmly established Lincoln as the leading Republican candidate for president. The address, which was delivered to an enthusiastic crowd, would quickly and repeatedly be published in pamphlet format by newspapers in Illinois and New York within days. After Lincoln secured the Republican Party nomination, the Republican Executive Congressional Committee also published an eight-page pamphlet of the Cooper Address. This was followed by Charles C. Nott of New York, who informed Lincoln that the Young Men's Central Republican Union wished to publish "a new edition in larger type & better form, with such notes & references as will best attract readers seeking information."[8] As with the publication of the Lincoln-Douglas Debates, Lincoln served as proofreader and editor to the expanded edition.

Proofreading his own work was something Lincoln was no stranger to. In *The Eloquent President*, author Ronald C. White recounted how Lincoln "made friends with newspaper reporters and editors. Lincoln, who in his debates with Douglas spoke without a full text of a manuscript, was beholden to newspaper reporters, who acted as stenographers in recording his own speeches. After an event he would often wander over to the newspaper office to check and revise the proofs before they were printed in the next edition."[9]

By mid-September, Charles Nott was able to deliver 250 copies of the new edition to Lincoln. At that time the edition would stand as the best-published work attributed to Lincoln. This fact was not missed on its author. "Lincoln was undoubtedly pleased by the production. The handsomely printed thirty-two page edition, [was] encased in a durable cover,

[and] featured thirty-five copious source notes."[10] Historian Harold Holzer observes that the edition was also a work of passion. "The result, the editors contended, was not just a pamphlet but a true "historical work—brief, compete, profound, impartial, truthful—which will survive the time and the occasion that called it forth, and be esteemed hereafter, no less for its intrinsic worth than its unpretending modesty."[11]

Holzer notes that Lincoln's Cooper Union address was significant because it "unleashed a tidal wave of celebrity nationwide" for the struggling candidate and allowed Lincoln to successfully campaign for president "without violating mid-nineteenth-century taboos against personal campaigning."[12] And perhaps most important, with the publication of his Cooper Union address, Lincoln "managed to electrify the media in the media center of the nation."[13]

It is pleasant to imagine Lincoln living past April 1865, and perhaps authoring a memoir after leaving office. If he had, it might have been compatible to Grant's published *Memoirs*. What Lincoln has left us can today be found in such works as *The Complete Works of Abraham Lincoln* (by John Nicolay and John Hay, 1894), and *The Collected Works of Abraham Lincoln*, which was edited by Roy P. Basler and published by the Abraham Lincoln Association in 1953. Basler had previously published *Abraham Lincoln, His Speeches and Letters*, in 1946, which included a Preface from Carl Sandburg. In it, Sandburg lamented the absence of a definitive collection of Lincoln's writings:

> Not yet has there been compiled and annotated a complete collection of the speeches and writings of Abraham Lincoln. No definitive work in this field has as yet come into existence. If there were such a work it would be heavy to use, it would be loaded with repetitious material, it would be cumbersome, definitely lack convenience, certainly not a handy volume. Of course such a complete and definitive collection of Lincoln utterances is wanted and needed. There are those students of Lincoln who give themselves the assignment of reading every last available word written or spoken by Lincoln.[14]

Basler's collection is noteworthy for anyone desiring to understand Lincoln as a writer. His wonderful essay, "Lincoln's Development as a Writer," which was included in the 1946 edition, is considered essential reading.

Today there are numerous volumes and editions covering Lincoln the writer. In 1991, as an example, Applewood Books published a slim volume titled *The Poems of Abraham Lincoln*.

In 1928, the *Atlantic Monthly* magazine, hungry for anything possibly authored by Lincoln, published a previously unknown cache of letters titled "Lincoln the Lover." The letters, claimed to be written by Lincoln to Ann

Rutledge, his first love, were ultimately revealed to be fakes, thus predating the most famous literary hoax of all time: the infamous 1984 "Hitler Diaries."

Historian David D. Anderson summed up Lincoln's essence as a writer. "Lincoln's greatness as a writer defies categorization because he did not become a great writer in any conventional sense. Rather he became a great writer because in himself he incorporated all of the American experience and its ideological basis, because he distilled both through his own intrinsic rationality and emotion, and then, in a few clear, concise, pregnant statements, he gave voice and meaning to the combination of harshness and hope, materialism and faith that is the foundation of his country."[15]

Andrew Johnson

In assuming the remainder of Lincoln's second term, Andrew Johnson witnessed a turbulent administration dealing with Reconstruction as well as an attempt at impeachment. After losing his party's nomination in 1868, Johnson returned to his native state of Tennessee. In 1875, shortly before his death, Johnson returned to politics as a United States Senator from Tennessee. Johnson had always maintained that his successful return to political life was the only vindication he needed to clear his name and silence his critics. From 1869 to 1875, however, Johnson was approached numerous times with the suggestion that he write his memoirs, or at least an account of his administration for the sake of history. Johnson had always disregarded the idea of authoring any such book, despite James Buchanan doing so in 1866. Whether Johnson was familiar with Buchanan's *Administration on the Eve of Rebellion* is not known, but if he had read it, Johnson most likely would have sided with the majority of historians who dismissed the book and considered it of little value towards properly assessing Buchanan's administration.

Letters show that Johnson was approached by J. Scott Payne on May 3, 1869, less than two months after leaving office, with a plea to furnish material for a proper biography.

Dear Sir,

Being desirous of writing a biography of yourself, and a history of your public services I find myself unable to proceed in the performance of this task without *reliable data*, of your early life personal—and public, and am unable to procure the same, without personal application, to yourself. I therefore respectfully request that you will furnish such material as will be useful, in the compilation of such a work as I desire to present it to the public—a work which I desire to make complete, including, your whole history up to the termination of your administration, on the 4th day of March 1869.

If my proposal meets with your favorable consideration (which I ask—) I would be pleased to adopt any suggestions you might feel inclined to offer, in the way of advice. I especially desire such data, as will give me a full & complete history of the formation of the state of government of Tennessee & the part you took therein. This is a subject on which but little light is thrown, by and history of the times, I have been able to procure.[1]

Paul Bergeron, who edited the *Papers of Andrew Johnson*, noted, "There is no evidence that Johnson responded or that Payne proceeded further with this project."[2] Johnson was later approached by William W. Hicks, publisher of the *XIX Century*, in the hopes of getting Johnson to contribute articles for the magazine:

> Now, my dear sir, honor us with one of your able papers. Let us have the honor of publishing a series of papers over your own signature to the people of the United States.
>
> We circulate everywhere, and are your unflinching friends. At this juncture, words from you, sir, would go far towards consolidating the masses against radical corruption, and we, of the people, will thereby be able to present you again to the people for what we are proud to feel is your proper place.
>
> If your time is too occupied to write, would you dictate to our stenographer such articles as would appear to you proper to publish at this time.
>
> My Dear Sir, Gov. Perry and all your friends would hail your advent in our pages with delight and hope, and the case of the South and West will be at once secured.[3]

As with J. Scott Payne's earlier letter, William Hicks' solicitation was also met with no response from Johnson, despite the offer of a paid stenographer. In June 1871, Johnson received a letter from Joseph S. Fowler, suggesting that Johnson write a speech to defend his administration and then publish it in the newspapers. "You should make a speech some place on your administration as military governor and as president, contrasting your purposes and policy with that since. This speech should be carefully written condensed so as to give a history of your administration in a form that will do to publish in the Newspapers & after the style of your messages. This should be prepared with great care. I would seriously recommend the preparation of such a speech. Let this be the effort of your life."[4]

As with the previous efforts, Johnson failed to reply, and in the following February Fowler once again wrote the former president. "Have you commenced writing up your Administration? The work besides vindicating your course would vindicate all who have been condemned with you. It would be useful to the country. It would be of great use in the coming conflicts between consolidation and Union."[5]

There appears to be a pressing urgency for Johnson to defend his administration in the letters of Hicks and Fowler. This was apparently from criticism stemming from the Grant administration. Johnson and Grant were adversaries, and Grant would later openly criticize Johnson's policy regarding reconstruction in his *Personal Memoirs*. In the end, Johnson avoided defending himself by writing any newspaper and magazine articles. He also never authored any autobiography or memoir of his administration. It was against his nature to write from the heart. So much so, that when a cholera epidemic struck Johnson in 1873, historian Paul Bergeron noted that being "seriously ill and not certain of surviving, he committed his inner thoughts to paper, an extraordinary rare action for him."[6] With his 1875 election, or "vindication," as he referred to it, Andrew Johnson played out the final days of his life not on the written page, but on the floor of the United States Senate.

Ulysses S. Grant

> If any one had suggested the idea of my becoming an author, as they frequently did, I was not sure whether they were making sport of me or not.[1]
>
> —Ulysses S. Grant

Following Grant's two terms as president from 1869 to 1877, the very thought of writing a personal memoir was the furthest thing from the former general's mind. Finally free of the responsibilities that came with the nation's highest office, Grant traveled the globe with his wife and received a warm welcome everywhere they went.

At the 1880 Republican Convention there was a movement to draft Grant's name for the presidential nomination. Though Grant had tired of politics, he admitted he would accept the nomination if offered. This caused a brief deadlock in the balloting process, but eventually Grant's name fell through, and James Garfield won the nomination. Grant had little faith in Garfield, and was constantly giving him unsolicited advice. After Garfield's assassination, Grant badgered Chester Arthur as well. Around this same time, Grant began investing heavily in the stock market and became a silent partner in the Wall Street firm of Grant & Ward. Grant proved to be naive regarding financial matters, and quickly lost the family fortunes.

Having little left to their name, the Grants spent the summer of 1884 in a cottage at Long Branch, New Jersey. The three-story cottage, partly owned by newspaper publisher George Childs and railroad magnate George Pullman,

Ulysses S. Grant writing his *Personal Memoirs* on the porch of his cottage at Mt. McGregor in 1885. Despite a race against cancer, Grant was able to deliver the finished manuscript to Mark Twain, who published it shortly after Grant's death (Library of Congress).

was intended for Grant's use whenever he felt necessary. While at Long Branch, Grant was approached by Robert Underwood Johnson, an editor at *The Century Magazine*, who proposed that Grant write a series of articles describing his Civil War battles for publication. Grant had received prior offers to write, but had always rejected them. Like Andrew Jackson, Grant preferred to have others write for him. An example was Adam Badeau, who had served as Grant's secretary during the Civil War. In 1868, Badeau had published the *Military History of General Grant*, which had comprised three volumes, and left Grant feeling they were the superior reference.

While Grant's reading preferences were not known, he did admit in his *Memoirs* that while a cadet at West Point Military Academy, he read mainly novels instead of books related to his studies. "It is difficult to know how important this world of imaginative literature remained for Grant. In later life he disliked discussing literary matters, perhaps because of his lack of formal training or possibly because he liked the books themselves better than the talk about them."[2] Grant went as far as to avoid such conversation even if it helped him appear intelligent. In a letter to wife Julia, Grant recalled a dinner guest who attempted to discuss literature with him. "After a while, he made some allusion to a character of Dickens. I was equally ignorant of poor little Oliver. So the old gentleman gave me up, and I enjoyed the rest of the evening."[3]

There were several other reasons why Grant had avoided writing for publication up to this time. One was his spelling. Author Richard Goldhurst noted how Grant's "spelling was notorious, even subversive."[4] Goldhurst's biography went on to suggest that perhaps yet another reason why Grant had always shunned writing his memoirs was that Grant had a superstitious nature.

> He dreaded retracing his steps. He had developed this peculiarity as a boy and it stayed with him all his life. Once he started to go anywhere or do anything, he would not turn back or stop until he had accomplished the thing intended. In later years he explained, "I have frequently started to go places where I had never been and to which I did not know the way, depending upon making inquiries on the road, and if I got past the place without knowing it, instead of turning back I would go on until a road was found turning in the right direction, take that, and come in by the other side." He carried this superstition to obsessional lengths. One night in Virginia while fighting Lee, Grant and his retinue lost their way. Grant steadfastly refused to return to his headquarters by the way he had come. Finally, in exasperation, one of his aides pointed out they were about to run into the Confederate picket lines. The general also amazed several friends in New York when he would not reenter his 66th Street house to reclaim an umbrella he had forgotten. With no servant in sight, Grant insisted on walking around the block before going back in. This fear had kept him from describing his personal military history. Recapturing the past is retracing one's steps. Now he had a reason for writing—his desperate need of money—more compelling than any reason for not writing. Like a soldier who does not relish his orders, he began planning what help he would have to recruit in order to charge over the ground again.[5]

Johnson offered Grant a proposal to write four articles at $500 per article, and Grant agreed immediately. Grant quickly devoted himself to the project, writing for several hours every day, with Johnson returning to Long Branch at times to "coach the General in what was wanted."[6] Johnson also discovered that Grant possessed "one gift that a writer cannot be taught: clarity. As President, he had written all his policy papers, and though not always politic, they were always clear."[7] Grandson Ulysses S. Grant III also recalled his grandfather's approach to writing:

> Instead of finding the work tiresome or boring, he found the recollections of victories won pleasant and interesting. It is true that the first draft of the article on Shiloh was completed in four pages and that was all the general intended to say about it, feeling that he had told the essential facts and that the public must know the rest of the story. However, with the family's and [Adam] Badeau's urging, he realized that there might be interest in some of the incidents and how he felt toward them—for instance, that his sword had been hit by a bullet and a horse killed under him. There were other incidents, which he was persuaded to write about, and in writing of them he became interested and was led to add comments and other people's actions. Having cast off the requirements of formal detachment that he imposed upon himself in all his official writings, he now found some interest in describing the picture more completely. And so he produced an article of reasonable size, which, with the one that followed on Vicksburg, was interesting enough to the public. In fact, he was surprised at his ability to produce something with so much human interest.[8]

Goldhurst also noted how "Grant was discovering that writing agreed with him. He had long been in awe of generals who could write their own books; now he found he too had this facility. The General worked in an upstairs room on a white pine table usurped from the kitchen, his materials spread before him. Julia came often and sat in a wicker chair to watch him pore over maps with the old intensity."[9]

The zeal that Grant had thrown himself into over writing the *Century* articles did not go unnoticed, and soon Grant found himself being entertained by company president Roswell Smith. It was Smith who suggested that Grant write a book. Sitting on the cottage's veranda, Smith pitched the idea to a skeptical Grant by comparing him to Napoleon Bonaparte.

It was about this time that Grant was paid a visit by literary figure Mark Twain. The two had met before, and got along well. Like other publishers, Twain suggested that Grant try his hand at writing. With pressing financial concerns now upon him, Grant agreed to give it a try. Although Twain had a pleasant visit, Grant never brought up his recent business with *Century*. In his autobiography, Twain recalled how he learned of Grant's dealings with the magazine:

> I was reading one night in Chickering Hall early in November 1884, and as my wife and I were leaving the building we stumbled over Mr. Gilder, the editor of the *Century*, and went home with him to a late supper at his house. We were there an hour or two and in the course of the conversation Gilder said that General Grant had written three war articles for the *Century* and was going to write a fourth. I pricked up my ears. Gilder went on to describe how eagerly General Grant had entertained the proposition

to write when it had last been put to him and how poor he evidently was and how eager to make some trifle of bread and butter money and how the handing him a check for $500 for the first article had manifestly gladdened his heart and lifted from it a mighty burden.

The thing which astounded me was, that, admirable man as Gilder certainly is, and with a heart which is in the right place, it had never seemed to occur to him that to offer General Grant $500 for a magazine article was not only the monumental insult of the nineteenth century, but of all centuries.... Gilder went on to say that it had been impossible, months before, to get General Grant to write a single line, but that now that he had gotten started it was going to be as impossible to stop him again; that, in fact, General Grant had set out deliberately to write his memoirs in full and to publish them in book form.[10]

Twain visited Grant the next morning, and Grant confirmed Gilder's story. Twain asked whether a contract had been signed, and when Grant said no, asked if he could read it, since he himself "had a long and painful experience in book making and publishing," and believed his opinion might be of use.[11] When Grant read the terms of the contract, Twain "didn't know whether to laugh or cry."[12]

Whenever a publisher in the trade thinks enough of the chances of an unknown author's book to print it and put it on the market, he is willing to risk paying the man 10 per cent royalty and that is what he does pay him. He can well venture that much of a royalty but he cannot well venture any more. If that book shall sell 3,000 or 4,000 copies there is no loss on any ordinary book, and both parties have made something; but whenever the sale shall reach 10,000 copies the publisher is getting the lion's share of the profits and would continue to get the lion's share as long thereafter as the book should continue to sell.

Now, here was a book that was mortally bound to sell several hundred thousand copies in the first year of its publication and yet the Century had the hardihood to offer General Grant the very same 10 per cent royalty which they would have offered to any unknown Comanche Indian whose book they had reason to believe might sell 3,000 or 4,000 or 5,000 copies.

I told General Grant that the Century offer was simply absurd and should not be considered for an instant.[13]

Twain suggested Grant request a royalty of 20 percent, or 70 percent of the profits after costs had been met. He told him Century should accept this, but if not to shop the manuscript around to other publishers. Should no other publisher agree to the terms, Twain asked that he be allowed to publish Grant's book. At the time he was preparing to publish his own book, *Huckleberry Finn*, under the imprint of Charles L. Webster & Co., which Twain believed to be "the best-equipped subscription establishment in the country."[14] Twain admitted, "I wanted the General's book and I wanted it very much, but I had very little expectation of getting it. I supposed that he would lay these new propositions before the Century people, that they would accept immediately, and that the matter would end."[15]

Twain then left for a western speaking tour, instructing Charles Webster, his business partner, to stay in touch with Grant. Subscriptions for *Century* increased after the magazine advertised Grant's articles and Twain estimated the articles were worth $100,000. Perhaps suspecting that Grant would soon realize that his talents as a writer were undervalued, Century sent Grant an additional check in the amount of $1,000. This only caused Twain to confirm his suspicions that Century was taking advantage of Grant. Richard Goldhurst notes that Roswell Smith did not attempt to "secure the book [earlier] because he was a gentleman publisher, which is to say he was a cautious businessman."[16] Roswell even "thought advances [were] bad policy," which no doubt hurt his chances after Twain had talked to Grant.[17]

With Grant's son, Fred, now on his side, Twain watched from the sidelines as publishers such as Century and American Publishing Company easily matched the terms Twain had laid out for the former president. Grant now understood how close he had come to accepting a bad deal, and was inclined to let Twain properly publish the book. To say that Twain was generous in his dealings with Grant is an understatement.

> In the course of one of my business talks with General Grant he asked me if I felt sure I could sell 25,000 copies of his book and he asked the question in such a way that I suspected that the Century people had intimated that that was about the number of the books that they thought ought to sell.
>
> I replied that the best way for a man to express an opinion in such a case was to put it in money, therefore, I would make this offer: if he would give me the book I would advance him the sum of $25,000 on each volume the moment the manuscript was placed in my hands, and if I ever got the $50,000 back again, out of future copyrights due, I would never ask him to return any part of the money to me.
>
> The suggestion seemed to *distress* him. He said he could not think of taking in advance any sum of money large or small which the publisher would not be absolutely *sure* of getting back again.... This was just like General Grant. It was absolutely impossible for him to entertain for a moment any proposition, which might prosper him at the risk of any other man."[18]

During the course of finalizing his contract with Grant, Twain was approached by Fred Grant and asked whether it would possible to advance his father some badly needed cash. Twain was aware of the Grant's dire financial circumstances and quietly agreed to the request. Twain went as far as to include language in the publishing contract transferring the book to Grant's wife, Julia, so Grant's creditors could not seize the book's proceeds. In his autobiography, Twain described the $1,000 check written out to Grant as "a circumstance which I have never spoken of and which cannot be known for many years to come, for this paragraph must not be published until the mention of so private a matter cannot offend any living person."[19] Twain went to great lengths to suppress the extent of Grant's financial problems from the public, thus sparing the former general and president much embarrassment.

Twain found it difficult to let go of his criticism over Grant's dealings with Century, and constantly railed against what he considered an insensitive publisher. "It was a shameful thing that the man who saved this country and its government from destruction should still be in a position where so small a sum—so trivial an amount—as $1,000, could be looked upon as a godsend. Everybody knew the General was in reduced circumstances, but what a storm would have gone up all over the land if the people could have known that his poverty had reached such a point as this."[20]

Robert Underwood Johnson, who had first approached Grant successfully as a writer for *Century Magazine* wrote, "The General, who knew nothing of the customs or etiquette of the publishing business, had been won over by the humorist. It was not a time for a contest, nor was it a book to be contended for in the customary fashion, and Mr. Roswell Smith, pocketing his disappointment, wrote a polite and generous letter to the General conveying our regrets that we were not to be associated with so distinguished an enterprise and our cordial wishes for its success."[21] Twain, a "Grant-intoxicated man," had won.[22]

It was during the writing of his *Memoirs* that Grant was diagnosed with throat cancer in the summer of 1884. At first Grant kept the news even from his wife, but eventually discussed it casually among friends. Ulysses S. Grant III recalled a conversation Grant had with some old acquaintances. "Shortly after this exchange the general took out his cigar case and said: "Gentlemen, this is the last cigar I shall ever smoke." He continued, "The doctors tell me I will never live to finish the work on which my whole energy is centered these days if I do not cease indulging in these fragrant weeds. It is hard to give up a cherished friend that has been your comforter and solace through many weary nights and days. But my unfinished work must be completed, for the sake of those that are near and dear to me."[23]

Twain would pay Grant a visit at Grant's New York City home in February 1885. By then, Grant's condition had become well known and was being reported in the newspapers. Twain recalled the visit in his *Autobiography*:

> After the 21st of February General Grant busied himself daily as much as his strength would allow in revising the manuscript of his book. It was read to him by Colonel Grant very carefully and he made the corrections as he went along. He was losing valuable time because only one-half or two-thirds of the second and last volume was as yet written. However, he was more anxious that what was written should be *absolutely* correct than that the book should be finished in an incorrect form and then find himself unable to correct it. His memory was superb and nearly any other man with such a memory would have been satisfied to trust it. Not so the General. No matter how sure

he was of the fact or the date, he would never let it go until he had verified it with the official records. This constant and painstaking searching of the records cost a great deal of time, but it was not wasted. Everything stated as a fact in General Grant's book may be accepted with entire confidence as being thoroughly trustworthy.[24]

It was a few days after Twain's visit that Grant formally signed the publishing contract with Charles L. Webster & Company on February 27, 1885. Prior to signing the contract, the subject of allowing the *Century* articles to be incorporated into Grant's *Memoirs* was brought up. Having navigated publishing rights before, Twain felt a proper inquiry should be performed and looked into the matter.

> Some time after the contract for General Grant's book was completed, I found that nothing but a verbal understanding existed between General Grant and the Century Company giving General Grant permission to use his century articles in his book. There is a law of custom which gives an author the privilege of using his magazine article in any way he pleases after it shall appear in the magazine, and this law of custom is so well established that an author never expects to have any difficulty about getting a magazine copyright transferred to him whenever he shall ask for it with the purpose in view of putting it in a book.[25]

Twain, Charles Webster, and their lawyer then met with Roswell Smith at Century's offices where the mutually agreed upon understanding was formally put in writing. It was while there that Twain made another discovery. Century produced a signed receipt from Grant stipulating the sum of $500 as payment for the magazine articles, as well as for use in a future book published by Century. Hence, *Century* had considered Grant's articles fully paid for, and reprinting them in a book of their own would not entitle Grant to any additional payment or royalty. Twain considered this to be "the sharpest trade I have ever heard of," and added that Century were "buying ten-dollar gold pieces from General Grant at twenty-five cents apiece," while not finding anything unfair about it.[26] During the course of the meeting, Roswell Smith also disclosed that the reason Century did not agree to the terms of Grant's contract was that they would not insure the sale of 25,000 sets. "I wouldn't risk such a guarantee on any book that was published," he told Twain.[27] Twain wrote that such a remark was "more evidence that the Century people had no more just idea of the value of the book than as many children might be expected to have."[28]

While Twain and Grant's lawyers nailed down any loose contractual language, Grant continued to write. By now, Grant was in pain and was being seen by Dr. John Hancock Douglas, a throat specialist. Douglas treated Grant with cocaine, which was applied topically with a brush to the cancerous area in the back of Grant's throat. After consulting with other doctors, it was agreed that medical procedures would be useless. Therefore, Grant's inoperable tumor would continue to grow and discharge mucus while Grant struggled to finish the manuscript. Biographer William E. Woodard described Grant's diminishing health in his final months:

> The uncertain physicians, doubtful of their own knowledge, came and went, while the General sat in an armchair in his library and talked huskily to a stenographer. His face was lean and drawn into deep lines of suffering; now and then he would have to stop his dictation because of pain. As the disease progressed he huddled more deeply in his chair under a pile of shawls and blankets. After a month or two of dictation his voice failed. Thereafter he sat with a writing board on his lap and wrote with a pencil on large sheets of paper.[29]

In the spring of 1885, the Grant's accepted an invitation to escape New York City and spend the summer at the Mount McGregor estate of Joseph Drexel, of Drexel, Morgan & Company. Mount McGregor was located in an area known as the Adirondacks, and Drexel's cottage was about the size of a Queen Anne house and featured a wide piazza on three sides, a feature that most likely appealed to Grant as he enjoyed sitting outdoors. So Grant could remain comfortable during the trip, William Vanderbilt loaned his private New York Central rail car. At Mount McGregor, the writing of *Memoirs* became "a race with death."[30] Grant's wife, Julia, wrote how the manuscript "occupied every leisure moment. He even wrote at night sometimes when sleep would not come to him. It was a happy thought that suggested that book. He worked on and on in his labor of love, his health gradually failing."[31] Mrs. Grant also found Drexel's cottage a welcome change from the city, and noted how it rallied her husband's spirits.

> This cottage was not only comfortable but elegantly, yet simply, furnished with everything that one could wish for. Within five hundred yards of the cottage was a fine new hotel, from which our table was daily served.
> How grateful it was to the General, as he sat resting from his writing on the wide, cool piazza, to see the hundreds of people who daily passed the cottage with uncovered heads, all anxious to get a glimpse of him.... The General could not be induced to rest long on the piazza. He was so anxious about his book, so afraid of not being able to finish it. After sitting awhile with us, he would take out his little tablets and write, "It is very pleasant to be here, but I must go to my writing or I fear my book will not be finished.[32]

In late April, the *New York World* published a story that stated that Grant had not written his own book. The newspaper had apparently received its information from General George P. Ihrie, who had served with Grant in Mexico. It was Ihrie who had "inadvertently remarked to a Washington columnist that [Grant] was no writer."[33] The *World* took the remark as fact and declared in their April 29 editions that "The work upon his new book about which so much has been said is the work of General Adam Badeau. General

Grant has furnished all of the material and all of the ideas in the memoirs but Badeau has done the work of composition. The most the General has done upon the book has been to prepare the rough notes and memoranda for its various chapters. He is so great that he can well afford to have the exact truth told about him."[34]

Twain was outraged at the accusations that he wrote to Fred Grant and considered suing for libel. After having his lawyers look into initiating a suit, Twain observed that the *World's* damage had not been repeated in any other publication, and wrote Charles Webster to let the matter drop stating, "I recognize the fact that for General Grant to sue the *World* would be an enormously valuable advertisement for that daily issue of nonmedicated closet-paper."[35]

Grant himself became embroiled by the libelous claims and addressed the matter in a letter to publisher Charles Webster. In the letter, Grant responded to the charges of Adam Badeau doing most of the writing. The letter was leaked to the press, and several newspapers published it along with statements supporting the general's claims. Badeau, however, viewed the recent events from a different prospective and used the opportunity to address several issues with Grant.

Badeau had in fact been working with Grant on the *Memoirs*, but as an assistant. Badeau, who mainly provided editing services, had a signed agreement with Grant that he would receive $5,000 out of the first $20,000 made from the book, and an additional $5,000 if it made $30,000. As an author himself, Badeau claimed to have put aside his own work that caused his income to suffer. This was all noted in a long letter Badeau left with Grant before he could open it. Also contained in Badeau's letter were seemingly spiteful feelings towards Grant. "Your book is to have a circulation of hundreds of thousands, and the larger its circulation the greater its importance—the more completely it will stamp out mine…. Yours is not and will not be the work of a literary man, but the simple story of a great general. Proper for you, but not such as would add to my credit."[36]

In this short passage, Badeau reveals the jealously that must have been pressing upon him for sometime. He knew Grant's book would surely injure further sales of his own *Military History of U.S. Grant*, which up until then was considered the essential Grant biography. Badeau also touted himself as being an accomplished author while dismissing Grant as a simple storyteller. Badeau wanted his contract with Grant rewritten to include a monthly salary of $1,000 as well as an overall percentage of the profits. Badeau was said to be "an arrogant man, often discourteous" and "the strangest of the strange men who were close to Ulysses Grant."[37] Biographer William S.

McFeely believed that "Badeau was probably a homosexual," and despite his "regularly irregular" habits, was "very intelligent."[38]

Grant would have none of it, and imagined Badeau tinkering with the book long after his death, while being paid $1,000 a month. Having been on the blunt end of bad business deals long enough, Grant fought any idea of making Badeau a partner and taking a percentage of his family's desperately needed profits. Unwilling to re-negotiate, Grant ended the professional relationship, but let Badeau know he would always be welcome as a friend. Badeau replied with a polite letter reaffirming Grant's authorship of *Memoirs*, and stating that he would send for his belongings. In his 1981 biography of Grant, McFeely attempted to understand the relationship between the two:

> It was hard indeed to know why Grant was drawn to Badeau; the 105 letters that Grant wrote to him—and that Badeau proudly printed in *Grant in Peace*—are devoid of any hint of intimacy. But apparently Badeau was one of the members of Grant's staff who somehow managed to make Grant comfortable without in any way being a threat to him, one of those who could perhaps sense his power (and think they understood it), but were not in any way a psychological obstruction to him.... And the critical clue to understanding the difficult relationship between the two men is that both were writers.[39]

McFeely also felt that "Badeau did not pick up Grant's oblique hint that he was doing his own work; instead, he arrived hoping to win immortality by putting into literary form the words of the dying general. It did not occur to him that Grant could write a book."[40] In the end, Badeau's jealously and resentfulness became apparent, especially regarding Twain's involvement as his business manager. Twain's undivided attention to Grant's financial well being and seeing that he received a more-than-fair publishing deal must have stung an established author like Badeau, who most likely had to navigate his own way around the publishing business.

In May 1885, Twain visited Grant at Mount McGregor. Grant was no longer able to eat, and his appearance was thin. He was also unable to speak, and communicated by notes. Despite his pain, Grant gave no indication of his discomfort and continued writing. Ulysses S. Grant III noted that "Dr. Douglas feared the worst day would be when the general had finished his book, evidently fearful of the general's succumbing to his illness when he had accomplished the mission he had set for himself."[41] In a note to son Fred, Grant gave his thoughts concerning the manuscript, writing, "I feel much relieved this morning. I had begun to feel that the work of getting my book together was making but slow progress. I find it about completed, and the work now to be done is mostly after it gets back in galleys. It can be sent to the printer faster than he is ready for it. There [are] from one hundred and fifty to two hundred pages more than I had intended. Will cut nothing out of interest. It is possible we may find a little repetition. The whole of that, however, is not likely to amount to many pages."[42]

Julia Grant claimed Grant finished work on the book on July 19. He insisted the publisher's deadline be kept and that nothing interfere with the book's progress. In one of his last communications Grant wrote how he "hoped the book will live."[43] Four days later, on the morning of July 23, 1885, Ulysses S. Grant died. When told of his death, Twain remarked he believed working on the book had kept Grant alive.

Prior to Grant's death, Twain had orders for 100,000 sets of the two-volume book. By the end of September sales of 250,000 sets were reported by subscription. With Grant now dead and no further obstructions standing in the way of final publication, *Memoirs* was sent to the printer and released to the public. In the book's preface, Grant gave a brief explanation of the book's origins, noting, "Although frequently urged by friends to write my memoirs I had determined never to do so."[44] Grant briefly explained his financial problems, along with the appearance of *Century Magazine*, and how he found writing a pleasant experience. Most notably, Grant did not want the book to reopen any bad feelings left by the war, adding, "In preparing these volumes for the public, I have entered upon the task with the sincere desire to avoid doing injustice to anyone, whether on the National or Confederate side."[45]

Despite its two volume bulk, *Memoirs* only briefly deals with Grant's boyhood years. Although the Mexican-American War is covered, *Memoirs* largely deals with the Civil War, and does not concern Grant's presidency. The book is remarkable by Grant's ability to recollect minute details despite being in the heat of battle, such as in this passage:

> The shells and balls whistled about our ears very fast for about a minute. I do not think it took us longer than that to get out of range and out of sight. In the sudden start we made, Major Hawkins lost his hat. He did not stop to pick it up. When we arrived at a perfectly safe position we halted to take an account of damages. McPherson's horse was panting as if ready to drop. On examination it was found that a ball had struck him forward of the flank just back of the saddle, and had gone entirely through. In a few minutes the poor beast dropped dead; he had given no sign of injury until we came to a stop. A ball had struck the metal scabbard of my sword, just below the hilt, and broken it nearly off; before the battle was over it had broken off entirely. There were three of us; one had lost a horse, killed; one a hat and one a sword-scabbard. All were thankful that it was no worse.[46]

Grant also went to great lengths to express respect and admiration for General Robert E. Lee, despite being his adversary. In writing *Memoirs*, Grant avoided dissecting the Civil War as scholars and historians would have, and stayed true to his own voice. The end result was a story told with humility and void of nonessential data. Grant wrote history not only as he remembered it, but also how he felt. One hundred years later, author Shelby Foote would best convey what Grant felt while writing his multi-volume epic, *The Civil War*, noting how there was "a satisfaction to be gotten from surrounding a historical event, assimilating it so to speak, and making it your own. It belongs to you thereafter, and when you go and stand on the ground, you feel and hear it all around you."[47]

Julia Grant's first royalty check from Mark Twain was in the amount of $200,000. *Memoirs* would soon earn Grant's estate a total of half a million dollars, and repay Grant's debts. Twain was also satisfied with the finished book, and only expressed second thoughts in a humorous exchange with Henry Beecher Ward. When asked whether Grant included any references to his drinking in the book, Twain realized the impact it could have made, and wrote, "I wish I had thought of it. I would have said to General Grant: "Put the drunkenness in."[48]

Not only did *Memoirs* become a then-contemporary best seller, it remains among the classic histories of the Civil War. Biographer William S. McFeely noted the book's "conciseness, totality, and strength, but what is perhaps most striking is the timeless quality of the prose."[49] So exceptional are Grant's *Memoirs*, that when former President Jimmy Carter expressed a desire to write his memoirs, he was advised to study Grant's book. "Rosalynn and I both agreed to write memoirs after leaving the White House, and we went determined to make them both interesting and commercially successful. The historians we consulted warned us not to be defensive or attempt to rewrite history. They also told us it was generally agreed that the best autobiographical work ever written by a president was the memoirs of Ulysses Grant."[50]

Speculation remains whether Grant used his illness to help sell his story. The fact that Grant wrote much of the manuscript in full view of the public, while sitting on a porch exposed to endless rounds of gawking tourists, remains unique. Most writers prefer to be left alone and undisturbed while working.

Another question is whether Grant's use of medicinal cocaine enhanced his performance as a writer. Numerous medical journals note the drug's ability to produce a lucid state of being and to aid memory. In *Cocaine: An Unauthorized Biography*, author Dominic Stratfeild observed that "when you're on it you're up, fast and running. You're feeling pretty much invincible and fear of embarrassment or failure simply does not feature."[51] The fact that cocaine supplied the user with a seemingly endless supply of adrenaline and enabled them to participate in marathon sessions of physical, as well as mental, activity has later aided many an artist and writer. Novelist Stephen King became addicted to cocaine in the late 1970s and despite the danger, acknowledged its powers. "Cocaine was my *on* switch, and it seemed like a really good energizing drug. You try some and think, "Wow, why haven't I been taking this for years?' So you take a bit more and write a novel and decorate the house and mow the lawn and then you're ready to start a new novel again."[52]

While Grant's doctors authorized and supervised his medicinal use of cocaine, its pharmaceutical use was not as regulated as is today. Grant was even permitted to self medicate at times. The fact that he was writing a book using personal memories while taking the drug could have enhanced or colored his recollections. It could have also eradicated his earlier fears that any attempt at writing would have exposed him to folly.

Memoirs became the first best seller authored by a president, and changed the way publishers did business with former, as well as future office holders. Unlike most of the rambling, self-serving, political notions and opinions authored by some of his predecessors, Grant's recollection of the American Civil War was something almost every American wanted to read, and could.

Rutherford B. Hayes

> There is a world of useful information on public affairs in J.Q.A[dam]s' Diary.[1]
> —Rutherford B. Hayes

Rutherford B. Hayes joins John Quincy Adams and James Knox Polk as presidents who kept an active diary while in the White House. While this would become a common practice in the mid-twentieth century, Adams, Polk, and Hayes's diaries stand out because they were written within the first century of the establishment of the office of president.

In 1964, T. Harry Williams edited the manuscript of the diary, which was housed among the collections of the Rutherford B. Hayes Library in Fremont, Ohio. Williams included only the portions of the diary that were written while Hayes was the Republican nominee, president-elect, and president. This 1964 edition was given the title of *Hayes: The Diary of a President 1875–1881*. Prior to this edition, the Ohio State Archaeological and Historical Society had published the *Diary and Letters of Rutherford Birchard Hayes* in five volumes from 1922 to 1926. In the preface of the 1964 edition it is noted, "Although the collection has some merit, it contains serious flaws and does not measure up to modern scholarly standards. The diary entries are incomplete, practically no notes are supplied, and Mr. [Charles R.] Williams chose to edit freely the language of the diarist. From the viewpoint of readability, much was lost by interspersing sections of the diary with letters from Hayes's correspondence."[2]

T. Harry Williams did away with a great deal of the clutter from the 1922–26 edition, and noted the fact:

> Obviously, a presidential diary can be a very valuable and interesting document. The Hayes diary is both. It is written in a sprightly style and contains all kinds of information. Unfortunately it is not a full diary, that is, maintained from day to day. In periods of great activity, such as campaigns, Hayes wrote sparingly or not at all. Thus, the diary is only fair for the campaign of 1876 when Hayes was a very busy man, but it is excellent for the dispute after the election when he was largely a passive figure.... It is, in fact, one of the best accounts penned of the social and routine life of a President.[3]

Hayes's diary is a disappointment in the fact that large gaps were not recorded. As an example, because of the dramatic events concerning the Electoral College, Hayes left Ohio for Washington on March 1, 1877, not knowing whether he was elected. En route to the capital Hayes learned he had been elected president. Since inauguration day fell on a Sunday, it was suggested that Hayes allow himself to be secretly sworn in. Hayes was then again sworn in the following day. Hayes originally left the period of February 27 to March 14 unrecorded, and only recorded his remembrances of the historical events in a single paragraph on March 14.

Editor T. Harry Williams, however, is correct in pointing out that Hayes's *Diary* was "one of the best accounts penned on the social and routine life of a President."[4] This is evident in the December 30, 1877, entry by Hayes in which he devotes three pages to a baby christening held in the Blue Room. Hayes also forbid liquor to be served in the White House during his administration. While Hayes instituted the ban out of respect for his wife, he did not share the strong opinions held by many in the growing temperance movement, and confided his thoughts in his diary: "It is said Gen Garfield will restore wine and liquor to the White House. I hope this is a mistake. I am no fanatic on this subject. I do not sympathize with the methods of the ultra temperance people.... If Gen Garfield rejects the practice I have inaugurated, he will offend thousands, and drive them into the hands of the Temperance demagogues."[5]

The passage is revealing in the fact that while Hayes banned liquor out of personal opinion, he was well aware that the temperance movement was becoming a growing and dangerous political machine. Hayes also sought an end to Reconstruction policies still in place from the Civil War, most notably voting rights.

Hayes never intended the diary to be published, and after completing his single term, retired from politics as well as any additional publishing endeavors.

James A. Garfield and Chester A. Arthur

James Garfield possessed a natural literary curiosity early in life and began keeping a journal at the age of seventeen in 1848. While attending Williams College he became editor of the school's literary periodical, the *Williams Quarterly*, and published examples of his own prose and poetry. Years later, the *Atlantic Monthly* published an essay penned by Garfield which led to speaking engagements and eventually the Republican nomination in 1880. Books always surrounded him and his tastes ranged from history and literature to economics, religion and government. Predecessor Rutherford B. Hayes once remarked, "If he were not in public life he would be equally eminent as a professor in a College, as a lecturer, as an author, an essayist or a Metaphysician."[1] Garfield was also ambidextrous, and perhaps his most unusual trait was the ability to write two different languages simultaneously.

Four months into his term, Garfield was assassinated. Had he survived and eventually retired from politics, Garfield probably would had made a good author.

Vice President Chester A. Arthur succeeded Garfield. When he had fulfilled the remainder of Garfield's original term in 1885, Arthur returned to his native home in New York State to resume his law practice. There, his health quickly began to fail and Arthur died in November of 1886. Arthur was not working on any manuscripts at the time of his death, and had never expressed any interest in authoring a book.

Benjamin Harrison

Benjamin Harrison is best remembered as being the president who served one term between Grover Cleveland's two non-consecutive terms.

Shortly before the 1892 election, Harrison's wife died. Soon after that,

Harrison was defeated for a second term. By the time his term ended the following March, Harrison was happy to be relieved of the presidency. At first the former president was unsure what to do with his free time. He returned to practice law on a limited basis and accepted an offer from Stanford University to deliver six lectures for $25,000. Harrison soon found the research and writing needed to be "long and tedious," but completed them by early 1894.[1] These lectures were later revised for publication and appeared in book form in 1901, under the title *Views of an Ex-President*.

Harrison declined offers to lecture at other colleges, and instead found enjoyment by traveling. During this time Harrison also turned down offers to be a bank president, as well as a professor's chair at the University of Chicago. He did, however, accept a contract for writing articles for *Ladies' Home Journal*. The contract called for nine articles at 3,000 words each for a total of $5,000. The articles were later incorporated into a book, *This Country of Ours*, which was published in 1897. The book sold well and was translated into five languages. Biographer Harry J. Sievers noted, "Harrison was satisfied that his writings had "promoted an interest in our public institutions," particularly in view of the wide circulation."[2]

Soon after having completed the articles for the *Journal*, Harrison remarried. In his final years, Harrison was content practicing law and once again being a husband. He did not author any additional magazine articles prior to his death in 1901.

Grover Cleveland

Grover Cleveland remains unique in presidential history with his two distinctively separate terms of office, 1885–1889 and 1893–1897. After the completion of his second term, Cleveland retired to Princeton, New Jersey, financially comfortable. Biographer Allan Nevins pointed out, "while it was unnecessary for him to earn money, he would have found a life of idleness intolerable. At first his only employment was as an occasional consultant in legal cases for large corporations. But he soon began to write."[1]

The writing began in 1899, when Cleveland accepted a speaking position in the Henry Stafford Little Lectureship on Public Affairs. Expected to produce one to two lectures per year, Cleveland delivered his first Princeton lecture in April 1900. Its title was "The Independence of the Executive," and was followed by "The Venezuela Boundary Controversy." These lectures, along with "The Government in the Chicago Strike of 1894," and "The Bond Issues," were incorporated in what would become his first book in 1904.

Presidential Problems was published by The Century Company and contained revisions of previously published lectures. Cleveland's writing was as stiff and formal as the subjects of his lectures, and "the composition of these discourses cost him protracted anxiety and toil."[2] Originally, Cleveland wanted nothing more to do with politics, but by penning essays on them he soon found himself mired in what he originally wished to avoid. Biographer Nevins also noted that Cleveland's attempts at writing were "nevertheless disappointing. He wrote not intimate personal narratives but formal historical discourses embodying numerous official documents; they contain all too little of what Cleveland alone could give, and all too much of what any competent annalist could supply by a little research."[3] Yet, Cleveland had found something to keep himself busy, and the money was good. Between 1900 and 1906, Cleveland wrote a total of eighteen articles for the *Saturday Evening Post* alone, and was paid as much as $2,500 per article. His was a long way from Ulysses S. Grant's $500 per article for four articles written for *Century* magazine in 1884.

Cleveland supplied articles to *Century* as well, along with stories published in *Collier's*, the *Atlantic*, and *Ladies' Home Journal*. As with *Presidential Problems*, some of these magazine articles found their way into what would become his second book, titled *Fishing and Shooting Sketches*. Published by the Outing Publishing Company in 1906 and illustrated by Henry S. Watson, the book was unlike the recent memoirs authored by former president Grant, and definitely written for sportsmen. With chapters such as "A Duck Hunting Try," and "The Serene Duck Hunter," *Fishing and Shooting Sketches* could have been a refreshing collection of outdoor stories, but failed to win an audience due to Cleveland's inability to excite the interests of the reader. "They had a pleasant sometimes a dry humor, while they showed expertness in the craft of the sportsman; but they lacked keen observation of natural scenery and wildlife, and there was no salt of originality in them."[4]

When the Carrell Publishing Company published *The Writings and Speeches of Grover Cleveland* at Cleveland's consent in 1892, editor George F. Parker observed in the introduction that "Cleveland's writings and speeches have little of the personal or autobiographical element," in them.[5]

It was during Cleveland's presidency that Grant's *Memoirs* were first published, opening the floodgates for former presidents who felt they had a story to tell. Despite the fact that *Memoirs* had done well and assisted Grant in regaining his historical stature, Cleveland never considered such an impact.

For a time, Cleveland believed that the nation was "bitterly hostile to him," and that the appearance of an autobiography would "invite abuse and ridicule."[6] As for his place in history, Cleveland felt that his administration would speak for him. "My official acts and public career are public property. There is nothing to say about them. What I did is done and history must judge of its value, not I."[7] Regarding his private life, Cleveland added, "my private life has been so commonplace that there is nothing to write about."[8]

Professor and friend Andrew F. West once even badgered Cleveland to write a short autobiographical sketch, perhaps worthy of newspaper or magazine publication, to which Cleveland replied, "I won't do it and I'll tell you why. The moment I began, the newspapers would cry: 'There goes the old fool again.'"[9] Despite his skepticism, there were times that Cleveland entertained the thought of writing his autobiography and he once confessed to a friend that "I honestly think that there are things in my life and career that if set out, and *read* by the young men of our country, might be of benefit to."[10]

Any speculation that there was anything left of a writer in Cleveland ended in 1905, when publisher S.S. McClure of *McClure's Magazine* offered him $10,000 for twelve articles. Cleveland came back with the suggestion that he instead sit for a number of autobiographical interviews with a writer who could then craft them for proper publication. McClure rejected the offer, thus closing the door on any further attempts at an autobiography. This brought some sadness to the former president, who was simply too tired to do it himself at that point, and confided he to a friend, "There is a circle of friends like you, who I hope will believe in me. I am happy in the conviction that they will continue in the faith whether an autobiography is written or not. I want my wife and children to love me now and hereafter to proudly honor my memory. They will have my autobiography written on their hearts where every day they may turn the pages and read it. In these days what else is there that is worthwhile to a man nearly sixty-eight years old?"[11]

In the last year of his life, Cleveland's health failed considerably, which kept him confined. This resulted in the broadening of his reading interests, which included novels, poetry and history. It was said that he took great interest in *The Federalist Papers*, written largely by Alexander Hamilton and James Madison, but that it left him with "a sense of inadequacy about his own efforts."[12] In his 2002 biography of Cleveland, author Henry F. Graff suggested that had he written his autobiography, Cleveland probably would have only disappointed the reader. "In putting pen to paper, Cleveland may have had in mind Harrison's recent book, *This Country of Ours*, or even Buchanan's self-serving account of the secession crisis."[13]

It is also possible that Cleveland avoided authoring anything autobiographical because Grant's *Memoirs* would have overshadowed it. Cleveland's story would have definitely paled when compared to Grant's military exploits, and perhaps he was aware of this.

William McKinley

In September of 1901, just six months into his second term, William McKinley was assassinated. Prior to his presidency McKinley was unpublished. Biographer Margaret Leech noted, "Though he lacked the gift of literary composition and the gestures of dramatic delivery, McKinley had gained an unrivaled reputation as a compelling orator."[1] In other words, while McKinley was a skilled public speaker, his words languished on paper.

McKinley's presidency covered an interesting time in American history. It witnessed the age of imperialism, the gold standard, and protectionism. Should he have written about it, the subject matter would have proved interesting. Unfortunately, McKinley left no diaries or manuscripts at the time of his death. While many historians rate his presidency as above average, McKinley's legacy was eclipsed by his successor, Theodore Roosevelt.

Theodore Roosevelt

> I am not learned. I know about some subjects which have interested me and which I have studied. Between them are immense gaps.[1]
> —Theodore Roosevelt

With Theodore Roosevelt, America once again had a literary executive in the tradition of Thomas Jefferson and John Quincy Adams. In the introduction to his *Selected Letters of Theodore Roosevelt*, historian H.W. Brands noted, "If Roosevelt was one of the most literary of presidents, he was also most active of American writers. Even if Roosevelt had not written a sentence worth the reading, he did plenty worth the writing."[2]

Roosevelt's literary career was launched while a student at Harvard University. It was there that he began work on a manuscript of the Naval War of 1812 during his senior year. After graduating, Roosevelt was elected to the New

Theodore Roosevelt authored dozens of books ranging from naval histories, the American West, hunting and nature, essays, political biographies and even an autobiography. He was also skilled in matters of publishing and maneuvered his way through book contracts without the aid of a literary agent (Library of Congress).

York State Assembly at the age of twenty-three, and on December 3, 1881, turned in to G.P. Putnam's Sons the five hundred page manuscript, which he titled *The Naval War of 1812*. Published the following year, the book "immediately established the author as a notable historian, and the book has endured, generation after generation, as a classic in the canon of American naval history."[3]

Roosevelt's attraction to the sea seemed natural for a boy who grew up in Manhattan. As a youth, Roosevelt was no stranger to both rowboats and yachts, and the manuscript absorbed him. Friend Owen Wister recalled Theodore's work habits:

> He finished his *Naval History of the War of 1812* mostly standing on one leg at the bookcases in his New York house, the other leg crossed behind, toe touching the floor, heedless of dinner engagements and the flight of time. A slide drew out from the bookcase. He knew that when a ship's course was one way, with the wind another, the ship had to sail at angles, and this was called tracking or beating. By exhaustive study and drawing of models, he pertinacious got it right, whatever of it came into the naval engagements he was writing about.[4]

The Naval War of 1812 received good reviews in America and Great Britain. It went through two printings, and a third was added the following year, in which Roosevelt added a preface and an additional chapter dealing with the Battle of New Orleans. Sales were helped by the fact that "by [naval] regulations adopted in 1886, at least one copy" of the book "was to be placed on every vessel in the U.S. Navy."[5] Roosevelt's intention in writing *The Naval War of 1812* was to present a balanced account of the conflict to both American and British readers. In the Modern Library edition of the book, author John Allen Gable wrote, "Those with an interest in military history or naval tactics and strategy will discover a rich and rewarding experience in reading this classic volume. *The Naval War of 1812*, of course, cannot be ignored by any serious student of Theodore Roosevelt's life and work."[6]

As for Roosevelt's opinion of his first book, he later came to voice some regret concerning some of his work habits. In his autobiography, which would be published in 1913, he came down hard on himself as a young author. "Before I left Harvard I was already writing one or two chapters of a book I afterwards published on the Naval War of 1812. Those chapters were so dry that they would have made a dictionary seem light reading by comparison. Still, they represented purpose and serious interest on my part, not the perfunctory effort to do well enough to get a certain mark; and corrections of them by a skilled older man would have impressed me and commanded my respectful attention."[7]

Roosevelt followed up on his book on naval history with a volume on living the ranch life in the American West. He had purchased a Dakota ranch and became genuinely interested in conservation. This interest became the basis for *Hunting Trips of a Ranchman*, which would be published in 1885. Biographer H.W. Brands wrote, "Compared to his *Naval History* [sic], this kind of writing required little effort or thought, consisting chiefly of personal observations supplemented by a modest amount of research in similar writings by other hunting types."[8] Roosevelt wrote the manuscript in a manner almost approaching Ernest Hemingway's big game exploits. "He made himself the hero of the tale," Brands noted, "but a hero with endearing imperfections."[9]

The reason Roosevelt was able to abruptly shift his subject matter and be successfully published was hidden in the fact that he had purchased a share in a publishing house. Brands noted how the book

> entered a publishing field crowded with similar accounts of frontier adventures. While some other authors had to hunt for publishers with almost the same tenacity as they pursued the big game of the mountains, Roosevelt avoided the problem by the neat expedient of having purchased an interest in a publishing house. In 1884, before leaving New York for the West, he signed a partnership contract with G.P. Putnam's Sons, the house that had issued his *Naval History* [sic]. His twenty-thousand-dollar investment guaranteed him a share of the firm's profits for three years—and presumably a home for whatever books he authored during that time.[10]

Roosevelt soon turned G.P. Putnam's Sons, one of America's largest publishing houses, into his own vanity press. This was reflected in the fact that the initial press run of *Hunting Trips of a Ranchman* was only 500 copies. Roosevelt himself seemed to have his doubts about it, admitting in a letter "the pictures will be excellent—as for the reading matter, I am a little doubtful."[11]

A biography of Missouri senator Thomas Hart Benton soon followed, with a publishing contract with Houghton Mifflin arranged through Henry Cabot Lodge. Roosevelt worked on the manuscript in New York as well as on his Dakota ranch, transporting books and research materials into the western wilderness as needed. In a March 1886 letter to Lodge, Roosevelt admitted, "Writing is horrible work to me; and I make slow progress. I have got some good ideas on the first chapter, but I am not sure they are worked up rightly; my style is very rough and I do not like a certain lack of sequitur that I do not seem able to get rid of."[12]

Some of problem was that by working on the manuscript in Dakota, Roosevelt had isolated himself from the great eastern libraries he was accustomed to getting research material from. He would end up seeking Lodge's help in securing such material, even going so far as inquiring whether he knew of a good research assistant. Roosevelt would end up rushing the manuscript out to the publisher in August, only to confide to Lodge that "I hope it is decent, but lately I have been troubled with dreadful misgivings."[13] Roosevelt's "misgivings" were rooted in the fact that he hardly revised anything once put to paper. Author H.W. Brands observed that "Roosevelt didn't have to rewrite ... indeed, he rarely rewrote anything. The perfectionism of a diligent reviser was foreign to Roosevelt's nature; he was too eager to get done and on to the next project."[14]

Published in 1886, *Thomas Hart Benton* received favorable reviews. The Benton book led to another biography from Houghton Mifflin on the life of Gouverneur Morris. Morris, who was known as "America's financier" during the War for Independence, became a burden for Roosevelt once he realized he was not as interesting as Benton. This is evident in the book's preface, where Roosevelt writes that Morris "was too unstable and erratic to leave a profound mark upon our political developments."[15] Between his biographies on Benton and Morris, Roosevelt published a second collection of Western frontier stories, titled *Ranch Life*. The book, which was illustrated by artist Frederick Remington, captured what it was like to live in the American West, which was still very much a wilderness. In a passage concerning simple travel, Roosevelt wrote of the hardships.

"Occasionally it is imperatively necessary to cross some of the worst parts of the Bad Lands with a wagon, and such a trip is exhausting and laborious beyond belief. Often the wagon will have to be taken to pieces every few hundred yards in order to get it over a ravine, lower it into a valley, or drag it up a cliff. One outfit, that a year ago tried to take a short cut through some of the Bad Lands of the Powder river, made just four miles in three days, and then had to come back to their starting-point after all."[16]

Author David McCullough noted that Roosevelt "wrote of the cowboy with an appreciation not to be found in the work of previous writers. He was, as [Owen] Wister said, the pioneer in taking the cowboy seriously. He wrote of their courage, their phenomenal physical endurance. He liked their humor, admired the unwritten code that ruled the cow camp."[17]

After *Ranch Life* was published, Roosevelt expressed a desire to write something worthy of the ages. It appears safe to say that up until this point the only book he was proud of was his *Naval War of 1812*. The biographies of Benton and Morris were rushed, and his two collections of ranch stories were treated somewhat as curiosities. In a February 1887 letter to Henry Cabot Lodge, Roosevelt dropped a hint that a deep and personal literary shift had occurred, and that something major was on the horizon. "If I write another historical work of any kind—and my dream is to make one such that will be my magnum opus–I shall certainly take more time and do it carefully and thoroughly, so as to avoid the roughness and interruption of the Benton."[18] In a similar letter, Roosevelt expressed the same feelings. "My literary work occupies a good deal of my time; and I have on the whole done fairly well at it; I should like to write some book that would really rank as in the very first class, but I suppose this is a mere dream."[19]

That April, Roosevelt wrote a letter to Francis Parkman, outlining what he intended to do. At the time, Parkman was one the most prominent historians in America. His major works included *The Oregon Trail*, and a seven-volume history, *France and England in North America*.

Roosevelt's enthusiasm, which at times reads like a fan letter, tells of the vast expansion of western history he hopes to properly capture on paper, all in the name of his idol.

> I am engaged in a work of which the first part treats the extension to our frontier westward and southwestward during the twenty odd years from 1774 to 1796–the years of uninterrupted Indian warfare during which Kentucky and Tennessee were founded and grew to statehood.... I have gathered a good deal of hitherto unused material, both from the unpublished Mss. of the State Department, and from the old diaries, letters and memorandum in various private libraries.
>
> This first part I have promised the Putnam's for some time in 1889; it will be in two volumes with such titles as "The Winning of the West and Southwest," and perhaps as a subtitle "From the Alleghenies to the Mississippi."
>
> I would like to dedicate this to you. Of course I know that you would not wish your name to be connected in even the most indirect way with any but good work; and I

can only say that I will do my best to make the work creditable. William Everett, John Morse or Cabot Lodge can tell you who I am.[20]

The Winning of the West, as it came to be known, would span four volumes, and become known as the "magnum opus" Roosevelt so dearly longed for. In his 1958 book, *The Seven Worlds of Theodore Roosevelt*, author Edward Wagenknecht referred to the work as a "gigantic fragment," noting that while it was "not as good as Parkman, but Parkman made the writing of history his lifework; Roosevelt produced his *magnum opus* during breathing spaces in a very active career. He did not exhaust available source material, but he did open up new areas of it, unknown to most of the writers of his day; his vision was penetrating and his method of procedure sound."[21]

The "breathing spaces" Wagenknecht refers to was the accelerated political career Roosevelt stepped into during the course of time it took him to write the multi-volume study. From 1889 to 1896, he held the position of New York City police commissioner, assistant secretary of the United States Navy, formed the Rough Riders and fought in Cuba, and served as governor of New York State. He had also become active in the Republican Party on a national level, and after remarrying in 1886, had a growing family.

In his 1995 foreword to the University of Nebraska's edition of *The Winning of the West*, historian John Milton Cooper, Jr., noted, "The wonder of them is that they got written at all. If nothing else, *The Winning of the West* stands as another monument to Roosevelt's preternatural energy and powers of concentration. No other active statesman in the English-speaking world, not even Winston Churchill, produced such a solidly scholarly work of history while he was, as the Romans said, *in medias res*—in the midst of things."[22]

The book also received it share of criticism. Historian James R. Gilmore publicly claimed that Roosevelt could not have written the lengthy work by himself, and that he borrowed heavily from other previously published histories. Roosevelt would not only refute Gilmore's charges that he did not write it, but promised a reward of $1,000 to anyone who could prove he wrote it with a collaborator.

During the time Roosevelt was writing *Winning of the West*, he was acutely aware that it would be a monumental task, and there would no doubt be distractions. In a 1890 letter to publisher George Haven Putnam, he admitted that he was juggling other uncompleted manuscripts as well, but intended to carry on with it as best he could:

> I think you are absolutely right about the western history. As I told you last winter, I was foolish enough to promise 18 months ago Professor Freeman, of England, a volume on New York for his Historic-Town Series, and that promise I shall have to keep. Outside of this I shall not go into any literary work excepting the *Winning of the West*. I

have already collected most of the material for my third and fourth volumes, and have outlined the first few chapters. I realize perfectly that my chance of making a permanent literary reputation depends on how I do this big work, not on doing a lot of little booklets, and I need hardly say that I infinitely prefer all my book to come from your press, and that you will always have hereafter first chance at any book I may write.[23]

The New York history which Roosevelt makes reference to was published in 1891. Given the simple title *New York*, the book made up a part of a histories-of-historic-towns series. Biographer Edmund Morris exquisitely noted the "rodent-like life of a professional historian," Roosevelt must have gone through while compiling information for *Winning of the West*:

> He burrowed through piles of ancient letters, diaries, and newspapers in Tennessee, and unearthed many long-forgotten documents in Kentucky, including six volumes of Spanish government dispatches, and some misspelled but priceless pioneer autobiographies; he inquisitively searched some two or three hundred folios of Revolutionary manuscripts in Washington, and ferreted out thousands of letters by Jefferson, Madison, and Monroe, untouched by previous scholars; he devoured the published papers of the Federal, Virginia, and Georgia governments in New York, and pestered private collectors as far away as Wisconsin and California to send him their papers.[24]

Roosevelt was still working on the *Winning of the West* when publisher Putnam suggested he write a book on naval hero John Paul Jones. Roosevelt politely begged off, citing it would distract him from completing the current manuscript. Roosevelt was still working on the *Winning of the West* in 1897, as evident in a letter to publisher Putnam. As President McKinley's assistant secretary of the navy, Roosevelt expressed that within the next six months "I want to begin to get the materials together for my next volumes of the *Winning of the West*. As you know, there are to be four of them. If I could get four, or even two (but by preference all four) done shortly after I leave this office—on the supposition that I shall be left here until the end of President McKinley's term–I should very much like it."[25]

The multi-volume *Winning of the West* was completed and published one volume at a time. It was met with immediate success, with first editions being sold out within a month of their release. The book proved to be everything Roosevelt had strived for. If he had never been elected vice president and succeeded to the presidency after McKinley's 1901 assassination, the name of Theodore Roosevelt would have been easily remembered in literary circles simply from this one book.

Roosevelt continued working on other manuscripts while attempting to complete *Winning of the West*. One of these, a collection of essays, was titled *American Ideals*. In letters to his publishers, Roosevelt often expressed doubt regarding manuscripts that had been submitted while working on his western history. Roosevelt apparently felt they were inferior to the multi-volume *Win-*

ning of the West, and gave publishers ample room to reject publishing them. Among the other books that saw publication during the time he worked on his western history were *The Wilderness Hunter, American Big Game, Hero Tales from American History, Hunting in Many Lands, Some American Game,* and *Trail and Campfire*. Three of these, *American Big Game, Hunting in Many Lands*, and *Trail and Campfire*, were co-authored with George Bird Grinnell.

In 1857, when Grinnell was seven years old, his father moved his family to an area of Manhattan called Audubon Park. John James Audubon, who had become famous for his nature paintings, particularly of birds, had originally owned the tract of land. Grinnell quickly became fascinated with Audubon, who had died only six years before. After graduating from Yale with a degree in paleontology, Grinnell developed a love for the American West, and had begun a series of expeditions and hunting trips there in 1870. In 1874 Grinnell accompanied Col. George A. Custer as a naturalist for Custer's Black Hills expedition. Two years later, in 1876, Custer would invite Grinnell, along with the famed 7th Calvary, on another expedition. Grinnell, however, was unable to accompany Custer. This was fortunate for Grinnell, because the expedition would end in the Battle of Little Big Horn.

During this time, Grinnell was also writing for *Forest and Stream* magazine, and eventually became owner of the publication in 1881. In 1886, Grinnell proposed the formation of what would become the Audubon Society, and was one of America's foremost naturalists. It was in the July 1885 edition of *Forest and Stream* that Grinnell published a review Roosevelt's book, *Hunting Trips of a Ranchman*. Grinnell's review was politely worded, but critical, especially to Roosevelt's eyes. "Mr. Roosevelt is not well known as a sportsman, and his experience of the Western country is quite limited, but this very fact in one way lends an added charm to his book," Grinnell wrote.[26] "We are sorry to see that a number of hunting myths are given as fact, but it was after all scarcely to be expected that with the author's limited experience he could sift the wheat from the chaff and distinguish the true from false."[27]

Roosevelt could not accept Grinnell's criticism, and swiftly paid the editor a personal visit at the *Forest and Stream*'s offices. A lengthy conversation ensued and the two men discovered they both shared a deep love for the outdoors. That they both came from wealthy New York families did not hurt either, and a lifelong friendship was quickly established. Roosevelt would come to appreciate Grinnell's expertise from past expositions, and Grinnell realized that Roosevelt possessed the political influence that could be beneficial to the struggling conservation movement and the Audubon Society. Choosing to co-author three books with Grinnell proved a wise move for

Roosevelt. Grinnell was no novice, and his experience as an editor was an added bonus for Roosevelt, who hated to revise anything.

During the late 1890s, Roosevelt was authoring so many books and he hardly had time to digest the publishing contracts he had signed. In letters to his publishers he sometimes sought clarification regarding contractual language and royalty figures. These letters are remarkable and revealing in that up until this point Roosevelt had not secured the services of a literary agent. Attempting to navigate this process alone by any other individual while engaged in a growing political career would have been unheard of, but it is a prime example of Roosevelt's lifelong characteristic of multi-tasking.

In 1898, the battleship USS *Maine* exploded in Havana harbor in Cuba, prompting the Spanish-American War. Roosevelt resigned his naval post and joined the fight. He was appointed commander of a regiment that would become known as the "Rough Riders." The regiment would secure their place in American military history for their charge up San Juan Hill, and give Roosevelt something more to write about. By the time *The Rough Riders* was published in 1899, Roosevelt was elected governor of New York State. Vice president Garret Hobart would die in November, creating a vacancy on the upcoming 1900 presidential ticket with McKinley. Roosevelt would be nominated for vice president at the Republican Convention that year, actively campaigning while McKinley remained at home in Canton, Ohio.

Despite traveling 21,000 miles and making 673 speeches in 24 states, he found time to publish a biography of Oliver Cromwell, as well as a collection of essays. In a letter to publisher Charles Scribner, Roosevelt reflected on the manuscript, as well as his historical opinion of Cromwell, stating that while Cromwell was "a great statesman" he failed because "he lacked the power of self-repression by Washington and Lincoln.... The More I have studied Cromwell, the more I have grown to admire him, and yet the more I have felt that his making himself a dictator was unnecessary and destroyed the possibility of making the effects of that particular revolution permanent."[28]

Oliver Cromwell would be the last of Roosevelt's three biographical efforts. After *Thomas Hart Benton* and *Gouveneur Morris*, it is surprising that he would even consider penning another biography. Roosevelt would later admit most of his biographical efforts were hurried. Yet another collection of essays, *The Strenuous Life*, referred to the personal experiences he endured in overcoming childhood health issues such as asthma, and encouraged Americans to make the most of life.

In September 1901 President McKinley was shot and killed. Upon becoming president, Roosevelt found himself at an odd loss for words, admitting to Henry Cabot Lodge "I shall not try to give you even in barest outline the history of the last two weeks."[29] As chief executive, Roosevelt's academic writing underwent a sabbatical. Hunting titles became the main theme while Roosevelt was president. These included *The Deer Family* (1902), *Outdoor Pastimes of an American Hunter* (1905), and *Good Hunting* (1907). During this period G.P. Putnam's Son also published a collection of Roosevelt's writings, *The Works of Theodore Roosevelt*, which amassed fifteen volumes.

Upon leaving the presidency in 1909, Roosevelt returned to writing. Among the titles were *African Game Trails, American Problems* and *The New Nationalism* (1910), as well as *Realizable Goals* and *The Conservation of Womanhood and Childhood* (1912). These constituted a mixed bag of outdoor writing as well as political issues. It was Roosevelt's outdoors and big game hunting writings that excelled during this period. In his 1971 book, *Theodore Roosevelt, Outdoorsman*, author R.L. Wilson wrote that Roosevelt never failed to revitalize himself when hunting. "His observation of animal life in Africa reinforced his avid belief in Darwinian evolution. It also reaffirmed a long-standing conviction of his: Life itself was a continual struggle and only those able to adapt to changing conditions were capable of survival. Roosevelt reveled in Africa because he believed it was as close as one could get to the natural world as it existed at the dawn of creation."[30]

In 1909, *Outlook Editorials* were published, which were a collection of articles culled from Roosevelt's contributions to the magazine, *The Outlook*. It was during the writing of *Outlook Editorials* that Roosevelt began toying with the idea of an autobiography. In typical fashion, he doled out chapters that were regularly published in the magazine, while at the same time serving as president of the American Historical Association. Finally, in 1913, *An Autobiography* was properly published in book form.

Roosevelt seemed to have enjoyed himself writing it, at times looming as large as he wished, and being free to include or leave out anything he desired. There were wonderful passages that revealed Roosevelt as the unashamed lifelong book-lover that he was, and their connection with his love of nature.

> There are men who love out-of-doors who yet never open a book; and other men who love books but to whom the great book of nature is a sealed volume, and the lines written therein blurred and illegible. Nevertheless among those men whom I have known the love of books and the love of outdoors, in their highest expressions, have usually gone hand in hand. It is an affectation for the man who is praising outdoors to sneer at books. Usually the keenest appreciation of what is seen in nature is to be found in those who have also profited by the hoarded and recorded wisdom of their fellowmen. Love of outdoor life, love of simple and hardy pastimes, can be gratified by men and women who do not possess large means, and who work hard; and so can the love of good books—not of good bindings and of first editions, excellent enough in their way

of sheer luxuries–I mean love of reading books, owning them if possible of course, but, if that is not possible, getting them from a circulating library."³¹

Yet to some *Autobiography* was a disappointment. H.W. Brands wrote that the book "read like an extended campaign speech: part homily, part platform, part defense of past actions."³² While David McCullough noted how it was "particularly interesting if read with a view to all that is left out."³³ Author Patricia O'Toole also dismissed the book, and what might have been:

> A pastiche of memoir, apologia, position paper, and sermon, TR's account of his life is an indispensable introduction to the man, his times, and the worldwide view of the elite who governed with him. The book is partial in both senses of the word; opinionated and incomplete. Victorian gentleman did not parade their sorrows, so there's no surprise in his decision to exclude his first wife, the grotesque Valentine's Day when she and his mother died, and his brother's alcoholism and early demise. But autobiography asks an author to muse on the personal significance of the events he chooses to count, and Roosevelt's lifelong aversion to self-reflection put him at a disadvantage in the genre. Without the reflective dimension, readers are deprived of autobiography's chief reward, the joy of coming to know the workings of another heart.³⁴

Roosevelt himself seems to have known he was not up to the effort, for in a letter to his sister he admitted having written it with "heated unintelligence."³⁵ The truth was that he had over-extended himself once again, for in a one-month period at home, he had "barreled through a half-dozen magazine articles and read the proofs of three books that would be published while he was away: the autobiography, the volume on African game, and a collection of his literary essays."³⁶

It was also during this time that Roosevelt felt it necessary to answer a charge of libel that had appeared in print. George A. Newett, the editor of *Iron Ore*, a weekly newspaper, had called Roosevelt a drunkard. Roosevelt sued merely to clear his name, and sought no monetary attachment. After spending $40,000 in legal fees, he was successful. A cousin, Ellen Roosevelt, then "had the trial transcript printed in book form and deposited in a number of libraries around the country. Bound in black leather, with *Roosevelt vs. Newett* stamped in gold on the cover, the volume had the look and heft of a Bible," and must have made an unusual oddity among Roosevelt's authored works.³⁷

After publishing his autobiography, Roosevelt occasionally dove into the political arena with his writing. These efforts include *Progressive Principles* (1913), *America and the World War* (1915), *Social Justice and Popular Rule* (1917), *National Strength and International Duty* (1917), and *The Great Adventure* (1918). Roosevelt could never completely withdraw from politics, and admitted that it seemed as if he was always running for something. He resisted running for a third term only after publicly denouncing the thought early in his presidency, and walked away from the White House in a grudge, even after personally selecting Taft as his successor. His hunger eventually led him to form the Progressive (or Bull Moose) Party in 1912. In a 1915 letter to a friend, he wrote, "Have you seen a copy of the little book I have published, called 'America and the World War?' I believe you will like the stands I there take. I am sick at heart over the actions of Wilson and Bryan."[38]

Books concerning his love of the outdoors and big game hunting overshadowed Roosevelt's political essays. These works would ultimately leave the legacy familiar to future generations. These include *Through the Brazilian Wilderness,* and *African Game Animals,* which were both published in 1914. Years earlier, the *New York Nation* praised such writing, as well as his qualifications to do so:

> Probably no American is better qualified than Mr. Roosevelt to write on such a subject as this, for he has himself hunted and killed every variety of game native to the United States, has lived on our so-called frontier, has known the particular life, thought, and action of its people, and, above all, possesses a true appreciation of nature, animate and inanimate, and the literary ability to relate what he has seen.... Our country still has the unexplored places, the peculiar life, and strange characters, not to be found in the earth's older regions, which belong to a nation's youth and are so dear to romance and adventure, and Mr. Roosevelt has seen and written of these things in a straightforward style, without either coolness or sentimentality, devoting most of his time to action, and leaving the romance to others.[39]

In his 1920 biography, *Theodore Roosevelt and His Time,* author Joseph Bishop recalled Roosevelt's method of writing while hunting in Africa. "He was a model of promptness and efficiency. When he promised a manuscript for a certain date, the promise was kept absolutely, no matter what intervened. Before he left for the African wilderness in 1909 he had written to the publishers of Scribner's Magazine the entire book known as "African Game Trails," including the Preface. One of the men who was with him said that, no matter how arduous the day in the hunting-field, night after night he would see him seated on a camp-stool, with a feeble light on the table, often with his head and face covered with mosquito netting, and gauntlet gloves on his hands, to protect him from the insects, writing the narrative of his adventures. Chapter by chapter this narrative was sent by runners from the heart of Africa. Two copies were dispatched at different times. When he got to the headwaters of the Nile one of the chapters was sent from Nairobi and the duplicate was sent down the Nile to Cairo. The blue-canvas envelopes often arrived much battered and stained, but never did a single chapter miss."[40]

In a 1917 letter to son Quentin, Roosevelt expelled the virtues of capturing the moment and the experience on paper, no matter what. "Write no matter how tired you are, no mater how incontinent it is, write if you're smashed up in a hospital; write when you are doing your most dangerous stunts; write when your work is most irksome and disheartening; write all the time!"[41]

Roosevelt's last published book on hunting game was 1916's *A Book-Lover's Holiday in the Open*. The book, which took place in the American west, closed the door on Roosevelt's larger-than-life persona. The year 1919 would see publication of *Theodore Roosevelt's Letters to His Children*, a light and airy small volume worthy of its title. It would be the last book Roosevelt would see published. On January 6, 1919, Roosevelt died in his sleep at home. At the time of his death, he was working on articles for several magazines, and had worked eleven hours at writing the day before his death.

In death, Roosevelt's legacy grew even larger, mostly thanks to his nature writings. In the second edition of Harper Collins' *Reader's Encyclopedia of American Literature*, published in 2002, Roosevelt's entry contained the observation that; "Of all the American presidents, with the possible exception of Woodrow Wilson, Roosevelt was probably the most deeply interested in books and the nearest to being a professional writer.... He often talked about books in public, and his endorsements could make a best seller. His own books sold well, especially *The Winning of the West*. He felt that historical writing must be vivid as well as accurate."[42]

Two collections of gathered works were widely published. These are *The Works of Theodore Roosevelt*, and *The Complete Writings of Theodore Roosevelt*. These multi-volume sets contained his many books, and were printed from the time of his presidency until well after his death. The "Elkhorn Edition" of *The Complete Writings* is considered the most desirable.

In 1925, a small volume of Roosevelt's early work was privately reprinted. Titled *The Summer Birds of the Adirondacks in Franklin County, N.Y. with Notes on Some of the Birds of Oyster Bay*, the five-page chapbook became the first printing of his two volumes on birds. Roosevelt had originally published *Summer Birds of the Adirondacks* with Henry Davis Minot in 1877. His *Notes on Some of the Birds of Oyster Bay* was originally published in 1879, and was originally distributed as a broadside. These two short titles, in reality a catalog of birds sighted in the area at the time, are not by any means considered definitive works on the subject. In fact, they are rarely ever mentioned in Roosevelt biographies, and are typically only known within book-collecting circles.

Nearly one hundred years after his death, Roosevelt's staggering literary output still amazes biographers and historians. While his *Naval War of 1812* and multi-volume *Winning of the West* are considered by many to be definitive studies, Roosevelt's true legacy remains ensconced within his nature writings. Not merely content to write about nature and its creatures, Roosevelt used the full measure of his executive authority to create multiple national parks while president, forever preserving the land from exploitation, as well as from the rising tide of westward expansion he personally witnessed during his many western trips.

In his 2009 book, *The Wilderness Warrior*, author Douglas Brinkley put into perspective how Roosevelt's published work endures in modern-day America:

> Besides overlooking his inherent conservationist attitude in *The Wilderness Hunter*, recent environmental historians have mocked Roosevelt as a weekend warrior, an urbanite with money to burn who bought himself a ticket to the wilderness for a few weeks and then returned home. At face value this analysis is true. But from the perspective of 2009 Roosevelt's desire to connect with nature to rejuvenate himself has proved ahead of its time. Today only 1.9 percent of Americans are living in rural areas, compared with 40 percent when *The Wilderness Hunter* was published, so Roosevelt was anticipating a modern trend. As of 2008 Jefferson's agrarian vision and the homesteading of the West were kaput. Even Thoreau's back-to-nature ethos, based on self-reliance, which had a revisionist run in the 1960's, had become cultist at best, a matter of a few survivalists holed up in forlorn mountain cabins in the Sierra Nevada or Appalachians. But Roosevelt's notion of extreme wilderness experiences in short fixes has become widespread. Shooting the rapids, mountain climbing, rappelling–Americans crave an extreme fix from nature in hundreds of different ways. Whole cities such as Boulder, Eugene, and Asheville cater to consumers of nature like Roosevelt: claustrophobic city dwellers and suburbanites desperate to encounter a rare bird or cypress grove or desert ecosystem before it all vanished.[43]

William Howard Taft

William Howard Taft is not remembered as an author mainly because most of his published works pertained to law and legal subjects. And while Taft found some pleasure in writing, he was not very good at it. Biographer Henry F. Pringle, who authored what is considered the most comprehensive biography ever written on Taft, the two-volume *Life and Times of William Howard Taft* (published in 1939), wrote of Taft's literary shortcomings. "Taft was not, in any sense, a literary craftsman and this, curiously, was despite the fact that he enjoyed writing.... His letters lacked style or grace, however. They were too verbose and rarely had charm. He had no flair whatsoever for the turning of a phrase, for brief analysis of a technical subject."[1] Pringle eventually concluded that Taft "had a through mind rather than a facile or brilliant one."[2]

Biographer Carl S. Anthony, however, mentioned Taft's ability to express himself on paper. Taft, he wrote, "showed a deft skill with the language. Spoken or written, he handled words like clay to make tangible shape of his conceptual notions on justice, equality, and morality."[3] Prior to his single presidential term, Taft served as an Ohio judge, secretary of war, and governor of the Philippines. It has been noted by many biographers that Taft found little pleasure in the presidency, and he ran for office mainly as a favor to Theodore Roosevelt, who considered him his handpicked successor. As a candidate, Taft dreaded writing campaign speeches, much less having to deliver them.

Upon leaving the presidency in 1913, Taft returned to Yale University, where he served as Kent Professor of Law and Legal History. "I do not retire to the practice of law; I retire to the academic shades of Yale to teach it, and this very act takes me out of the maelstrom of politics. It is a dignified retirement."[4] It was during his time at Yale (1913–1921) that most of Taft's literary output as an authored occurred.

Taft often wrote in an academic and formal manner. Many of his subjects were written in the tone of a monotonous address, and rarely did words jump off the page. Much of what he wrote concerned judicial matters, which reflected Taft's first real love. This is evident in *Ethnics in Service* (1914), in which Taft presents a lengthy discourse on the history of lawyers. *The Anti-Trust Act and the Supreme Court* followed a year later.

Taft also wrote about the legal powers of the presidency under the constitution. *The Presidency: Its Duties, Its Powers, Its Opportunities, and Its Limitations,* along with *The Chief Magistrate and His Powers* (both published in 1916) could almost be considered bookends. In *Liberty Under Law: An Interpretation of the Principals of Our Constitutional Government* (1922), Taft almost dissects the constitution, offering personal revisions along the way. Of all of his books, only *Service with Fighting Men; An Account of the Work of the Young Men's Christian Associations in the World War* (1922) had nothing to do with law.

Taft often expressed his desire to someday become chief justice of the Supreme Court. This wish came true in 1921, when President Harding appointed him to the nation's highest court. Because of his tenure as chief justice, Taft did not retire from public office as most of his predecessors had, and therefore did not pen an autobiography or memoir. Taft would hold on to his position on the high court until his health forbid him, and was dead a little more than a month after resigning in February 1930. Much of what is remembered of Taft's writing is from his time as chief justice. He seemed to enjoy writing opinions handed down from the court, and perhaps excelled more as an author in that arena. Author Jonathan Lurie weighed both sides of the coin in his 2012 biography on Taft. "Taft could not find elegance in his writing, be it either in judicial decisions or in affairs of state. The occasional eloquence of Louis Brandeis and the epigrammatic wit of Oliver Wendell Holmes, two of Taft's future colleagues on the High Court, will not be seen in Taft's written work. On the other hand, even as early as his superior court tenure, his opinions were carefully crafted, thoroughly researched, [and] well grounded in precedent."[5]

Taft's reluctance to write an autobiography or memoir rested in his belief that history would remember him kindly. Like Andrew Jackson, Taft felt confident enough to dole out the task to journalist (and friend) Gus Karger. However, Karger unexpectedly died in 1924. After Taft's 1930 death, wife Nellie Taft (who had written her own memoir) delegated family members to hire an official author to wade through the former president's papers. Henry Pringle was chosen, although he would have nothing to do with the project. Instead, Pringle authored his two-volume *Life and Times of William Howard Taft*.

Surprisingly, Pringle barely touched upon Taft's writing life. While he mentioned Taft occasionally penning articles for magazines, he never delved further. In fact, many of Taft's biographers fail to mention any of his numerous published works as an author.

Woodrow Wilson

> I have—almost unwittingly—taken the lead in a very great work.[1]
> —Woodrow Wilson

Woodrow Wilson was perhaps the most academically educated man ever to hold the office of president. Wilson was president of Princeton University prior to becoming governor of the State of New Jersey, which led him to the office of president of the United States.

Few are aware, however, that long before becoming president of the university, Wilson was a student at Princeton, and contributed essays that were published in the campus publication, the *Nassau Literary Magazine*. It was also while at Princeton that Wilson discovered Walter Bagehot, an English author who provided him with "a model for his criticism of American political institutions."[2] Wilson would later remember Bagehot as being "my master," along with being "the most vivacious, the most racially real, of writers on life—whether the life be political, social, or separately intellectual."[3]

Woodrow Wilson authored several books on political science and his writing could best be described as academic. A biography on George Washington was a failure, and may have caused Wilson's reluctance to write his autobiography (Library of Congress).

Biographer Arthur Walworth wrote that "Bagehot's essays on the English Constitution set Wilson to analyzing his own nation's Congress in similar terms, and the Englishman's frankness gave the young American courage to speak his mind."[4] Bagehot's inspiration would soon lead Wilson to write a 1878 essay titled "Cabinet Government in the United States," which would be published in the highly acclaimed *International Review*. Other Wilson biographers also agree that Bagehot's influence shaped Wilson's political thought. "Wilson thought Bagehot had, beyond anyone before him, made the British government more intelligible to ordinary citizens. Similar treatment, if applied to the American Constitution, Wilson thought, would produce a measure of revelation for those who were still reading *The Federalist* as an authoritative constitution manual," wrote author Phyllis Lee Levin.[5] Levin would also note that Bagehot "was perhaps the principal literary figure who held Wilson in thrall and to whom he was indebted for the thrust of his own work."[6]

Wilson's early success as a writer would cause his father, a Presbyterian minister, to lament that his son was "born halfway between the Bible and the dictionary."[7] Wilson would later place additional articles in publications such as the *New York Evening Post*, but insisted upon "reputation, not quick money."[8] During his time at Princeton, Wilson also served as editor of the student paper, *The Princetonian*, which fueled his desire to write.

After graduating, Wilson enrolled at Johns Hopkins University. It was there that he became exposed to noted historians such as John Franklin Jameson, who recognized Wilson's literary talents. Eighteen eighty-five saw the publication of Wilson's' first book, *Congressional Government*, which was published by Houghton Mifflin. Professor Mario R. Dinunzio, who later edited Wilson's *Essential Writings & Speeches*, observed that the "Publication by a prestigious house and the good reviews that followed were an enviable achievement for a student still short of his Ph.D."[9]

Congressional Government was released to positive reviews and established Wilson's credibility. This was followed by offers to teach and lecture from numerous institutions. He would ultimately choose an offer to teach history and political science at a college for women, Bryn Mawr College. At the age of twenty-nine, Wilson had "found that he had achieved a degree of fame unusual to one so young."[10] In a letter to wife Ellen, Wilson attempted to come to terms with what he had done, and what the future could hold. "I have—almost unwittingly—taken the lead in a very great work. My book succeeds because I have taken the lead; and now, the opening having been made, I must come up to my opportunities and be worthy of them. That is enough to sober—as well as enough to inspire—anyone!"[11]

Wilson was very much in love with Ellen, and considered her the inspiration for the challenge to undertake such an endeavor. Upon receiving his first copies of the book, he rushed off a heartfelt letter, pointing out, "if the book fails, I have your love to enable me to forget the failure, and to strive to retrieve it; if it succeeds, I shall have the delight of knowing that the success is sweet to you, of knowing that I have so far achieved the absorbing desire of my heart—the desire of making my precious little sweetheart happy."[12] Houghton Mifflin was apparently generous with Wilson's publishing contract. "They have actually offered me good terms as if I were already a well-known writer," he wrote to Ellen.[13]

Critics and reviewers alike found the book important and noteworthy. In *The Presidency of Woodrow Wilson*, Kendrick A. Clements wrote that the gist of *Congressional Government* "was not primarily that Congress was corrupt but rather that Congress, which then supervised administration as well as legislating, was trying to do too much."[14] Author Mario Dinunzio observed that the book was "his analysis of the American system reflected [by] his admiration for British parliamentary government in which the prime minister and cabinet officers served in the legislature. The absence of such executive leadership in Congress was one of his targets, and he saw the American presidency as a weak office."[15] Later, as president, Wilson would use *Congressional Government* as a guidebook. "One of the most remarkable aspects of Wilson's presidency, at least during his first administration," wrote Kendrick Clements, "was his ability to dominate the government without antagonizing Congress."[16]

In 1883, two years before the publication of his first book, Wilson had the foresight to purchase a Caligraph, which was an early model of typewriter. Wilson quickly adapted to using the device for composing manuscripts, and considered it an asset for someone who desired to be a prolific writer. Wilson had also taught himself shorthand, and admitted that he "composed entire paragraphs and even longer passages in his mind before putting them down on paper."[17]

During this time, Wilson worked on a manuscript titled *A History of Political Economy in the United States*. Co-authored with a fellow graduate student by the name of Richard Ely, the proposed textbook never saw publication because of Ely's inability to finish his half. Still, seventy pages of text prepared by Wilson survive today.

The year 1889 saw publication of *The State: Elements of Historical and Practical Politics*. As a college textbook, it required Wilson to learn German in order to be able to translate badly needed sources, which his wife, Ellen, was brought in to do. Wilson would later regret the commission to author the book, calling it "a fact book ... a plebian among books ... [and] vulgar looking."[18] Although he was able to produce the volume under contract, the experience left a bad taste in his mouth, and he thereafter swore always "to be an author—never more a book-maker."[19] Yet, the book was a success, became required reading in universities for many years after, and saw several translations.

By the end of the nineteenth century, numerous universities that offered enticing teaching and administrative positions were entertaining Wilson. Biographer Arthur Walworth contends that during this period Wilson personally wrestled with the attraction of a literary career versus an administrative one. Walworth writes that Wilson "seemed rather to withdraw from administrative affairs and to wrap himself in literary work and to retire into a world of historical truth," adding "writing was the escape most accessible to him."[20]

It was during this time that Wilson's literary pursuits turned to history. With the publication of *Division and Reunion: 1829–1889*, in 1893, Wilson made his mark as an historian. A short work aimed for the general reader, the book earned praise from northern historians who had considered Wilson a southern writer. Some criticism was aimed at Wilson's writing style, such as one historian who thought that Wilson "was more occupied with brilliance of style than with the presentation of facts."[21]

Author Edwin A. Weinstein felt that the book marked a drastic change in Wilson's writing. He rarely pored over obscure sources anymore, instead content to keep with the flow of the book. Because of this, "Wilson was sometimes careless with the facts and gave the impression that he regarded digging for them as a routine task for lesser minds. After *Division and Reunion*, he rarely consulted primary sources. Too much knowledge, he warned, would break the spell of the imagination."[22]

Two books followed; *An Old Master and Other Political Essays*, and *Mere Literature*. These volumes contained essays on Wilson's political and educational philosophy, and would be sandwiched between his largely historical writings.

Wilson's interest in American history soon led him to an offer, from *Harper's* magazine in 1895, to author a serialized biography of George Washington. Published in book form one year later, *George Washington* would be roundly criticized for its inferiority. Biographer John Milton Cooper wrote, "*George Washington* was a bad book, written in an affected style with the saccharine, moralizing tone of contemporary children's books such as *Black Beauty* and *Little Lord Fauntleroy*."[23] Historian Arthur Link went as far as saying the book were "the lowest point in his literary career."[24] Biographer Edwin Weinstein, who also held a degree in neurology, noted that Wilson was under physical and emotional strain when he wrote it, yet refused to let him off lightly. "By any literary or scholastic standard, the book is his most mediocre work. It is a mixture of fact and fancy—in this respect like any other popular biography of its day. Contemporary critics were surprised that someone of Wilson's eminence should have descended to writing a potboiler.

In fact, Harper and Brothers, the publishers, claimed that the book would put Wilson into the rank of novelist."[25]

Wilson's relationship with *Harper's* produced *A History of the American People*, which would be published in 1902. Originally published in twelve serial installments at $1,000 apiece, the book sales brought in almost $30,000. Years later, Wilson would confide that he had "never been proud of that history," and "wrote it only to teach myself something about our country."[26] At the time, Wilson complained to historian John Franklin Jameson that "the editors of the popular monthlies offer me such prices nowadays that I am corrupted."[27]

Professor Mario Dinunzio noted that after the success of *History*, Wilson intended to write "a work on the philosophy of politics, which he intended to be his masterpiece."[28] In June of 1902, however, Wilson accepted the presidency of Princeton University. "This new turn ended his serious work as a scholar," and "the book was never written."[29]

In 1913, Wilson produced a book of speeches taken from his successful 1912 presidential campaign. In the book's preface, however, Wilson was quick to point out its true intentions. "[This] book is not a discussion of measures or of programs. It is an attempt to express the new spirit of our politics and to set forth, in large terms which may stick in the imagination, what it is that must be done if we are to restore our politics to their full spiritual vigor again, and our national life, whether in trade, in industry, or in what concerns us only as families and individuals.... The New Freedom is only revived and clothed in the unconquerable strength of modern America."[30]

Decades later, in 1956, the book was revised and expanded as *A Crossroads of Freedom*, and edited by John Wells Davidson. In his introduction, Davison noted that the book "has performed a valuable service by acquainting the public with the general principals of Wilson's political and economic program. But for the historian, as well as the interested layman, it is tantalizingly incomplete."[31]

The New Freedom would be Wilson's last book prior to his presidency.

During his two terms as president, Wilson's health seriously deteriorated. Wilson had health issues such as waking up blinded in one eye, and being almost unable to write. As president, Wilson was known to suffer at least one significant stroke that left him temporarily incapacitated. These health problems would erode his writing capacity after leaving office in 1921, even though offers to write would continue to pour in. One such offer was an offer to write of the Paris peace negotiations for $150,000. Other offers included newspaper columns, and a *Ladies' Home Journal* serial on the life of Jesus Christ. Inquiries about a possible autobiography were met with a blunt "There ain't going to be none."[32]

The George H. Coran Company went as far as to offer Wilson "the rights to any book by Wilson on the period of his presidency, and particularly the past five years ... $100,000 in advance and $100,000 on delivery of a manuscript of not less than 150,000 words and 20 percent on all books sold in the United States, with foreign royalties to be adjusted."[33] Wilson rejected the offer.

In the spring of 1923, Wilson decided to attempt to write again. An essay titled "The Road Away from Revolution," which George Creel, a literary agent and friend, considered inferior when compared to Wilson's past work, was offered. Wilson insisted on placing the article in a magazine, while Edith Wilson and Creel weighed the consequences: Negative reviews would certainly crush the already ill former president, but positive reaction would boost his sagging spirits. Creel quietly placed the article in the August issue of *Atlantic Monthly* for $200. It would be the last published work of Wilson to appear in his lifetime.

At Wilson's personal request, *The Road Away from Revolution* was quickly reprinted in a "small (almost a miniature) book."[34] Biographer August Heckscher wrote that "It was well accepted by the public, which raised no questions about the author's competence—and certainly was without conception of the agony in which it had been produced."[35]

Woodrow Wilson died February 3, 1924. The autobiography that publishers often begged for, but Wilson denied, never came to fruition. Edith Wilson, however, would publish *My Memoir* after his death, but the reviews were harsh. In her memoir, Mrs. Wilson noted that Wilson planned to author a book on government, but could never get past the dedication page.

Warren G. Harding

Warren G. Harding is notable as being the last president to never write anything significant that was published before, during, or after his presidency. In short, Harding did not author any books in his lifetime, nor have any appeared after. This is peculiar, because prior to being elected to the United States Senate, Harding was the editor and publisher of an Ohio newspaper, the *Marion Star*. Harding published the *Star* under the Harding Publishing Company, which published nothing else except the newspaper.

Although Harding frequently authored editorials in the *Star*, his writing suffered, and this is evident in a speech written in 1912: "Progression is not proclamation nor palaver. It is not pretense nor play on prejudice. It is not personal pronouns nor perennial pronouncement. It is not the perturbation of a people passion-wrought, nor a promise proposed."[1] Harding's attempts at speech writing were so poor that H.L. Mencken labeled it "Gamalielse" (Harding's middle name was Gamaliel), and his handlers no longer allowed Harding to author his own speeches. After Harding's sudden death in office, Florence Harding burned much of his personal papers, perhaps fearing scandal. Nothing notable, such as any attempt of a memoir, was known to be among them.

Calvin Coolidge

America's first exposure to Calvin Coolidge came in 1914, with an address known as "Have Faith in Massachusetts." Coolidge was a Massachusetts state senator at the time, and the popular and widely reprinted speech led him to the office of governor. While serving as Governor of Massachusetts, Coolidge received national recognition with his handling of the 1919 Boston police strike. His quotable "There is no right to strike against the public safety by anybody, any time, anywhere," led to *Have Faith in Massachusetts* being published in book form along with other speeches. The following spring, Coolidge was being touted as a Republican candidate for president, and Frank Sterns, a friend from Massachusetts, saw to it that every delegate received a copy of Coolidge's book. At the Republican Convention that summer, Ohio Senator Warren G. Harding received the presidential nomination, with Coolidge nominated as his running mate.

Harding's sudden death in August of 1923 brought Coolidge to the presidency. He was afforded a full term in his own right in 1925, refused to seek an additional term in 1928, and retired from public office. By the time he left office in March 1929, book publishers and magazines that sought to secure the rights to his memoirs and magazine articles were courting Coolidge. An offer from the *Cosmopolitan Magazine* and Book Corporation promised five dollars per word and contracts were signed. Coolidge set up an office in Northampton, which was primarily used as a "downtown loafing place."[1] It was there he most likely wrote much of what would become known as his autobiography with the aid of a stenographer. Coolidge "kept at it diligently, faithfully to the end," before sending it off to Cosmopolitan for the $75,000 plus price that the manuscript would bring him.[2]

Coolidge finished the manuscript so quickly that the Cosmopolitan Book

Corporation was able to bring the first edition of *The Autobiography of Calvin Coolidge* in late 1929, only months after he had left office, a rare feat in the publishing world. Coolidge's endearing simplicity is reflected in the book's unadorned title, and its absence of a preface or foreword. Despite its title, *Autobiography* was rarely personal or confessional. In *A Puritan in Babylon*, biographer William Allen White wrote that Coolidge's *Autobiography* "was not an intimate biography. One would hardly expect ribald details from Calvin Coolidge."[3]

After finishing *Autobiography*, Coolidge never wrote another book. What little writing he did was confined to a "short Ben Franklinesque daily comment on passing things" syndicated in newspapers and magazines.[4] By the end of the publishing contract, Coolidge had grown tired of writing and chose not to renew it. "I am afraid I am all burned out. But I am very comfortable," he admitted.[5] Coolidge died of a heart attack in January 1933.

Herbert Hoover

I want to write a better book.[1]
—Herbert Hoover

Herbert Hoover became a published author long before he was elected president in 1929, and was still being published long after he left office in 1933.

In 1891, at the age of seventeen, Hoover started attending at California's Stanford University where he soon obtained a temporary position as an assistant in an Arkansas Geological Survey. This was followed by similar positions for official United States Geological Surveys in California and Nevada. By the time he graduated in 1895, Hoover had met Miss Lou Henry, who would eventually become his wife. Hoover left Stanford with an engineering degree and found work in Nevada and Colorado gold mines as a laborer, working his way up to assistant manager. In 1897 Hoover landed an engineering position in an Australian gold mine. Two years later he found himself in China, and by 1908 was earning a living as an international free-lance engineer. In addition to free-lancing, Hoover accepted an invitation from Stanford to deliver a series of lectures to the student body. These went over so well that Columbia University in New York offered him the same invitation.

Soon after speaking at Columbia, Hoover compiled the lectures into manuscript form and offered them to a publisher. The publisher, W.R. Ingalls, was no stranger to Hoover as he had previously submitted articles to Ingalls' publication, the *Engineering and Mining Journal*. Hoover's articles had been published as early as 1903 and were largely related to the industry. Biographer David Burner wrote that during this period "Hoover did a good deal of writing—much of it concerned with specific, limited problems of finance or management—that touched on the character of those who are in charge of modern industry."[2] Ingalls accepted Hoover's manuscript, and in 1909 published it under the title *Principles of Mining*. The book became a standard textbook in the study of engineering, and is still consulted today. In his later published *Memoirs*, Hoover recalled that the book "came into large demand, and has been reprinted several times over, and is still used in the engineering schools."[3] Reviews of the book were mixed; with one praising its "straightforward style" and lack of "miners' jargon," while another complained of its "cumbersome sentences, careless punctuation, and abruptness."[4] Publisher Ingalls, however, remembered Hoover's manuscript being a mess. "It was atrociously bad—bad in handwriting, in spelling, in grammar and syntax, and in composition."[5] As a result, Ingalls had to spend time professionally editing it, with Hoover

In 1912, Herbert Hoover published the first English translation of the 1556 mining classic, *De Re Metallica*, a serious undertaking. Although many considered his presidency a failure, Hoover would redeem himself through numerous books concerning political and social issues (Library of Congress).

hardly bothering to look at the proofs. If he considered authoring a published book a badge of honor, it did not show, for years later Hoover was said to have told a "startled and unappreciative Stanford professor that writers were worth a dime a dozen."[6]

Perhaps the worst damage to arise from *Principals of Mining* were claims that Hoover used previously published work "almost verbatim, and without credit" to the rightful author.[7] Letters from Hoover are said to acknowledge the claims, but Burner came to the conclusion that the evidence was "too slim to charge Hoover with anything like plagiarism; he may simply have relied on the work of others in the same manner that many scholars do."[8]

Even while *Principals of Mining* was at the publishers, Hoover had been working on another book project. While traveling the globe doing freelance work he had begun accumulating an outstanding reference library. This included classic and modern writings in every language, as well as technical engineering manuals spanning centuries. One of the books that Hoover found irresistible was *De Re Metallica*, which had been published in 1556 by a German scientist named Georg Bauer (1494–1555), under the pen name Agricola. At the time of its publication, the book was considered the best work available on the subject of mining, and continued to be for over two centuries. Much of Agricola's expertise, however, became lost over time, as the book had been written in a vulgate Latin now considered a dead language. Latin scholars had long considered it to be incapable of proper translation, especially since Agricola used formulas containing language that did not exist at the time.

Biographer Eugene Lyons wrote that *De Re Metallica* was "a technological work, abounding in nomenclature and formulas that the Latinists could not decipher. Since there were no ancient Latin words to describe many medieval engineering processes, Agricola apparently had invented them or transliterated them from German and French expressions into a Latin of his own coinage."[9] Since it had been published in Latin, the church owned many of the only copies, and miners who wished to consult it had to obtain the services of a priest to translate it. Hoover knew little Latin, while Mrs. Hoover had a better understanding of the language. Therefore, she assisted him with the translation. With a world-class library at their disposal, the two decided to make an earnest attempt at translating the acclaimed work in 1907.

In his *Memoirs*, Hoover wrote of the book's history and recalled how he and his wife approached the mammoth undertaking:

> Sometimes the task amounted more to scientific detective work than to translation. Material A might start as an unknown substance but in different parts of the book Agricola would state its varying reactions when treated or combined with known sub-

stances B or C. Thus I could often have the meaning of his terms worked out in our laboratories. Often enough, when we discovered the meaning of a term we found that there was no modern word to express it because that particular process had been long abandoned. In any event, we grappled with it sentence by sentence, during our spare time, month after month, for over five years. We lugged the manuscript all over the world for odd moments that would be available for work on it.[10]

After five years and four revisions, the Hoover's had a translation that they were satisfied with. They then turned the manuscript over to a friend, Edgar Rickard, for publishing. Rickard could have easily set the manuscript in modern typeface and bindings, but felt the book merited special attention. Rickard knew an English commercial printer who shared his love of fine books and agreed to print the edition at cost. A papermaker was brought in to produce linen paper similar to paper used from the 16th century. Type was cast in the exact font used in the original. All this was done in an oversized folio and bound in white vellum. Hoover wrote an introduction, which included a biography of Agricola, as well as a listing of known editions. The entire translation received extensive footnotes covering the scientific processes as well as the translations. Hoover noted that despite years of hard work, as well as the expense of producing the fine edition, profit was not an ulterior motive. "Three thousand copies were printed and about 1,500 were sent as gifts to engineers and institutions. So that all engineers and others who were interested could obtain it, we placed 1,000 copies on sale through Edgar Rickard's publications, at a nominal price of $5, which hardly covered the binding."[11]

The price seems insignificant when one takes into account the years of traveling the couple spent pursuing the translation, as well as having paid over $20,000 for additional help. Hoover shared the book's 637-page translation credit with Mrs. Hoover, and dedicated the work to John Branner, a Stanford University professor. The beautiful limited edition quickly became a valuable collectors item. The couple also attempted a translation of Agricola's *De Natura Fossiliarum*, but was only able to complete a draft. Hoover would later also privately publish a bibliography of pre–1700 mining works.

By 1920, engineering and mining no longer captured Hoover's attention. This was evident in 1918, when President Woodrow Wilson appointed him to transform the Food Administration into a vehicle for European relief after suffering the ravages of World War I. Hoover was still revered in the field of engineering though, and in 1920 was elected president of the American Engineering Council. One of his major projects with the AEC was the issuance of a report titled *Waste in Industry*. Published in 1921, the 409-page report was written by a committee of which Hoover was a member. Hoover wrote the report's preface, which "became a milestone on the American road to greater efficiency and production."[12] At the time of its publication, Hoover had been appointed Secretary of Commerce by President Harding, and thus began a life in politics.

Early in his term as commerce secretary, Hoover wrote a book, *American Individualism*. Published in 1922, the book was considered controversial at the time for its opinion's on free enterprise and capitalism. Eugene Lyons commented that in spite of his published works, Hoover was still struggling as a writer. "Words were not Hoover's most effective tools. As a literary stylist he will certainly not be bracketed with Jefferson, Lincoln, or Wilson—to mention Presidents who, as Hoover, did their own writing. He was not elegant or scintillating; too often he relied on phrases worn thin from much usage. But he achieved his aim, which was not sensation but lucidity."[13]

American Individualism did not sit well among Harding's cronies, who had tried to keep Hoover out of the cabinet. Both Harding and Coolidge failed to heed his warnings that would eventually lead to the stock market crash of 1929, and Coolidge sarcastically referred to Hoover as a "wonder boy." Coolidge went as far to try to talk Hoover out of running for president by pointing out the petty annoyances of the job, but Hoover didn't listen and was elected in 1928. That same year, a volume of campaign speeches, under the title *The New Day*, was published.

With the October 1929 Stock Market crash Hoover's days in office were numbered, and he failed to win a second term.

Never a fan of the New Deal, Hoover wasted little time in writing his rebuttal of Roosevelt's practices. *The Challenge to Liberty*, published in 1934, was originally intended to be the former president's parting shot at politics. "I have long since resolved myself that just one final blast from me will register my concluding contribution to American life," he wrote a friend.[14] It is believed that Hoover had the manuscript finished by August, and had signed a contract with the *Saturday Evening Post* for the rights to two articles. Biographer Richard Norton Smith noted how "[Roosevelt's] name was not mentioned once in *The Challenge to Liberty*. Neither was the New Deal per se. But no one who read it could doubt the targets of Hoover's wrath, nor the fury that burned beneath a cool, philosophical deceptive surface."[15]

Reviews of the book were poor, with the *New York Times* calling it a series of "brooding, bitter essays," while the *San Francisco News* noted that it reflected Hoover's sense of defeat.[16] Despite being selected as a Book-of-the-Month Club offering, *A Challenge to Liberty* sold poorly, and at the beginning of December 1934, sales had amounted to 85,000 copies while the publisher had predicted 150,000.

The year 1938 brought *Addresses Upon the American Road*, which would eventually expand to eight volumes in later years. These volumes are filled with various essays, addresses, comments and letters relating to everything from foreign relations to fishing auguries. Stanford University Press published the later volumes. Hoover graduated from Stanford. It was also home to the Hoover Institute. Biographer Eugene Lyons noted the literary differences between Hoover and Roosevelt. "On the intellectual level, Roosevelt was a lowbrow who never voluntarily read a serious book, except about ships and navies, which were his hobby. Hoover [however] was avid for scholarly knowledge in all fields and himself the author of thoughtful books."[17]

In May of 1942, *The Problems of Lasting Peace* was published. Co-authored with Hugh Gibson, who had been private secretary to Charles Evans Hughes and holder of numerous foreign appointments before being dismissed by Roosevelt, the book was a political history lesson on how America got from the first World War to the second. Much of the gist of the book, as explained in its title, was addressed at maintaining peace after securing victory.

Despite its odd title, *The Problems of Lasting Peace* found Hoover at his best. Gone were the shackles of resentment concerning Roosevelt that had burdened him in his previous books, and he sincerely believed that he had something significant to offer.

On January 7, 1944, Mrs. Hoover unexpectedly died at their New York home. She had returned home to find her husband working, and not wishing to disturb him, went into another room where he later found her on the floor unconscious. Whatever grief Hoover held he kept private, choosing instead to bury it by co-authoring a follow-up with Hugh Gibson, *The Basis of Lasting Peace*, the same year.

With Roosevelt dead and Truman president, Hoover found a friend in the White House. This friendship led to the establishment of the Hoover Commission in 1947. Headed by Hoover, the Commission issued several reports. In 1953, President Eisenhower established what became known as the Second Hoover Commission. One of these reports, *The Necessary Steps for Promotion of German Exports, so as to Relieve the American Taxpayers of the Burdens of Relief, and for the Economic Recovery of Europe*, was published in 1955. Historian Eugene Lyons dryly observed how Hoover "had decided to pay the price of inelegant wording in order to compress his basic message into the very title."[18]

In 1951, the first two volumes of Hoover's three-volume autobiography were released, with the third volume published in 1952. *The Memoirs of Herbert Hoover* had actually been completed years earlier and were held back by

Hoover, who wished them published after his death. Hoover, however, had "outlived the bastards," and at the age of seventy-seven finally permitted the publication of his most autobiographical writings to date. Yet, *Memoirs* was hardly intimate, and much of the book was written in Hoover's traditional businesslike manner. Chapters with titles such as "Fascism Comes to Agriculture," and "The Expenditures, Accounting and Statistics: Index Numbers," really have no place in a memoir.

Perhaps wishing to surpass Ulysses S. Grant by volume, Hoover invested $70,000 of his own money towards printing costs for the three-volume set. Hoover did much of his own writing, and held a personal disdain for ghostwriters, but typically enlisted a staff of six to eight secretaries and researchers to assist him.

In 1958 Hoover published *The Ordeal of Woodrow Wilson*. As the first account of a president written by a fellow office holder, many claimed it was Hoover's best book, which was reflected by its appearance on the best-seller lists. Flush with his success at authoring political biography, Hoover considered a biography of Robert Taft, but the book never advanced past the synopsis stage.

Once Hoover had completed the Wilson manuscript, he returned to the project that he had left interrupted. The project, which would eventually bear the title *An American Epic*, told the history of American relief projects since 1914, and Hoover's involvement with them. As with *Addresses Upon the American Road* and *Memoirs*, *American Epic* would eventually require multiple volumes, in this case four. The first appeared in 1959, with the final being published in 1964. Biographer Eugene Lyons observed that it was a story only Hoover could tell, as he had been involved with it from the beginning. "Hoover had constantly emphasized America's instinct for compassion, its readiness to share with the needy the world over. These books provide the record in concrete terms. There are few nations that do not owe a debt of gratitude to the United States and therefore to its thirty-first President."[19]

In-between the volumes of *American Epic*, Hoover managed to publish two small books. The first of these was a book featuring letters to and from children and entitled *On Growing Up*. Published in 1962, the book included previously published letters as well as a few short essays, and was the shortest manuscript Hoover had submitted in decades. The book was actually therapeutic for the eighty-eight year old former president, as he acknowledged in the book's foreword, for he often sat up answering letters on nights that he could not sleep. Sensitive to suggestions that he did not author his own books, Hoover boasted, "The master file of this correspondence is available to demonstrate that these children's letters are genuine and that I have no ghost writer."[20] Hoover followed up with a small book on fishing. Written while he was restricted to bed due to illness, *Fishing for Fun, and to Wash your Soul* consisted of both new and old material related to fishing. It would be his last published work. By authoring a book on fishing, Hoover joined former President Grover Cleveland, who did the same in 1906 with *Fishing and Shooting Sketches*.

By then, Hoover had settled into a comfortable routine for both living and writing. Though his primary residence remained in New York City, summers were spent in California and the winters in Florida. He worked on his writing at a "small, uncluttered desk in the living room," at the Waldorf, where "stacks of files and books and printers' proofs overflowing on end tables and sofas" surrounded him[21] It would be here that Hoover would toil on his final manuscript.

Hoover had begun work on what would be his last manuscript sometime after World War II. Originally called "The Crucifixion of Liberty," and then "The War Book," Hoover eventually settled on the title of *Freedom Betrayed*. Hoover's secretaries referred to the manuscript as his magnum opus, and watched in amazement as he would work on it for up to ten hours a day. As with ghostwriters, Hoover had little use for dictating machines or even ballpoint pens, preferring the use of pencils instead. Sometimes Hoover would become so involved with writing that he would pass written research requests to the assistant who sat opposite him instead of asking verbally. *Freedom Betrayed* had gone through about a dozen revisions by the time the manuscript was completed, and was large enough to fill several volumes.

Although newspapers were eager to publish the serial rights, Hoover held back on publication and instead permitted a group of journalist friends to review the manuscript. The group came to the conclusion that publishing it would damage the credibility Hoover had since regained, as well as potentially expose him to libel. Hoover's son, Alan, eventually decided not to submit the manuscript to the publisher, and instead locked it up in the vault of the Hoover Institution.

Hoover died October 20, 1964. Like John Quincy Adams, Hoover had produced a substantial number of published works in his lifetime. Herbert and Lou Hoover are notable in the fact that along with Jimmy and Rosalynn Carter, they remain the only president and first lady to co-author a book.

In 2011, the Hoover Institute at Stanford University would finally publish *Freedom Betrayed: Herbert Hoover's Secret History of the Second World War and Its Aftermath*. Working from the original manuscript, the book was edited to 920 pages.

Franklin D. Roosevelt

While attending Harvard University in 1901, Roosevelt served as an editor for the Harvard University newspaper, the *Crimson*. His association with the paper was largely regulated to writing editorials concerning school matters. Much of what Roosevelt read was either history or nautical related.

In 1924 Roosevelt made his first attempt at becoming a serious writer by writing a book based on the life of naval commander John Paul Jones. While accounts differ on whether it was a biography or novel, Roosevelt never finished it. Biographer Nathan Miller noted that "Although [Roosevelt] had a strong sense of history, he lacked the staying power and concentration required to produce lengthy books."[1] Personal secretary Grace Tully once recalled that Roosevelt's fascination with Jones would later evolve into a "sketch for a movie" based on Old Ironsides, which was "submitted to a Hollywood studio, but never produced."[2] Ironically, cousin Theodore Roosevelt also contemplated writing a biography of Jones. Roosevelt, who found it difficult to even keep a diary, was perhaps aware of his limitations as a writer, and his "uncompleted writings became something of a rueful joke both to himself and his friends."[3] Biographer John Gunther noted that "FDR's choice of words was often somewhat effusive and effeminate, and his prose has little sustained pace or rhythm. He was much addicted to words and phrases like "fearfully," "horrid," "perfectly splendid," 'terribly," "awfully nice," and above all "thrilled."[4]

In the spring of 1925, Roosevelt wrote eight newspaper columns for the Macon *Telegraph* under the headline "Roosevelt Says." The subject matter, however, was often material previously presented in speeches, and was "bland and avoided controversy."[5] As a result, no other paper picked them up for syndication except for the Atlanta *Constitution*.

Roosevelt's stature as a published president is unique because he was actually published *while* president. The two books in question were titled *Looking Forward* and *On Our Way*. Both were basically overviews and histories of his New Deal programs. While Roosevelt was able to stir crowds with speeches, his words rarely crossed over into the intimacy needed as an author. Because of this neither book sold well.

Roosevelt's disappointments with publishing did not end with *On Our Way*, for in 1937 he pushed to get his public papers put into book form. Attorney Sam Rosenman, who would later help Harry Truman place his *Memoirs*, assisted Roosevelt in getting a contract with Bennett Cerf of Random House. Roosevelt threw himself into the project, even deciding upon the binding and typeface, but he failed to properly edit, which inflated production costs. When Cerf warned the president that former President Hoover's similar work had sold poorly, Roosevelt was said to reply, "Why, if Hoover sold 1,700, I'll sell a million!"[6] Roosevelt, however, failed to consider that in 1937 not everyone could afford $15 for a set of books. When the first volume was released, it sold 4,000 copies despite the publisher having printed up 25,000. Roosevelt had remained optimistic even after Cerf informed him that only 334 copies were sold in Washington, D.C. Cerf decided to cut his losses by offering the remaining volumes at remainder prices, which infuriated Roosevelt, as well as Rosenman, who "did not think that books by the President of the United States should suffer the indignity of being remaindered."[7]

Roosevelt's attempts to get his papers published into book form were probably the result of an earlier publishing fiasco. In 1935, Roosevelt outlined a book proposal for a novel under the title of *The President's Mystery Story*. Roosevelt presented the sketchy outline of a murder mystery involving a millionaire who simply wishes to disappear with five million dollars, without leaving a trace. Roosevelt quickly found a willing friend and publisher, Fulton Oursler of *Liberty Magazine*, to publish it in serial form. Roosevelt contributed little more than an outline, and allowed Oursler to "farm out" the piece to six writers. Farrar & Rinehart published *The President's Mystery Story* in 1936. Despite hiring writers to complete it, the book was a failure. In 1967 publishing house Prentice-Hall published a revised edition, under the title *The President's Mystery Plot*, with an additional chapter added. Oddly enough, the book was made into a short film with the title *The President's Mystery*. Another mystery novel attempted by Roosevelt was *Dark Masquerade*, which never made it past a synopsis.

When compared to an author, Roosevelt excelled as a speechwriter. It has been written that even working on a speech with Roosevelt was a trying experience, and often involved multiple drafts from several ghostwriters. Roosevelt most likely pondered writing his memoirs after leaving office. With a Great War and economic recovery under his belt, he might have expected nothing short of Grant's *Memoirs* to compete with. His sudden death in office on April 12, 1945, left any book projects unfulfilled.

Harry S. Truman

> If I had known how much work it is I probably would not have undertaken it.[1]
> —Harry S. Truman (on writing his *Memoirs*)

Harry S. Truman signing a copy of his memoirs at his Kansas City office in 1956. Truman enjoyed writing and was comfortable with writing in his own voice (courtesy Truman Library & Museum).

Truman succeeded to the presidency upon the death of Roosevelt in 1945, and was elected to a term on his own right in 1948. By the time Truman left Washington in January of 1953, he had a considerable number of corporations offering to pay him for his time. Truman felt it was beneath the dignity of a former president to lend his name for any commercial venture or lobbying influence, and refused to entertain such suggestions. Truman had not left office a wealthy man, and the presidential pension act did not become law until 1958. Therefore, Truman returned to the life, and financial circumstances, he had known before becoming president.

In his final presidential press conference Truman revealed he had received offers to write his memoirs, but admitted he was unsure whether they were worth writing. One month later, in February 1953, it was announced Truman had signed a book contract with publisher Henry Luce of *Life* magazine. In a letter to former Secretary of State Dean Acheson, Truman wrote, "I'm about to sell out a book for a fantastic sum. It's not worth it but I'm sorely tempted."[2] Although the amount was never publicly disclosed, it was later revealed to be $600,000. The contract was negotiated by lawyer Sam

Harry S. Truman at a 1960 book signing for his book *Mr. Citizen*. Truman enjoyed public book signings and became the first "modern-day presidential author" by doing so (courtesy Truman Library & Museum).

Rosenman and was to be paid in installments over the next five years. Despite signing a contract with *Life*, Truman fostered a personal dislike for Henry Luce that went back several years. Truman later claimed to have confronted Luce at a party arranged to celebrate the book deal. Sam Rosenman witnessed this and told Truman, "Harry, be careful. We haven't signed all the papers yet. If you make him mad, maybe he won't sign up."[3] This did not worry Truman, who felt Luce needed him more than he did

Before starting work on the book Truman took a vacation to Hawaii. Upon returning home to Missouri, however, Truman wished he had never signed the contract and confessed to Dean Acheson that he dreaded writing. The two exchanged ideas and Acheson ended up assisting Truman, who admitted he had "been working like a Turk."[4] Come fall, Truman was diligently working on the book. *Life*, however, had realized he was not a writer and would need a staff to assist him. Former speechwriters William Hillman and David Noyes were brought in to help craft the book. Both were said to be loyal and protective of Truman, who they still considered their boss. Biographer Merle Miller recalled Hillman being "a large, shambling man, a cigarette forever dangling from his full lips, [and] his ample stomach forever covered with ashes."5

Truman worked out of an office in the Federal Reserve Bank Building in Kansas City, Missouri. Truman would talk into a recording machine, which he hated, while a professor of journalism jogged Truman's memory for hours at a time. Everything was then fact checked and typed up. By late fall over 100,000 words had been transcribed. Truman was sometimes at odds with some of the staff, and this often led to departures during the progress of the book. Truman would often fix himself bourbon for lunch and sit in a comfortable chair while a staffer read him back the working manuscript, making verbal corrections.

In 1954 Truman began securing additional funding for his presidential library. This created a distraction when working on the book, and Truman brought in Dean Acheson as editor and proofreader. Acheson wielded great influence and Truman typically adhered to Acheson's recommendations. By January 1955 Truman admitted, "The damned thing is turning out much better than I thought it would, but I need your opinion badly."6 That summer, with the *Life* deadline approaching, Truman gave Acheson the daunting task of reviewing what had become the second draft of *Memoirs*, all 1,775 pages. The book would be separated into two volumes, and over the course of three months Acheson made forty-five pages of corrections and suggestions to the manuscript.

When Acheson came to the manuscript of the second volume, he felt Truman's ghostwriters were having their way with him. Author Merle Miller agreed, claiming "they had dejuiced and dehumanized him in everything that was written. They had laundered his prose, flattened his personality, and made him pontifical, which was the last thing I found him to be. Their mere presence in a room made him feel self-conscious, causing him to clean up his language and soften his opinions. With them around Mr. Truman came out bland."7

Year of Decisions, the first volume of *Memoirs*, was released in November 1955. This was followed by the March 1956 release of volume two, *Years of Trial and Hope*.

Prior to the release of volume one, Ken McCormick, the editor in chief of Doubleday and Company, proposed issuing a thirty-five dollar signed limited edition set. Truman rejected this outright, and instead proposed autographing as many copies as he could for Kansas City booksellers. He also refused to allow use of the Autopen when it came to his signature. "I cannot possibly enter into a program, which would look as if I were selling autographs instead of a book. I want the book sold on its merit. If it cannot be sold that way, then it's not worth having. I have a very strong feeling about any man, who has had the honor of being an occupant of the White House in the greatest job in the history of the world, who would exploit that position in any way, shape or form, I hope you understand the situation."[8]

On November 2, 1955, Truman signed about four thousands copies of *Memoirs* in five and a half hours. Kansas City bookstore owners attended the event, the first for a former president. In doing so, Truman had unwittingly ushered in the modern day age of presidential bookselling. After that, it would become common for ex-presidents to sit and sign their books for readers.

Perhaps the most unexpected shock following the publication of *Memoirs* was Truman's realization that the book had not become the financial windfall he had predicted. After expenses and taxes, Truman still had to pay sixty-seven percent on federal and state income taxes. What made this particularly sore for Truman was the fact that in 1949, then-general Eisenhower was able to claim a tax rate of only twenty-five percent on the $635,000 sale of his book, *Crusade in Europe*. Eisenhower had received the favorable capital gains rate on the grounds that he was not a professional author, along with the intervention of the Truman administration. With the shoe now on the other foot, Truman received no assistance from Eisenhower whatsoever. In *Off the Record*, editor Robert H. Ferrell notes "Because of the resulting outcry, Congress in 1950 passed the so-called Eisenhower amendment, which forbade any use of capital gains for writers whether professional or amateur."[9] Truman would later claim his net return from writing *Memoirs* "was about $37,000 over a five-year period. It was a package deal. I receive no royalties."[10] After the language of the 1958 Presidential Pension Act, however, Truman would have federal funding to provide him with a paid staff and office space.

Writing *Memoirs* would prove to be an ordeal for Truman. Despite complaining that he made little money, Truman learned a lot about the business of publishing. In correspondence with his publisher, Truman often used publishing jargon such as "galleys" and "advanced proofs." History had always interested him, and others told him he would have made a good teacher. Instead, Truman could now teach through writing.

Truman's next book was *Mr. Citizen*, which was published in 1960. After editing *Memoirs* Truman had a lot of unused material. Some of the manuscript probably made its way into *Mr. Citizen* as well as other books. The bulk of *Mr. Citizen* was culled from newspaper and magazine articles written after 1957. *Mr. Citizen* picks up where *Memoirs* left off, with Truman now once again a private citizen. In the book Truman revealed what happens to former presidents as well as what he thought they were still useful for. Another book soon followed, titled *Truman Speaks*. Published by Columbia University Press in 1960, this small book contained transcripts taken from a series of lectures Truman had given at Columbia University in April 1959.

On December 26, 1972, Harry S. Truman died at the age of eighty-eight.

In 1980, a new book of Truman's writings appeared. *Off the Record: The Private Papers of Harry S. Truman* contained an assortment of mixed writings. The book contained diary entries, letters, essays and other memoranda. The most significant of these were diary entries. Truman, along with Presidents Eisenhower, Nixon and Carter, were the only twentieth century presidents to have kept a diary. Truman made hundreds of entries while in the White House, and recorded Roosevelt's April 12, 1945, death and his swearing-in with extensive detail. Editor Robert H. Ferrell described Truman's diary as "frank, rambunctious, [and] full of life. It is, to put the case modestly, fascinating."[11]

In 1989, additional private writings of Truman surfaced in the form of *Where The Buck Stops: The Personal And Private Writings of Harry S. Truman*. Edited by daughter Margaret, *Where The Buck Stops* spurred new interest in the late president. Its origins can be dated back to the overflowing and abundant manuscript that became *Memoirs*. Although the 1953 *Life* contract with Henry Luce called for a manuscript of 300,000 words, Truman had written approximately two million by 1955. This was trimmed down to 580,000 by the time the book went to the printers.

What Truman did with these extra words is interesting. In a 1958 letter, Truman writes, "These memoirs of mine are not complete. I dictated over a million and a half words on the subject and we had to cut the number to about 520,000. I'm leaving the balance to Margaret, hoping it will be of some value to her and also an addition to the truth and the facts of the time."[12]

Dean Acheson seems to have planted the seed for *Where The Buck Stops* while helping Truman edit *Memoirs*. At the time, Acheson suggested that Truman remove certain passages pertaining to his predecessors, as well as his views on American history. "Take these pages out of the book. They don't belong here at all. Save them, and later on, when your income tax is not so much of a problem, do them over."[13] Margaret Truman acknowledged her father's personal style of writing, adding, "My father asked that [this] not be published until he and my mother had left us. He decided this because he wanted to feel free to say things about people and events in his usual frank and honest fashion. No words minced; no punches pulled."[14]

Where The Buck Stops was classic Harry S. Truman. He reviewed many of his presidential predecessors, sometimes in an insulting manner. This included his dislike of Dwight Eisenhower, and referring to Franklin Pierce as a "nincompoop." And while Truman revealed his love of Lincoln, he acknowledged, "my family were all against him and thought it was a fine thing he got assassinated."[15]

In 1973, author Merle Miller's book *Plain Speaking* was published. While not authored by Truman, it contained oral interviews from Truman transcribed into autobiographical form by Miller. *Plain Speaking* remains interesting because Miller was critical of William Hillman and David Noyes, who had assisted Truman with his *Memoirs*. After spending time with Miller and reading an advance copy of one of his articles, Truman wanted nothing to do with the book. Exerting his influence, Noyes encouraged the *Saturday Evening Post* to not publish any of Miller's pieces on Truman, so the disrespect was mutual.

In the end, Truman seemed to enjoy writing and was comfortable doing it in his own voice. He best summed up his legacy with the comment, "If I come out all right, I'm lucky."[16]

Dwight D. Eisenhower

> Revised or not, my writing had never threatened the standing of Twain or Hemingway.[1]
> —Dwight D. Eisenhower.

As Supreme Commander of the Allied Forces during World War II, Dwight D. Eisenhower's first brush with publication came in the form of a report titled *Report by the Supreme Commander to the Combined Chiefs of State on the Operations in Europe of the Allied Expeditionary Force, 6 June 1944 to 8 May 1945*. Published by the U.S. Army in 1946, the 123-page report was a technical record of U.S. Army movements from D-Day to the surrender of Germany. Though issued in Eisenhower's name, it was most likely compiled by a staff of officers and assistants. The report was written in a straightforward military style and does not contain any personal observations.

With the war now over, publishers with offers to publish his memoirs quickly approached Eisenhower. At first Eisenhower wanted nothing to do with writing. "To all of these proposals I turned a deaf ear. For one thing, I was really tired: I wanted nothing so much as the opportunity to loaf a while and then try to find out what to do with the rest of my life."[2]

Eisenhower took a liking to Richard Simon of Simon and Schuster, however, and was soon sending Simon examples of his writing to critique. Eisenhower doubted his abilities as an author, and Simon was experienced enough not to pressure him into a contract early. The possibility of a book brightened when Eisenhower secured a commitment from Arthur Nevins, a former staff member. By the summer of 1947 Eisenhower was deluged with publishing offers, and had turned away Nevins's offer. As a commander of the army-turned-president, many publishers were hoping a book from Eisenhower could repeat the success of Grant's *Memoirs*.

While many of the offers were generous, Eisenhower still occupied the office of Chief of Staff of the Army, and Eisenhower felt that attempting to write a book while serving on active duty was inappropriate and impossible. Eventually Douglas M. Black of Doubleday gained Eisenhower's confidence. Black maintained that Eisenhower owed the country, as well as history, his story. Black also presented Eisenhower with a simple book contract, or as Eisenhower put it, "a single package to cover the whole affair so that I don't have to argue with too many different people."[3] Black secured the deal with a current Internal Revenue Service ruling that permitted a book written by a non-professional writer to be sold with all rights, and then taxed as capital gains instead of earned income. To Eisenhower, this was as simple as selling a piece of property.

Eisenhower began work on the manuscript in early 1948, with a staff that included three secretaries and an army historian. He was encouraged to read Grant's *Memoirs* as homework. When Eisenhower brought in historian Stephen Ambrose as editor, Ambrose was surprised by Eisenhower's rough language. When Ambrose mentioned this, he was told that it showed that he had gained Eisenhower's confidence. "That shows he trusts you. He knows you will clean up his language."[4]

Doubleday & Company paid Eisenhower $635,000 for all rights to the book when completed. After paying $158,750 in capital gains, Eisenhower cleared a net profit of $476,250. *Crusade in Europe* was published in late 1948, and became a best seller. While the book continued to sell well long after signing the package deal, Eisenhower was not bothered with the additional income he would have received in a regular contract. Stephen Ambrose would note, "The real beneficiary of the deal was the publisher, not Eisenhower."[5] Despite any financial discrepancy, Eisenhower enjoyed working with Doubleday, and would go on to publish additional books with them.

As mentioned in the previous chapter, *Crusade in Europe* would later arouse bitter feelings from President Truman. When Eisenhower received the assurance of the Internal Revenue Service that they would accept his capital gains package deal with Doubleday, the Truman White House had quietly seen that the general be treated well. Five years later, with Eisenhower now president, Truman had signed an identical deal with the publication of his *Memoirs*, and expected similar treatment. Eisenhower, however, refused to become involved, and Truman was heavily taxed.

Eisenhower's next book, *Peace with Justice*, would be published in January 1961. By then he had retired from the army, been named president of Columbia University, and served two terms as president of the United States. Published by Columbia University Press, it contained thirty selected addresses given from 1950 to 1960. Upon leaving the presidency, Eisenhower was once again swamped with publishing offers. Thanks to the success of *Crusade,* his Gettysburg, Pennsylvania, farm was paid for, and through his government pension Eisenhower was "under no compulsion to hustle a dollar," from anyone.[6]

He would once again sign with Doubleday to write his memoirs in February. It was said that Eisenhower's books were "staff constructions: they were planned and shaped in committee, other hands drafted typescript, and Eisenhower's hand in the finished product was chiefly editorial, applied to striking out and interlineating as he searched for the satisfactory phrase."[7] It soon became apparent that Eisenhower's memoir would encompass two separate volumes. While the pair would become known as *The White House Years*, they would each have their own identity. Published in November 1963, *Mandate for Change* would become volume one. When Eisenhower received an advance copy in September it was the center of attention. One of his sons, John, would become an author in his own right, and knew how his father probably felt. "That moment—when a book comes out between covers—is the thrill of the writing game. I have experienced it now three times ... and whether the book sells or not, there is a satisfaction in a completed product that makes all the labor worthwhile."[8] Compared to his war memoir, *Mandate* would not sell as well and received mixed reviews. It reached number two on the *New York Times* best seller list before coming to an abrupt halt due to the assassination of President Kennedy two weeks later. With publishers scrambling to publish books memorializing Kennedy, sales of Eisenhower's book never recovered.

The following year would see publication of the second installment, titled *Waging Peace*. As with *Mandate for Change*, many reviews were critical concerning Eisenhower's writing. As an example, Eisenhower downplayed his 1956 stroke as if it were a simple cold. Perhaps the most revealing fact was found in the acknowledgments page where Eisenhower thanked his editors, writing, "In numberless ways they made my task easier—sometimes even enjoyable."[9]

After the completion of his largest book project, Eisenhower had no longer found writing to be enjoyable. It was surprising that Eisenhower's next book was another memoir. Published in 1967, *At Ease: Stories I Tell to Friends*, would be "accorded a far warmer reception than its predecessors," and widely read.¹⁰ *At Ease* was the memoir Eisenhower had tried to write, but was unable to with so many editors. Although he remained with Doubleday, the editorial assistance that Eisenhower had received for the *White House Years* was replaced. The book was written in a relaxed and narrative manner, and was at times even humorous. It was arguably his best book, despite oddities such as his recipe for vegetable soup in the appendix. Author Robert Ferrell called it "an autobiography, gracefully told."¹¹

Doubleday would approach Eisenhower with additional book proposals, but none caught his interest. With his health failing, Eisenhower's last real "literary effort" would be the medical diary suggested by his doctor to monitor his troubled heart. Although having suffered a serious heart attack in 1968, Eisenhower managed to produce one more book with Doubleday. *In Review: Pictures I've Kept* was published in early 1969. It was heavily illustrated with text drawn from his previously published books. Eisenhower's input appears to have been minimal, and aside from choosing photographs, it is hard to imagine him doing more. At the time Eisenhower was confined to the hospital since his last heart attack. It was there that Eisenhower died on March 28, 1969.

In 1981, W.W. Norton & Company would publish *The Eisenhower Diaries*, which were edited by Robert H. Ferrell. The December 27, 1935, to March 14, 1967, diary Eisenhower kept was sporadic, with gaps sometimes covering years. Although it contains White House entries, they were not published separately such as with later presidents, and are often overlooked.

John F. Kennedy

John F. Kennedy first became an author while still a student at Harvard University. While attending Harvard his father, Joseph P. Kennedy, served as ambassador to Great Britain. In 1939, John visited his father in London and witnessed firsthand England's entry into the Second World War. When Kennedy returned to Harvard in September, he began to work on a thesis paper for his political science class that was taught by Arthur Holcombe. A published author in his own right, Holcombe would later teach Henry Kissinger and Henry Cabot Lodge, Jr.

Kennedy chose to write his thesis on England's foreign policy since 1931.

Fortunately for him, he had his father's office at his disposal, and Kennedy was able to request and receive research materials directly from the embassy. With the aid of a typist the thesis was completed in early 1940. Kennedy submitted a copy to his father for his opinion and the ambassador showed the manuscript along to an old friend, Arthur Krock of the *New York Times*. Krock thought it to be publishable but cautioned the ambassador that it might injure his political career. Joe Kennedy disregarded Krock's advice and encouraged John, reminding him that becoming a published author would certainly help his stature. Krock even suggested the title of *Why England Slept*, which was a play on words from Winston Churchill's book, *While England Slept*.

Krock would spend two weeks editing Kennedy's manuscript remembering:

> It was mishmash, ungrammatical. He had sentences without subjects and verbs. It was a very sloppy job, mostly magazine and newspaper clippings stuck together. I edited it, and put in a little peroration at the end.[1] Gertrude Algase, who served as Kennedy's agent, then solicited the manuscript to several publishers. Harper Brothers and Har-

When senator John F. Kennedy's *Profiles in Courage* was awarded the Pulitzer Prize in 1957, research assistant Theodore Sorensen was rumored to have authored a substantial part of the book. Although both men denied the claim, rumors persist to this day (courtesy John F. Kennedy Library).

court Brace both turned it down, despite Algase suggesting that Joseph Sr. and Joseph Jr. could provide books as well. Eventually Wilfred Funk accepted it, on the condition that Henry Luce of *Time-Life* furnished the foreword. After putting so much work into the book Krock felt slighted at first, but realized Luce's association would garner great publicity.

With Luce's backing, *Why England Slept* received largely favorable reviews. It had it critics, however, such as Harold Lanski of The London School of Economics. Joseph Kennedy considered Lanski influential and presented Lanski with a copy to critique. But Lanski was not impressed with the book, and in a frank manner, expressed such to Joseph Kennedy. "I don't honestly think any publisher would have looked at that book of Jack's if he had not been your son, and if you had not been Ambassador. And those are not the right grounds for publication."[2]

Why England Slept would sell eighty thousand copies in the United States and England. With the forty thousand dollars he earned in royalties, Kennedy purchased a Buick convertible and donated his English royalties to the town of Plymouth, England, which had been bombed by Germany. In *A Question of Character*, author Thomas C. Reeves wrote that "to make the book a bestseller, the ambassador quietly purchased between thirty and forty thousand copies, storing them in the attic and basement of his Hyannis Port home."[3]

Friend Charles Spaulding remembered Kennedy being good at self-promotion, which would later prove to be an asset in politics. "It was just a sort of amusing pragmatism that he hadn't just written the book and then he was going to just disappear. He was going to see that it got sold. He was just laughing at his own success.... He was doing everything he could to promote it. And he was good at it. The interviews, radio programs, answering letters, autographing copies, sending them out, [and] checking bookstores."[4]

By the time Joseph Kennedy sent a complimentary copy to Prime Minister Winston Churchill, Kennedy's days as ambassador were numbered, but he still pressed copies of the book on anyone he thought could help sales or publicity. Despite this, John went to lengths to separate himself from his overbearing father. In the book's acknowledgments page he stated, "The views expressed in this book are my own, and for them I accept full responsibility."[5] It also put him ahead of his older and competitive brother, Joe Jr., who at the time, was expected to be the political torchbearer of the family. Ironically, it was John's success as an author that could have also led Joe Jr. to an early death.

In early 1939, Joe Jr. had taken a trip to Spain and attempted to write a book on the Spanish Civil War. The events in Germany and England would soon overshadow events in Spain, and the struggling author would abandon the project. In his autobiography of Joseph P. Kennedy, author Ted Schwarz wrote of the disastrous effect John's book had upon Joe Jr. "He knew little of history, had seen none of the fighting, and had talked to neither leaders nor the general populace. He was a brash young man who tried to turn a few days' sightseeing, coupled with opinions based on assumptions, into a treatise someone might buy. The problem was that Jack accomplished something Joe Jr. could not. Worse, Jack was able to utilize his father's letters and papers as resources; something Joe Jr. had not been able to do."[6]

After Harvard, John attended Stanford University. Since he was leaning toward a career in journalism Stanford was a good choice. John could have easily gone to Yale, but Joe Jr. was already pursuing law there, and the thought of attending the same school as his older brother was not an option. After Pearl Harbor, John joined the Navy and was given command of a PT Boat. After a Japanese destroyer rammed his boat in 1943, John became a war hero. Joe would join the Air Force, and after seeing his younger brother once again become the center of attention, signed up for a dangerous bombing mission in 1944, resulting in his death.

It was Joe's death that led John to his second book. While recovering from his war injuries he had begun gathering reminiscences and recollections of Joe from friends and family. Kennedy wished to collect the accounts and publish them in book form as a Christmas gift to his parents in 1944. The project, however, prove more demanding than Jack anticipated, and it was not completed until the spring of 1945. Eunice Kennedy later remarked that the idea of writing about Joe was discussed by the family, but "it was Jack who disappeared every evening from five to seven-thirty and wrote letters and made calls, and collected information, and wrote the book while the rest of us were still playing games."[7] Harvard University Press privately published the book, which was titled *As We Remember Joe*, in a limited edition of 360 copies. Each slim volume came with its own maroon slipcase. Two hundred and fifty copies were sent out to various relatives, friends, and service colleagues. While the book included an introduction written by Jack, most of it contained the memories of those who knew Joe. It was said Joseph Kennedy, Sr., was unable to read it.

Biographers Joan and Clay Blair noted that *As We Remember Joe* was "not really a book in the strictest sense."[8] Accounts of the book vary, with some describing it as a collection of anecdotes, and something of a eulogy. Regardless, it remains a collector's item. In his 1969 autobiography on Joe Jr., author Hank Searls claimed that although an additional five hundred copies "have been printed since, it is a rare book: Parke-Bernet Galleries in New York auctioned two copies for $1,500 each in 1945; in 1964, at another New York auction, a mysterious blonde who would not identify herself and said she was twenty-three but looked like a teenager bid $1,100 for another copy and won."[9] In 1976, authors Joan and Clay Blair quoted the book being "worth perhaps $2,000 a copy."[10] Copies continue to escalate, and today they typically range from $2,000 to $5,000. In 1965, Robert F. Kennedy printed up a small press run of the book, which he signed and distributed as Christmas gifts.

Now an author and war hero, Kennedy was elected to the House in 1946, followed by the Senate in 1952. Along the way he occasionally wrote articles that were published in magazines and newspapers. His chronic back pain caused by his war injury would lead would lead Kennedy to write his third book, *Profiles in Courage*. While recuperating from surgery in 1954, Kennedy had read Herbert Agar's *Price of Union*, and came away inspired. Kennedy wanted to remind readers that politics could be a noble pursuit, and began working on an article. Over the next several months, the article grew into a book, tentatively titled "Patterns of Political Courage." A draft was submitted to Harper's Magazine, with the publisher being interested in a possible book. Speechwriter Ted Sorensen worked closely with the senator, shipping him books and serving as chief researcher. Kennedy would dictate into machine that was then typed up by a stenographer. Kennedy would then edit by pencil, Sorensen recalled, and stayed clear of a typewriter. In 1955 Kennedy underwent additional back surgery. While recuperating at his Palm Beach home he would prop himself up in a chair and work on the manuscript. Assistant Dave Powers would remember Kennedy working on the book day and night, the only thing that helped distract him from his back pain.

By June 1955, most of the manuscript was complete. After sifting through numerous working titles, *Profiles in Courage* emerged. Kennedy now felt it was time to have the manuscript critiqued by an established author, and asked historian Arthur Schlesinger, Jr., to look at it. Asking Schlesinger to be candid and frank, Kennedy gave him free reign to dismiss or alter any part of the manuscript. Schlesinger replied that he found the manuscript "skillfully written and a genuine contribution to political discussion."[11] The correspondence between Kennedy and Schlesinger regarding the manuscript would eventually fill six pages when Random House published *The Letters of Arthur Schlesinger, Jr.,* in 2013. Schlesinger's assistance would prove to be priceless, and help keep the projected publish date of the book, then scheduled for January 1956, on track. It was also the beginning of a lifelong friendship.

Profiles in Courage was published January 1, 1956, and told the stories of eight senators. All eight had risked their political career at one time or another by placing themselves at odds with either their parties, constituents, or national region. *Profiles in Courage* received good reviews and quickly went to the top of best seller lists where it would remain for several months. In a shrewd business move, Kennedy had the publisher reinvest ten percent of the earnings back into the book's promotion, and matched it with his own royalties. The book became a tremendous asset to his political career, and earned him national stature. When the Democratic Party met for its National Convention in Chicago that summer, Kennedy's name was widely circulated for vice president. Although he failed to clinch the nomination, at that point Kennedy knew he could probably make a successful run for the presidency in 1960.

On May 7, 1957, the Pulitzer Prize Advisory Committee announced that John F. Kennedy had won the prize in biography for *Profiles in Courage*. While Kennedy was honored by the Committee's selection, it also became the source of much debate. Ever since the book was released in 1956, there had been claims that Kennedy had not been its primary author. Critics pointed to Ted Sorensen and his speech-writing ability, and believed that he was in fact the book's unacknowledged ghostwriter. Sorensen and Kennedy repeatedly denied the charges, but they refused to go away. Additional rumors included father Joseph Kennedy attempting to befriend members of the advisory committee.

On a December 1957 episode of ABC television's *Mike Wallace Show*, political columnist Drew Pearson was quoted as saying Kennedy's book had been ghostwritten. Kennedy phoned Sorensen and felt it was time for legal action. "This challenges my ability to write the book, my honesty in signing it and my integrity in accepting the Pulitzer Prize."[12] Sorensen would assist Kennedy and his attorney, Clark Clifford, by gathering up samples of the manuscript that showed Kennedy's handwriting. They also prepared a list of witnesses who had seen the senator work on the book. This list included secretaries, visitors to Palm Beach, and even publishers. At a meeting with ABC executives, Pearson was telephoned by ABC in the presence of Clifford and Kennedy, and when asked whether Sorensen authored the book, once again maintained what he had stated on Mike Wallace's program. Sorensen writes that after cross-examining him, ABC "finally agreed that the Senator was clearly the author of *Profiles in Courage* with sole responsibility for its concepts and contents, and with such assistance, during his convalescence, as his Preface acknowledged."[13] ABC even attempted to extricate themselves from the situation by claiming Sorensen had "privately boasted of being the author," and allegedly did so while intoxicated.[14]

After Kennedy personally attested for Sorensen's character, a deal was struck. Sorensen would furnish a sworn statement stating he was not the author of *Profiles*, and ABC would retract the story and issue an apology on the *Mike Wallace Show*. Despite this, rumors of Sorensen's involvement would continue to pursue Kennedy. In his book, *Jack: The Struggles of John F.*

Kennedy, biographer Herbert Parmet went as far to claim Sorensen had ghostwritten the book. Parmet cited his conclusion on sources available at the John F. Kennedy Library, which included working drafts of the manuscript as well as tapes dictated by Kennedy. Parmet's views were shared by other Kennedy biographers, such as Robert Dallek, who wrote "Jack did more on the book than some later critics believed, but less than the term *author* normally connotes. *Profiles in Courage* was more the work of a "committee" than of any one person."[15]

By June of 1957 the book had sold over 100,000 copies and had been translated into several languages. *Profiles in Courage* would be constantly reprinted through the years, and revised and expanded with new introductions and commemorative editions. Notable editions include the Inaugural edition of 1961, and the Memorial edition of 1964, which included a foreword written by Robert F. Kennedy. The book has never been out of print, and continues to find a new audience with every generation. *Profiles* would even find a television audience when NBC broadcasted twenty-six episodes in a mini-series from November 1964 to May 1965.

It has been pointed that Kennedy probably salvaged his political career by writing *Profiles* while convalescing from extensive back surgeries. These surgeries, of course, caused Kennedy to miss time from the Senate, and diminished his voting record. Because of the success of *Profiles*, however, Kennedy was considered politically untouchable at the time, and easily retained his Senate seat.

In 1958, Kennedy published his fourth book, *A Nation of Immigrants*. Compared to the huge success of *Profiles in Courage*, the book did not capture the same degree of readership, and today remains relatively forgotten. *A Nation of Immigrants* is a brief history of American immigration. Chapters include pre and post–Revolutionary immigration, as well as the immigrant's contribution to America. The book came about after the 1957 Displaced Persons Act, as well as the Refugee Relief Act, both of which Kennedy sponsored while in the Senate.

In 1960, Kennedy ran for president. That same year, a collection of his speeches was published in a book, *The Strategy of Peace*. The volume, published by Harper & Row, included an introduction by Professor Allan Nevins and an interview with journalist John Fischer. *Strategy* was basically a campaign tool, and was used to promote the Senator's views on domestic as well as global challenges. Biographer Michael O'Brien observed that the book was "the largest single effort by Kennedy's campaign to beguile the intellectuals and opinion leaders," of the day by sending personalized copies of the 233 page book to influential scientists, labor leaders, clergymen, and others.[16]

One year into Kennedy's term, Harper published *To Turn the Tide*. The 1962 book, which was edited by John W. Gardner, was a collection of statements and legislation that had been initiated or passed since Kennedy's inauguration.

After his November 22, 1963, assassination, publishers rushed countless literary tributes to the slain president into print. One of these was *The Burden and the Glory*, a collection of public statements and addresses made by Kennedy during his time in office. As with *Strategy of Peace*, the book was edited by Allan Nevins. The addresses and statements are characterized by topics such as race relations, economy, science, and international conflict. Of all the addresses included, perhaps the most memorable is Kennedy's "Ich Bin Ein Berliner," made in Berlin five months before his death. As a postscript, the volume includes the "Undelivered Speech for the Dallas Citizens Council," which he was scheduled to give in Dallas.

In a 1964 interview with Arthur M. Schlesinger, Jackie Kennedy revealed possible plans her husband had wished to explore after leaving the presidency. Although not published until 2011, Mrs. Kennedy stated he had considered becoming the "publisher of a great paper."[17] One newspaper he had in mind was the *Washington Post*.

In 2012, author David G. Coleman published *The Fourteenth Day*, his book documenting the Cuban Missile Crisis of 1963. Throughout the book, Coleman relied on notes and sources that included Kennedy's use of a Dictaphone. He particularly makes mention of a recording Kennedy made "sometime in 1959 or 1960–before he was president but after he had decided to run," in which Kennedy recited "a history of his political career and [explained] why he found elected office so important and personally rewarding."[18] Coleman went on to speculate that Kennedy was most likely laying the groundwork for what would one day have become his memoirs. "On this occasion, Kennedy was not dictating a letter or memorandum. It is not known precisely known when he made this particular recording or why. It is possible—even probable—that he was making notes for what would one day be the first draft of his memoir. He was, after all, already an accomplished and Pulitzer Prize–winning author, well versed in a historian's way of thinking. He made other, similar recordings later, while in the Oval office, that were almost certainly early notes for such a book, something for him to work on after leaving office."[19]

Of particular interest to readers of Kennedy's published writings is *The Kennedy Literature: A Bibliographical Essay on John F. Kennedy*. Authored by James Tracy Crown and published by the New York University Press in 1968, the book is a noteworthy study of Kennedy's writing style as well as a critical evaluation of his published works. No other president has been afforded the honor of an independent volume critiquing their literary abilities. Published five years after his assassination, Crown permitted Kennedy's popularity and public sentiment to settle down before judging Kennedy's literary standing among his predecessors. In a short essay titled "Kennedy as a Writer," Crown writes, "The question of where Kennedy ranks in regard to other presidential writers deserves at least passing mention. Kennedy was, of course, by far the best selling writer of any man who occupied the White House. The spectacular success of the writing of Ulysses S. Grant, incidentally, stands as proof that it is not necessary for a public figure to be an intellectual in order to write for a wide audience."[20]

The Kennedy Literature also includes a chronological bibliography of everything ever published by Kennedy, including books and magazine articles. Also included are reviews of Kennedy's books. Major biographies are also reviewed. Published articles listed under personal material, campaigning, and the presidency also appears. Twenty-five pages of twenty-nine publications dealing with the 1963 assassination are dissected by Crown as well. Crown, it appears, was among the skeptics when it came to believing the Warren Commission Report, citing that it "reads like a fairy story."[21] Finally, Crown suggests additional sources for further research.

Overall, *The Kennedy Literature* remains essential reading for anyone wishing to delve deeper into Kennedy's writings. Although the book has been long out of print, used copies can typically be located through Internet booksellers.

Lyndon B. Johnson

> What do you think this is, the tale of an uneducated cowboy? It's a presidential memoir, damn it, and I've got to come out looking like a statesman, not some backwoods politician.[1]
> —Lyndon B. Johnson

Lyndon B. Johnson had a gift that enabled him to reach out to the poor and underclass, but was best when left to his own devices, which involved ad-libbing. When it came to expressing himself through the written word, Johnson's talents diminished. Former speech-writer George Reedy recalled how "Johnson's inability to connect words with reality also produced nightmares for his speech writers." His only instructions were "Do me a speech," which really meant "Give me a script so I can entertain the audience."[2]

Johnson's only real experience at writing occurred while a student teacher in San Marcos, Texas, in 1929. It was there that Johnson was appointed summer editor of the *College Star* newspaper and wrote editorials that appeared under his byline. Johnson, however, did little of the actual writing. "Nearly all his editorials were written by his mother or a member of the staff he could command," recalled a fellow staffer.[3] This hardly mattered, as Johnson's editorials were based on "flaccid subjects" such as holidays, or "flattering biographies of administrators and faculty."[4] Throughout Johnson's political career as both congressman and senator, he never considered authoring a book, as John F. Kennedy did, which could have easily broadened his national appeal. Instead, Johnson chose to let his reputation in the Senate build his name up nationally.

Johnson's first book was published while serving as president. In 1964 Johnson addressed the graduating class of the University of Michigan at Ann Arbor, where in a speech, he outlined what became known as his vision of a "Great Society." Two years later, in 1966, Random House would set Johnson's words against photographs taken by noted photographer Ken Heyman. The end result was a 169-page book of text and photographs entitled *This America*. While Johnson was given full author credit, the folio sized book is largely exerts of speeches grouped with Heyman's black and white photographs. Aside from a brief Publishers Note, the book contains no preface or introduction from either Johnson or Heyman, instead allowing the text and photographs to speak for themselves. While Johnson's words are powerful, it is often Heyman's photographs that capture the reader's attention.

In March 1968, Johnson announced he would not seek another term. As the end of his presidency drew near, Johnson looked forward to retirement. In December, he disclosed his plans were "spending some time with Lady Bird, reading books that had been given him for Christmas, and then engaging in some teaching and writing."[5] It was about this time that Johnson secured a publishing contract with Holt, Rinehart, and Winston for his memoirs. Acting on Johnson's behalf was New York attorney Arthur Krim. Krim's clients included the Motion Picture Association of America, which placed Krim within the reach of Hollywood should anyone desire the book's film rights. Johnson soon realized that while he craved having a book authored under his name, he had no real literary ability or desire. "Sitting in solitude for long hours struggling with memory was not Johnson's cup of tea," biographer Randall Woods observed, and like former president's Truman and Eisenhower, "it was decided he would dictate."[6]

Johnson assembled a team of former White House aides to help prepare writing the manuscript. The most crucial appointment, however, was twenty-five year old Doris Kearns, who possessed a Harvard Ph.D. in political science, and was a former White House Fellow. With about a month remaining in his term, Johnson began a full-blown attempt to woo Kearns into coming down to Texas with him. Once there, his plans were to put her up in a cabin on his ranch and have her assist him in writing his memoirs. "I'll invite a millionaire to the ranch every weekend, and I'll buy you pretty clothes, and I'll put you on a diet and give you a fabulous salary so you can look beautiful all the time," Johnson told her, "Now, what girl in her right mind wouldn't come and work with the president of the United States under these conditions?"[7] Kearns, who wanted nothing except to return to Cambridge, knew she would be miserable in Texas. "Nothing would be mine, perhaps not even myself," she wrote.[8]

Kearns suggested she could assist Johnson on a part-time basis, and when Johnson told her it had to be all or nothing, she believed the subject would not come up again. So she was naturally surprised when Johnson called her to the

Lyndon B. Johnson inspecting a copy of his 1971 book, *The Vantage Point*. Johnson enjoyed telling his own story, but found writing difficult and preferred a competent biographer handle such matters. *Vantage Point* received poor initial reviews and discouraged further attempts at writing, so Johnson focused his energy towards his presidential library, which in the end became his other "book" (courtesy Lyndon B. Johnson Library).

White House on January 19, his last full day in office. Kearns met Johnson in the Oval Office, which she remembers being the only room in the mansion which had yet to be touched by movers. Johnson quickly got to the point:

> As soon as I get settled at home, I'm going to write my memoirs. Those memoirs are the last chance I've got with the history books, and I've got to do it right. I've got to get my story out from beginning to end. We've got to go through my papers, and diaries, and ask hard questions to jog my memory. I want you all to be like vultures with me, picking out my eyes and ears, tearing those memories and experience out of my guts, putting all my insides into your sacks so you can help me write my story. Then I'll go over your drafts again and again until I remember everything I want to say. Will you do it? Will you help me?[9]

This time, Johnson had wisely left the door open for Kearns to choose her degree of involvement. He would accept whatever help she could give, whether it be part-time, weekends, or even during vacations. Kearns felt she could not refuse the last request of a president in the waning hours of his presidency, and accepted. The fact was not lost on Johnson, who, despite possessing perhaps one of the most temperamental egos in the history of the presidency, now felt his power shrinking. "It's not so easy to get the help you need when you're no longer on top of the world," he confessed. "I know that and I won't forget what you're doing for me."[10]

Kearns later married, and under the name Doris Kearns Goodwin, authored several books on American history, one of them being *Lyndon Johnson and the American Dream*. In it, Kearns recollects her involvement in the Johnson White House, as well as post-presidency. The book, part biography and part memoir, is revealing in its behind-the-scenes story of the writing of Johnson's memoirs. Kearns would spend the next four years traveling between Harvard and Johnson's ranch in Texas to assist him on his book. This included weekends, her summer vacation, and winter holidays. Fortunately, the Johnson Library was nearby, and while it competed for the former president's attention, it proved to be a treasure trove of documents.

Johnson would dictate, often in the form of an interview, which would then be transcribed into written form, and rewritten into a rough draft by ghostwriters. After reading the drafts Johnson would suggest changes. Johnson's staff would be surprised to discover how he would freeze up and stiffen once he was being recorded for material, only to relax after a session was over. Kearns recalled that whenever the staff tried to incorporate anything Johnson said that had not been formally dictated into the manuscript, he would remove it and insist, "this was a presidential memoir and had to be written in a stately fashion."[11] She would later attribute Johnson's dictation anxiety to a lifelong fear of speaking in front of unfamiliar audiences.

Despite his aversion to dictation, Johnson still reveled in his storytelling abilities, even when they were false. Kearns recounted how Johnson told her his great-great-grandfather was killed at the battle of San Jacinto. "Later, I learned that Johnson's great-great-grandfather had not died at San Jacinto, or even been there," she recalled, "He was a real estate trader and he died at home, in bed."[12]

In 1971, Johnson's memoir was published. *The Vantage Point, Perspectives of the Presidency 1963–1969*, totaled 636 pages and began with his recollections of the Dallas presidential motorcade while being shielded on the floor of his limousine with a Secret Service agent atop him. In the book's preface, Johnson writes, "For better or worse, this is a book that only a President could have written. That is the sole excuse for its existence. I make no pretense of having written a complete and definitive history of my Presidency. I have not written these chapters to say, 'This is how it was,' but to say, 'This is how I saw it from my vantage point.'"[13]

Vantage Point was not well received, mainly because of Johnson's insistence that the language be cleaned up. By removing all of his folksy Texan anecdotes, Johnson authored an inflexible recollection of his presidency. Biographer Robert Dallek wrote, "The result was a sanitized book drained of the real LBJ."[14] In her own book recounting her association with Johnson, Doris Kearns also admitted, "this posturing would be disastrous for the memoirs" and "was clear from the time the first draft was completed."[15] Kearns adds that even Johnson knew the book was doomed to fail, but proceeded with the manuscript. "Johnson's insistence on distancing himself from the material made the book's failure inevitable. And he believed that, no matter how good his memoirs were, no matter how hard he worked on them, it wouldn't matter in the end. History was the real judge now, not the contemporaneous public, and he knew that there was no way for his memoirs to affect historical judgment."[16]

Johnson would confess to Kearns how, "No matter what I say in this book the critics will pull it apart."[17] Because of this attitude, Johnson would never attempt to author additional volumes, which had been suggested by his publisher, and which would have dealt with his childhood and his time in the Senate. Instead, readers are left with *The Vantage Point*, which resembles as an unfinished trilogy. A series of interviews with CBS reporter Walter Cronkite could have been seen by Johnson as a vehicle to unburden him from further writing commitments. The interviews, however, were unable to replicate a properly written memoir. Harry S. Truman had tried a similar route with Merle Miller, and in the end, Truman was unsatisfied with Merle's manuscript.

Johnson's final distraction from writing came in the form of the Lyndon Baines Johnson Library, which was dedicated on May 22, 1971. With his memoirs now completed, Johnson focused his remaining energies on the library, and even put the $1.2 million dollar advances he and Lady Bird had earned from writing their memoirs into the building. To Johnson, the Library became *the* book he had been unable to write. Doris Kearns recalled that although Johnson talked about her helping him with a book about his time in the Senate "it was clear he wanted nothing more to do with any formal writing about his life."[18]

In 1972 Johnson, who had a history of heart problems, suffered a heart attack. This, it seems, put to rest the possibility of further writings. Johnson had retired financially secure, and held multimillion-dollar holdings in bank stocks, land, and radio-television properties, and unlike Ulysses S. Grant, was not dependent on book sales and publishing contracts. In fact, Johnson had the foresight to invest in an early cable television system long before it would become a fixture in the average American home. Johnson would suffer a fatal heart attack at his Texas ranch on January 22, 1973.

Doris Kearns best summed up Johnson's attitude regarding writing. Kearns suggests that Johnson was well aware he was not a Kennedy, and would be condemned by the "literary province of the intellectual Northeast" no matter what he wrote.[19] Therefore, he felt entirely comfortable allowing a capable biographer to spend time with him, as she had, write the story in his words, and properly shape "the final verdict of [his] history."[20]

Richard M. Nixon

> It turned out to be the seventh major crisis of my life, and by far the most difficult from the standpoint of the mental discipline involved.[1]
> —Richard Nixon, on writing *Six Crises*.

As a child, Richard M. Nixon was an avid reader, and enjoyed classics such as *Tom Sawyer*. Years later, he could still recite entire passages from the book from memory. Nixon attended Whittier College and graduated with a B.A. in history, and found his voice on the debating team. Debating led him to writing, and in 1936 he contributed articles for *Law and Contemporary Problems*, which served as the literary quarterly of Duke Law School, where Nixon had won a scholarship. His published articles included such titles as "Changing Rules of Liability in Automobile Accident Litigation," which dealt with legal jargon and were hardly the stirring prose of a future politician.

Like many office holders, Nixon used his law degree to get into politics. In 1946 he won a seat in the House of Representatives, representing a district in California. His involvement in the 1948 espionage case against Alger Hiss led to national recognition, and secured him a seat in the Senate in 1951. In 1952, Nixon ran as vice president on the Eisenhower ticket, and won. At the conclusion of Eisenhower's second term, Nixon tried for the presidency in own right.

Nixon's first book, which appeared in 1960, was a typical campaign-style publication. Titled *The Challenges We Face*, it was published by McGraw Hill, and was compiled of speeches and essays. The back dust jacket of the book featured the famous photograph of Nixon with Soviet premier Nikita Khrushchev in their 1959 "Kitchen Debates." In the end *Challenges* did little for Nixon and even less for the campaign, which he lost to another author: John F. Kennedy.

After the election, Nixon found himself with time on his hands. Although he had no intention of writing another book, Adela Rogers St. Johns, who worked on his campaign (and was actually a Democrat) suggested he try it. St. Johns pushed Nixon, telling him that if he wanted a best seller for 1962 he had to get started. She also reminded him how *Profiles in Courage* had helped Kennedy, as if guiding him towards his next campaign. "Writing easily and fluently is something I have never been able to do," he admitted, and the failure of *Challenges* probably still haunted him.[2] Even a nationally syndicated newspaper column featuring his by-line seemed to be going nowhere.

Mamie Eisenhower, as well as John F. Kennedy, assured Nixon a book would do well and encouraged him. Kennedy went as far as telling him that every public official should author a book sometime. St. Johns acted as Nixon's agent and arranged for a meeting with for Ken McCormick of Doubleday to discuss the possibly of a memoir. McCormick had previously worked with Eisenhower on *Crusade in Europe*, and also secured the contract. Nixon presented McCormick with an outline for what would become *Six Crises*. Nixon remembers McCormick encouraged him as well, and sold him on writing. "He approved the concept, told me how easy and enjoyable I would find writing a book to be, and finally convinced me that I should undertake the venture."[3]

Six Crises would be framed with the help of researchers and ghostwriters. Journalist Earl Mazo, who worked with Nixon, described Nixon's writing technique. "He never goes near a typewriter, but with the facts and data gathered from him by his researchers, he scribbles notes and phrases on a large, yellow lawyer's pad, then dictates the finished product into a machine. [Rosemary] Woods did the typing. Often he went off alone, to Apple Valley, near Palm Springs, or to Trancas Beach to spend a week or so dictating. Like many writers, he would take long walks to collect his thoughts, becoming oblivious to everything around him."[4] Nixon would spend most of 1961 working on the book, which he admitted, "turned out to be the seventh major crisis in my life, and by far the most difficult from the standpoint of the mental discipline involved. My respect for those who write books, already high, has gone up a hundredfold."[5]

Doubleday would release *Six Crises* on April 1, 1962. The book dealt with six political crises during his time as Eisenhower's vice president. It is interesting to note that while Eisenhower downplayed incidents such as his oval office stroke in his White House memoir, Nixon's recollection was forthright and revealing. St. Johns kept her word, and *Six Crises* would make the best seller list, remaining there for six months and earning Nixon over $200,000 in royalties. Biographer Stephen Ambrose wrote how Nixon remained endeared with the book as time went by. "Nixon was proud of his first book. Decades later, he was still proud of it. *Six Crises* took on a life of its own, until Nixon began referring to it almost in the third person, as if he had nothing to do with its creation. During Watergate, he would constantly urge his aides to read *Six Crises* for inspiration and insight."[6]

It should also be noted the book makes a cameo appearance in 1978's *RN: The Memoirs of Richard Nixon*. It was 1972, and Nixon had just concluded his first historical meeting with Mao Zedong in China. "As we were leaving, Mao said, "Your book, *Six Crises*, is not a bad book." Looking at Chou, I smiled and shook my head and said, "He reads too much."[7]

In the fall of 1962, Nixon ran for governor of California. It was assumed that he would remain in the public eye as governor of an important state, and therefore make a future presidential run. Nixon lost and would later claim his heart was never really in it.

In 1963, Nixon was planning to move to New York to become a senior partner in a law firm. It appears that the success of *Six Crises* had rejuvenated him, and he was in demand. In the spring he signed a contract with *The Saturday Evening Post* for a foreign policy article. He also had the idea for another book.

Nixon had become intrigued with Theodore W. White and his book, *The Making of the President, 1960*. Nixon believed he could produce a superior version of the story, and intended to write the manuscript with speechwriter Stephen Hess. Hess and a staff of researchers would do much of the legwork, while Nixon would add valuable insight and comment. Most importantly, the book would keep Nixon's name in the political arena without having to run against Kennedy in 1964. Ironically, Nixon and Hess were scheduled to sign a book contract with Doubleday on November 22, 1963. Upon hearing of Kennedy's assassination, Nixon decided not to commit to a contract with Doubleday. Stephen Hess recalled how Nixon, "needed to keep his options open, which meant in these circumstances backing out of the Doubleday contract. Working on such a book would tie him down too firmly at a time when he needed to stay available for whatever might develop."[8]

Biographer Jonathan Aitken would refer to the years 1963 to 1967 as "The Wilderness Years" in Nixon's life. Much of his time was spent campaigning for others. Although this would have been the perfect opportunity to author another book, he chose not to. Instead, Aitken writes, "Nixon read widely and deeply during his wilderness years. Whenever possible he would put in three or four hours with a book before retiring for the night."[9] In a letter to Aitken, Nixon wrote "I can't say that any of this reading provided specific guidance for the foreign and domestic policies I developed during this period, but I have always believed that anyone in the political arena is better prepared to address controversial current issues if he immerses himself in history, biography and philosophy."[10] Aiken also noted Charles de Gaulle's 1960 autobiography, *The Edge of the Sword*, was the most heavily annotated volume in Nixon's library.

Nixon would return to national politics in 1968 by securing the Republican nomination for president. Instead of the usual campaign literature, a new edition of *Six Crises* was printed. It would prove to be the best testament to Nixon's career, and probably helped him win in November. While president, Nixon authored no books, instead personally laboring over his speeches. Author Richard Reeves noted how Nixon "took great pride in the fact that he wrote his own most important speeches, or edited speechwriters so much that their work became his."[11]

With the Watergate scandal quickly consuming all his energies, Nixon was forced to resign the presidency on August 9, 1974. In his resignation speech, Nixon quoted Theodore Roosevelt's "Man in the Arena" speech. Years later, he would use it as the title of a book. While Congress considered charging him, Nixon made the best of the situation. "All I'd need would be a good supply of books and a hard table to write on. Some of the best literature in history was written in jail—look at Gandhi and Lenin."[12] A September pardon from President Ford would dissolve Nixon's legal matters, and he once again considered writing a book. Life threatening health issues would sidetrack him in October, however, but by the end of 1974 he had begun working on an outline of a manuscript.

Nixon threw all his energies into the manuscript, eager to tell his side of the story. Books such as *All the President's Men* and *The Final Days*, both by Bob Woodward and Carl Bernstein, painted a harsh picture of the Nixon presidency, and Nixon himself called them "trash." Nixon would spend much of 1977 editing the manuscript, which had swelled to about 1.5 million words, with a handful of aides. One of these was Diane Sawyer. Sawyer had previously worked in Nixon's press secretary's office, and was an English major. She later became a news anchor with CBS and ABC. Most of Nixon's material for what would become his memoirs came from his diary. From 1954 to July 1974 Nixon kept a diary, most which had been dictated. Most of Nixon's presidential papers would become the center of a legal battle between Nixon and the U.S. Government. While the government claimed they were evidence, Nixon claimed they were personal property. In 1977 the Supreme Court ruled on the matter, and items considered personal in nature were returned.

The publishing contract Nixon signed with Warner Books provided a $2.5 million advance, along with $300,000 for "provable expenses." Nixon kept adding to the manuscript, which became a problem for Warner, who basically dealt with paperback reprints. Warner would solve the problem by selling the hardcover rights to Grosset & Dunlap for $225,000, against future royalties. Another concern was that while the book was to be released the following fall, Nixon had not yet covered Watergate. Diane Sawyer explained that they were leading Nixon through the manuscript in chronological order, and were hoping that by the time they reached Watergate, a rhythm would have been established and Nixon would open up.

Nixon became obsessed while working on the manuscript and went to great lengths to protect it until he was ready to let the world read it. This included locking it up in a vault every night. Throughout the writing process he continued working in the same professional manner he had since the beginning, even making himself available for work on Christmas day if needed. By early 1978 the manuscript was at the typesetters and being set in galleys. All that was left was the title. The publishers wanted *The Memoirs of Richard M. Nixon*, which was fine with him. Nixon, however, wanted a little more. One day he produced one of his ever-present yellow legal pads and scrawled a large "RN" encompassed in a circle. The mark was instantly identifiable to Nixon staffers, and was how Nixon typically signed-off or approved documents. From there on in the book's proper title became known as *RN: The Memoirs of Richard M. Nixon*. (Today, publishers and booksellers typically refer to the book simply as *RN*.)

Despite a boycott attempt with the catchy slogan "Don't Buy Books by Crooks," the hardcover edition sold out of its first printing within weeks of the May 15, 1978, release. It would debut at number four on the best seller list. Reviews were mixed. Some were openly hostile, calling Nixon a "liar" and the book "awful," while others claimed Nixon was just as good a writer as Truman and Eisenhower, if not close to Grant. *RN* was not only a best seller in America, but also worldwide. An extensive book tour followed, even appearing before the Oxford Union Debating Society in England as an honored speaker. One of the reasons Nixon threw all of his energies into the memoirs was that he was nearly broke like Ulysses S. Grant. Unlike Grant, who lost much of his money with bad investments, Nixon had incredible legal fees, which were coupled with back taxes, overdue mortgage payments, and medical bills.

With the success of *RN*, Warner had become interested in another book from Nixon. By the end of 1979, Nixon had delivered. The book, which Nixon had titled *The Real War*, dealt with the aggression and military escalation of the Soviet Union. Unlike his memoirs, the book came together quickly. By the summer of 1979, Nixon had completed the basic manuscript, turned it in to the publisher, received the page proofs at the end of the year, and returned them to Warner on February 14, 1980. On May 1, 1980, *The Real War* was released. It quickly sold out on both sides of the Atlantic and became a best seller. Nixon promoted the book, and made headlines when he said (in Europe) that there was "a 50/50 chance the United States would not exist" by the end of the century. Ronald Reagan, then the 1980 Republican Party candidate, was said to have read it with great interest. With the collapse of the Soviet Union in 1991, however, the book suddenly became outdated.

His next book, *Leaders*, was published in 1982. It was a series of biographies of world leaders he had known, such as Winston Churchill, Charles de Gaulle, Nikita Khrushchev, and Zhou Enlai. For Nixon, who graduated from college with a bachelor's in history, *Leaders* would be the closest to a historical biography he would ever write. Nixon was also shrewd at self-promotion. Even though his books were best sellers, he often used them as his international calling card. Thousands of copies of *The Real War* and *Leaders* were sent to kings, presidents and ministers, not to mention journalists and academics throughout the world.

In 1983, Nixon published *Real Peace*, which was considered a sequel to *The Real War*. It was said that Nixon was unhappy about President Reagan's performance, and that he "feared Reagan was following the advice of *The Real War* too closely."[13] Nixon had begun writing the book over the July 4 weekend, and, impatient with the long process of publishing, decided to publish the book himself. After sending out several hundred copies, Nixon let the book rights go up for auction. The *New York Times* bought the newspaper rights, and then sold the remaining rights to Little, Brown. During this time, Nixon wrote op-ed pieces for major newspapers and promoted *Real Peace* with a book tour. Nixon also videotaped an "electronic memoir," which was sold to a video production company, earning him $1 million.

In 1984 Nixon signed with Arbor House and published *No More Vietnams* in 1985. The book was praised in conservative newspapers and panned in liberal ones. It also surprisingly stayed on several best seller lists for eighteen weeks, proving that Americans were finally ready to properly digest a war they would much rather have forgotten. Biographer Stephen Ambrose wrote that "what was regrettable was that he could write such a big book on such an important subject, one in which he had played a leading role from

1954 to 1969 and the leading role from 1969 to 1973, without once asking himself difficult questions."[14]

The book *1999: Victory Without War* was published in 1988. Nixon had finished the manuscript on his seventy-fifth birthday and was now publishing under Simon & Schuster. As with his previous three efforts, Nixon chose to write about what many considered his strongest point, which was foreign policy.

In 1990 Nixon would publish *In the Arena: A Memoir of Victory, Defeat and Renewal*. Technically his third memoir (after *Six Crises* and *RN*), it remains notable for addressing Watergate much more than *RN* had in 1978. By 1990 Nixon was able to distance himself from the scandal, and look back upon it with more clarity. Nixon would also remember how writing helped regain a foothold on post-presidential life. "On my sixty-fifth birthday, January 9, 1978, I made a major decision. I had completed my memoirs, and fortunately the book turned out to be a best seller. I was in excellent condition physically and thought I was now in a condition to tackle other projects. I had to decide what to do with the rest of my life. In a sense, this was a life-or-death decision. If a person quits after defeat, he dies spiritually and will soon die physically."[15]

Nixon also writes of the pleasures of reading and how it was therapeutic in times of crisis. He even mentions how Theodore Roosevelt always took a book along no matter where he went, even in the jungle.

In the Arena was well received and has stood the test of time as one of Nixon's best, especially to his biographers. Conrad Black called it "a pastiche of themes and subjects, though quite interesting in places."[16] Stephen Ambrose wrote how it "was in many ways his best book since the memoirs."[17] Daniel Frick noted that "its real story [was] the presumption of Nixon's total rehabilitation; that he can offer advice on living, not just with the belief that those chestnuts will be accepted, but that, through his persistence, he has *earned* the right to assume the wise man's role."[18] And Jonathan Aitken called it "An uncharacteristically personalized volume of memoirs and advice."[19] Despite strong sales, Nixon was still not satisfied with the book. "I wrote *In the Arena* because I thought it would do some good," Nixon said in 1991, "you know, I thought it would be good to get my side out. But if I were doing it again, I would not include the Watergate crap because it's all the reviewers concentrated on, and they neglected everything else."[20]

Seize the Moment: America's Challenge in a One-Superpowered World, would be published in 1992. With the Soviet Union now firmly ensconced in the history books, the book was a strange reversal of his earlier books, *The Real War* and *Real Peace*. Yet Nixon maintained there was still much work to do, and that this was not a time to rest on our laurels. As was his custom, Nixon promoted the book. With the presidential election coming up, he also sent out autographed advance copies to Republican nominee George Bush, as well as Democrat Mario Cuomo, at the time a favored contender. Nixon playfully predicted, "Cuomo will read it; Bush might not have the time, but he should make the time. And he *should* thank me."[21]

In March 1992, Nixon appeared on C-Span's *Booknotes* and spoke about writing:

> Writing a book is very, very hard work. I know you interview writers on your program—I've seen them on occasion—and I must say I admire authors. I'm not saying that in the terms of myself, but it is a great ordeal for me. I don't write easily. I write outline after outline, then I dictate into a machine after I've done the whole thing so that it is the spoken word rather than the written word, which, as you know, is very formal. And then I have good people work with me. But when I finally get down to crafting the final product, it is a great, great burden, an ordeal, for me. Every time I finish a book, I say never again.[22]

In April 1994, Nixon was hard at work on the manuscript of what would become his final book, *Beyond Peace*. Monica Crowley, who served as editorial advisor and research consultant for *Seize the Moment* and *Beyond Peace*, worked with Nixon. *Life* magazine had secured the rights to serialize it, and Nixon was planning yet another book tour. Nixon was working on *Beyond Peace* when he was stricken with paralysis, unable to speak properly. Within days Nixon had slipped into a coma, and died April 22, 1994. *Beyond Peace* would be published posthumously the following month.

It was as an author that Richard M. Nixon vindicated himself and rose from the political graveyard. Just as Herbert Hoover once claimed to have regained his reputation by having "outlived the bastards," Nixon did so by writing.

In his book *Nixon's Enemies*, author Kenneth F. Kurz observed the political resurrection of Nixon at a time when his critics claimed that he could not even get elected as dogcatcher. "That was all right; Nixon had no desire to be dogcatcher. He preferred to write his books, to give to a body of work that distilled the perspectives of a lifetime's experience in politics and diplomacy. Just as the man himself was rife with paradoxes, so is his literary corpus. Nixon's books form a repository of wisdom, generosity, profundity, pettiness, and vengefulness. Probably without fully realizing how much he revealed, he left a written record of himself at best and worst."[23]

Even Nixon mused about his books. "My books will last only if the events beat out the predications and also the recommendations that I have set forth in them. But whether they have lasting value is something that I cannot judge. The jury's still out on that."²⁴

Gerald R. Ford

Gerald R. Ford's entry into the world of publishing remains unique. Over fifty years later, the first book for which Ford would serve as a contributing author remains controversial and traumatic for many of its readers: *The Warren Commission Report*.

Ford was a congressman from Grand Rapids, Michigan, when President Kennedy was assassinated on November 22, 1963. Ford recalled how he was driving home from a school conference with his wife, Betty, when they heard the news on the radio. Within the course of 48 hours Kennedy's alleged assassin, Lee Harvey Oswald, was also shot and killed. Days later President Johnson established a bipartisan committee to investigate the assassination of Kennedy and any possible conspiracies.

Chief Justice Earl Warren of the Supreme Court would chair the committee. Members would include former CIA Director Allen Dulles, former Chase Manhattan chairman John McCloy, Georgia Senator Richard Russell (D) and Kentucky Senator John Sherman Cooper (R). Congressman Hale Boggs and Ford would round out the committee.

Ford immediately accepted Johnson's appointment but realized he would need assistance.

Ford's assistance came in the form of John R. Stiles, who was Ford's first campaign manager and an old friend. More importantly, Stiles was a writer, and could assist Ford in drafting his share of the manuscript that would eventually become known as *The Warren Report*. Ford would later recall how he and other members of the committee would disagree at times, remembering his appointment was not ceremonial, and expecting his work to be thankless.

After completing the interviews of everyone considered essential to the investigation and reviewing their testimony along with the evidence, the Commission began drafting the manuscript. Writing and editing the final report proved to be a tedious process for everyone involved, and in Ford's case, one of his contributions to the text would later prove controversial, particularly the "single bullet theory."

In early September 1964 the manuscript was composed in page proofs and was ready for printers when Senator Russell refused to sign the report. Apparently Russell had doubts concerning the single bullet theory. Chairman Warren insisted the report be unanimous, and to satisfy Russell, commissioner McCloy "fashioned some compromise language" that satisfied everyone.[1] With Russell's objections now out of the way, the remainder of the September 18, 1964, meeting was spent on "housekeeping items and innocuous motions, seconded and carried, about the numbers of copies of the report to be released, who was to get leather-bound copies of the report and accompanying volumes of hearing with their names stamped in gold, and similar inconsequential matters."[2]

On September 24, 1964, the Warren Commission presented its report to President Johnson. For unknown reasons, Johnson delayed the report's release to the public until the following Saturday. *The Warren Commission Report* would quickly become a best seller and was widely debated. Because the report is officially a government document and written while Ford was drawing a salary in Congress, he was not, as were the other members of the Commission, entitled to collect royalties against book sales. The Commission's role in constructing the report was similar to "write for pay" contracts. It should be pointed out, however, that members of the Commission had their expenses covered while working on the investigation. Because the publication of the Report was a joint effort of the members and their respective staff–Gerald R. Ford is acknowledged as one of its authors.

It is interesting to note that Ford's involvement with drafting *The Warren Report* did not harm his ability to easily win re-election to his congressional seat in 1964. Electoral Records show Ford maintained a steady 60–68 percent margin of victory since first winning his seat to Michigan's 5th Congressional District in 1948. If anything, Ford's role on the committee increased his national stature, much like John F. Kennedy's did when he published *Profiles in Courage* as a Senator. Amazingly, Ford missed only one roll call vote between October 1963 and September 1964.

With the *Warren Report* now published, one would think Ford would have been relieved to have the burden of the investigation behind him. Ford, however, did just the opposite by writing his own book on the assassination. In 1965 Ford and John R. Stiles would publish *Portrait of the Assassin*. Stiles, who assisted Ford with the *Warren Report* manuscript, had tried his hand at writing fiction but was unsuccessful. Stiles would never abandon his dream of becoming a published author, and appears to have approached Ford about writing a book together. Ford Biographer Bud Vestal wrote that *Portrait of the Assassin* "was Stile's idea; writing was his first love, especially historical writing. [Stiles] wrote much of the book, but Ford worked hard at it, too."[3]

Earl Warren of The Warren Commission presents a copy of *The Warren Report* to President Lyndon B. Johnson as Gerald R. Ford (fourth from left) looks on. Despite dozens of published conspiracy theories, Ford stood by the commission's findings for the rest of his life (courtesy Lyndon B. Johnson Library).

Portrait was essentially a reworking of the *Warren Report* into a nonfiction novel. In the book's foreword, Ford and Stiles laid out the book's purpose. "The present account is not intended to take issue with the conclusions of the Commission. It is hoped, however, that this book will reach many readers who, for lack of time or other reasons, may have not read and analyzed the massive content of the Report and its 26 volumes of testimony and exhibits. The narrative is organized in the style of a novel. It lives and breathes with the emotions of those who suffered through the events."[4]

From the writing style of *Portrait*, Vestal appears to have been correct in his claims that Stiles was the predominant author. The book's dramatic and novel-like form was not consistent with Ford's character, and in writing it Stiles finally fulfilled his dream of becoming a published author. The book did not perform well, and the only money Ford and Stiles would ever see from it would be the publisher's ten thousand dollar advance. Ford and Stiles never wrote another book together, and *Portrait* remains John Stiles' sole literary effort.

As with *The Warren Commission Report*, *Portrait of the Assassin* would attract its share of controversy. Critics claimed that Ford had used his stature as a member of the Warren Commission for personal profit. Ford dismissed the complaints, but in the numerous pro-conspiracy books that had been published since the *Warren Report*, various authors were harsh concerning Ford's role in the Commission. In his 1985 book *Reasonable Doubt*, author Henry Hurt notes that the controversy remained as late as 1973:

> It is ironic that Gerald Ford, certainly one of the most resolute defenders of the Warren panel, should be the one commissioner who violated the top-secret classification of certain commission proceedings. The breach, which is a violation of federal laws, occurred in 1965, when he published his book called *Portrait of the Assassin*. Ford, who earned at least $15,000 for his literary efforts, was asked about this by the Senate Rules and Administration Committee in 1973, during his confirmation hearings after Richard Nixon appointed him to the position of Vice-President. Ford told the Senate committee: "We did not use in that book any material other than the material that was in the 26 volumes of testimony and exhibits that were subsequently made public."[5]

Fate would have it that Gerald Ford would become the last surviving member of the Warren Commission. Despite the opportunity to revise or repudiate anything in the Report, Ford never strayed from the published edition. It was said that Ford "still bristled whenever somebody like Hollywood director Oliver Stone floated JFK conspiracy theories for mass consumption."[6]

In October 1973, Vice President Spiro Agnew resigned and President Nixon nominated Ford to serve out Agnew's term. Ford was confirmed by the Senate and sworn in December, becoming the first vice president to be seated under the 25th amendment. As Watergate accelerated, it appeared Nixon would face impeachment. Nixon resigned on August 9, 1974, and Ford became president. Ford would serve out the remainder of Nixon's term, but would fail to win a term in his own right.

Ford began working on his memoirs soon after leaving office in January 1977. From his past experiences with the *Warren Commission Report* and *Portrait of an Assassin*, Ford remembered writing as a difficult and lengthy process. Ford avoided writing so much that his wife, Betty, published her memoir a year before his.

In 1979, Harper & Row released Ford's autobiography, *A Time to Heal*. Ford acknowledged Trevor Armbrister's assistance in the book, and many considered him to be its ghostwriter. Armbrister was a Washington bureau correspondent for Reader's Digest, whom Harper & Row had a business relationship with, and was most likely how the two met. Armbrister would spend two years working on Ford's book.

A Time to Heal begins in early August 1974, in the days leading up to

Nixon's resignation and Ford's swearing in. Ford's unique place in history as the only appointed president is told well. In the present day world of post–9/11 security, some of his recollections almost seem surreal. As an example, there was no official residence when Ford was vice president and he was still living in the same Alexandria, Virginia home that he had lived in for decades as a congressman. Ford tells of watching Nixon's resignation speech on the television in the family room and walking outside to make a statement in a drizzling rain to the reporters who had gathered outside the front door.

A Time to Heal sold well, and with a best seller finally to his name, Ford eventually authored additional books. In 1987, Arbor House published *Humor and the Presidency*. *Humor* evolved from a symposium held at the Ford Presidential Library. Comedians, political cartoonists, and politicians spoke at the event, which led to Ford's idea for another book. Ford reminisced about the humor poked at him while president, and how other presidents dealt with it. The book also included a collection of political cartoons dating back to Thomas Nash. Written in a lighthearted manner, *Humor* was far from the serious nature of most presidential and political memoirs, and reflected Ford's good-humored nature.

In 1998, Ford co-authored a book on his hometown of Grand Rapids, Michigan. Titled *Grand Rapids: The City That Works*, the book was collaborated with photography editor John Corriveau. Ford's chief contribution to *Grand Rapids* was a sixteen-page autobiography of his life as a Grand Rapids resident, which reads like a fond reminiscence. The book is heavily illustrated and includes profiles of area corporations and businesses, professional groups, and community service organizations. Overall, Ford's presence in the book is minimal, and resembles community/business oriented reference books often published by the local Chamber of Commerce.

The dramatic and legally contested Bush/Gore presidential election in 2000 induced Ford to once again to take up his pen. Ford co-chaired a National Commission with successor Jimmy Carter dealing with election reform. The commission, known as the National Commission on Federal Election Reform, issued a report titled *To Assure Pride and Confidence in the Electoral Process*. Numerous policy recommendations were made in the report, which was co-chaired by Lloyd N. Culter and Robert H. Michel. Filled with statistics, charts and scenarios dealing with issues such as early voting, voter registration, and absentee voting, *To Assure Pride and Confidence* is not light reading. Published by the Brookings Institution Press, it did not sell well and failed to capture the public's imagination.

In Ford's final years, Lord John Press, a limited editions publisher, printed several of Ford's addresses and speeches. These were numbered and signed by Ford, and introduced into the limited editions market. While these slim hardbound volumes are of interest to collectors, they should not be confused with Ford's other published works.

Ford's final book would be a reprinting of the 1964 *Warren Report*, along with a new foreword written by Ford. Published by Flatsigned Press in 2007, *A Presidential Legacy and the Warren Commission* contained Ford's final words on the Kennedy assassination and his involvement in the Warren Commission. Written shortly before his death, Ford was the last surviving member of the Commission, and addresses this in his opening statement. "I am sad to say that, as of this writing, I am the last member of the Warren Commission. My voice, therefore, must speak for seven on this fortieth anniversary of our findings."[7]

In his twenty-nine-page foreword, Ford debunks countless conspiracy theories that have appeared in book and film. He stands behind the Commission's findings and contends that America has allowed itself to be swept up in these theories, and it is time to sit down and once again revisit the facts, noting "America needs to get a grip on this hysteria."[8] Ford closes with a plea for Americans to reconsider the presented facts, and to re-read the *Warren Commission Report*. "Your biggest contribution as an American citizen would be to read the *Warren Commission Report*. I know that reading a technical report can be very daunting and boring, but I can assure you that this one is quite captivating, although some of the more squeamish readers may want to skip over the graphic medical procedures."[9]

And so by returning to his involvement with the Warren Commission, Ford had come full circle in his writings as a published author.

It should be noted that the fiftieth anniversary of the assassination of John F. Kennedy in 2013 produced several noteworthy books. Among these were several that focused on the *Warren Report*. That year, Howard P. Willens, the only surviving member of the three-person supervisory staff of the Commission, published his offering, *History Will Make Us Right*. The book reaffirmed the Commission's findings and dismissed the endless tide of conspiracy books claiming otherwise. Willens was kind to Ford, and recalled Ford's underlying commitment to the Commission despite being at odds with Chief Justice Warren.

"Even as the commission began to gain momentum, it was not an entirely unified team. Gerald Ford continued to chafe under Warren's style, although he was the only member who aired such complaints. Decades later, he still thought the chief justice ran a "one-man commission" and was not responsive to the views of other commission members. He characterized Warren as "pretty categorical in his views ... there was no deviation from his schedule and his scenario. He treated us as though we were on a team, but he was the captain and the quarterback." Notwithstanding his reservations, Ford made a very substantial commitment to the commission's work."[10]

Willens also recalled how Ford denied letting anyone, including President Johnson, rush the report's findings, despite being unable to meet the original July 1964 deadline.

While Ford's presidency remains memorable by the unique manner in which he attained it, his legacy as an author also remains unique by his association with the *Warren Report*. Overall sales of the book remain remarkable, considering it is officially a government document. The only other government document that saw similar printings was the *9/11 Commission Report*, published in 2004.

Jimmy Carter

> This book is my own work, typed by me on my trusty word processor.[1]
> —Jimmy Carter

As a young boy growing up on a farm in Georgia, Carter read constantly, and in the third grade won an award for having read the most books. Carter's mother, who would affectionately be known as Miss Lillian, "stressed the importance of the children saturating themselves in good literature," and regarded reading "of paramount importance in the Carter household."[2] Carter's sister, Gloria, remembered the entire family even reading at mealtime. "We always took a book to the table, at least everyone except Daddy, and we never talked at the table."[3] Miss Lillian confirmed that books were always permitted anywhere, anytime, and anyplace in the home. "I'm an avid reader. I made them read. I allowed them to read books at the table, especially if they had a few minutes before the school bus."[4]

Reading at mealtime would become a lifelong habit with Carter. Author Kandy Stroud wrote how Carter remembered, "There's hardly a meal ever gone by that we were in the privacy of our own home that we didn't take something to the table to read."[5] Carter also recalled asking for books at Christmas, and at the age of twelve reading *War and Peace*. Other favorite authors were James Agee and William Faulkner, both southerners.

After high school Carter pursued a career in the Navy, and kept a diary while stationed on a submarine. He felt obligated to return to the family farm after the death of his father, and through his business entered politics. After being elected to the Georgia state senate and governor, Carter made a run for the presidency.

To help his campaign as an underdog Carter began writing a campaign autobiography in 1974. Carter would write the book, titled *Why Not the Best*, entirely himself and publish it in 1975. Unfortunately, Carter believed the book contained every answer anyone would have about him, and that it could even replace press interviews. This would lead to an uncomfortable encounter with reporter Elizabeth Drew who asked him about his plans. "It's in the book, how I decided to run for the Presidency, and the plans are in the book. There's no point in our talking about these things when they're in the book." When Drew explained that her staff was attempting to locate a copy for her, he replied icily, "It's in the stores."[6]

In 2003 Jimmy Carter published the first work of fiction ever authored by a former president. As is his custom, Carter promoted the book with a national book tour that included book signings (private collection).

Why Not the Best would prove to be an asset to the 1976 campaign, and get Carter badly needed name recognition. It sold nearly one million copies, sometimes distributed hand to hand, one at a time, in an almost grassroots manner. Carter helped personalize the book by signing copies, sometimes dozens at a time, for campaign workers to distribute.

Broadman Press, a religious publisher located in Nashville, Tennessee, would publish the book. Carter was originally considering writing something of a religious nature, but when he revealed his intention for an autobiography, Broadman quickly accepted. Instead of an advance, Broadman paid Carter with free copies. Attorney Bob Lipshutz, who served as campaign treasurer, stressed "Carter was less interested in making money than in receiving exposure for *Why Not the Best*."[7] Once released, Broadman was unable to meet public demand, and Bantam Books were contracted to issue a paperback edition, which went into repeated printings.

Carter would defeat Gerald Ford for the presidency in November 1976. In early 1977, *A Government as Good as Its People* appeared. It contained a mixture of speeches, interviews, and comments made by Carter during the campaign, and would represent what his incoming administration would be.

The Carter presidency would only endure a single term. Upon returning home to Plains, Georgia, in 1981, Carter discovered his peanut warehouse business, which had been placed in a blind trust since becoming president, had acquired more than $1 million in debt. Financially strapped, Carter did what Ulysses Grant and Richard Nixon did in times of trouble, and signed to write his memoirs.

Literary agents Marvin Josephson and Lynn Nesbit represented Carter, and were able to secure a multimillion-dollar book deal with Bantam. Carter originally wanted to write about his Middle East peace efforts at Camp David, but was persuaded to do a memoir first, as it would offer a bigger advance. Carter agreed, but placed a strict one-year timeframe to complete the book. Carter knew what he did and didn't want the book to be. "I hope to make it highly personal in nature, not a definitive history. I'm not going to try to write an apology or rationalization of what we did."[8]

Keeping Faith: Memoirs of a President would originate from Carter's White House diaries. In the book's foreword, Carter writes,

> Immediately after returning home from the White House on January 20, 1981, I unpacked eighteen large black volumes of diary notes, which I had accumulated during my four years as President. These highly personal papers—some five thousand pages of them—have been the primary source of this book, augmented by my own memory and the official records of my administration.
>
> This book is my own work, typed by me at home on my trusty word processor. There are times when I had other responsibilities or when I yielded to the temptations of my nearby woodworking shop or a convenient fishing place, but I have spent most days and nights of the past year [1981] on this project.[9]

Carter received a considerable amount of knowledge by working with Steve Hochman, a research assistant, historian, and apprentice of Dumas Malone. Hochman had worked with Malone during the writing of Malone's six-volume Pulitzer Prize biography of Thomas Jefferson, and was invaluable to Carter, often working eight to ten hours a day. *Keeping Faith* would become a best seller, and launch Carter on to what would become a successful post-presidential career as an author. Incidentally, the diary entries that Carter would use to shape the book would eventually be published as *White House Diary* in 2010.

Carter's next book, *Negotiation: The Alternative to Hostility*, was published in 1984. Delivered as a lecture for the Inaugural Lecture Series of the Carl Vinson Memorial at Mercer University in Macon, Georgia on April 28, 1983, the slim volume dealt with Carter's experience as a negotiator. Originally published by Mercer University Press, it quickly fell out of print and became something of a collector's item. It has since been reprinted and can be purchased from the Carter Presidential Library.

In 1985 Carter published *The Blood of Abraham: Insights into the Middle East*. This was the manuscript Carter originally wanted to publish after first leaving office, but he was held back by his agent. *The Blood of Abraham* dealt with the then-present Middle East situation. It included a chronological history of events going back to 9000 B.C., the journey of Abraham, the birth of Israel, and the fight for a Palestinian State.

The year 1987 saw the publication of *Everything to Gain: Making the Most of the Rest of Your Life*. This book is unique among Carter's published efforts by the fact that it was co-authored with his wife, Rosalynn. "We live in such a remarkable time that it is difficult for us to comprehend the changes that have taken place in our lifetimes," they write in the book's introduction.[10] "At different times in our lives we have voluntarily made some radical changes, moving from the U.S. Navy to a small family business, then into local, state, and national politics. We have also had to accommodate some involuntary changes, the most traumatic of which was leaving the White House in 1981."[11]

Everything to Gain was essentially Carter's third volume of memoirs. If *Why Not the Best* regarded his pre-presidency and *Keeping Faith* dealt with his presidency, then this volume picked up life after the presidency. The book dealt with the life remaining after completing a major accomplishment, and the inevitable question of "what do I do now?"

As previously mentioned, the book was co-written with Rosalynn Carter. While Jimmy worked on his presidential memoir, Rosalynn was writing her autobiography. Both recalled working on them simultaneously. "Not long after we came home we got two new word processors and enjoyed using them. We both knew how to type, and although we had not done so for years, the skill came back and we enjoyed using our fascinating new machines. It is not an exaggeration to say that we were like children with new toys."[12]

The book revealed how Carter set up an office in what originally was a garage, while Rosalynn used a small bedroom at the other end of the house. It is hard to imagine the former president writing his memoirs out of what was once a garage, but he did. Rosalynn also received valuable advice about writing her autobiography. "When I began working on my own book, Edmund Morris, one of the country's leading presidential biographers, said to me, 'Don't try to make your place in history. It's already made.' Suddenly I realized that I didn't have to 'set the record straight,' in some combative way as I had originally intended. The events were all there for everyone to see.... I was free to write my own story, the story of my life, and so my book became an autobiography."[13]

It deserves to be pointed out that *Everything to Gain* was the first book to be co-written with a first lady since Herbert and Lou Hoover's translation of *De Re Metallica* in 1912.

In June of 1988, *An Outdoor Journal* was published. Subtitled *Adventures and Reflections*, it would be Carter's only book on his love of fishing, hunting, and hiking. The book recalled a few confrontations with poisonous snakes, such as rattlesnakes. One instance recalled Carter hunting with an uncle when still a youngster, and coming upon a rattlesnake. "It was coiled to strike, and its rattlers began to sing as we stood, amazed within striking distance. A shock, almost of paralysis, went through my body. Uncle Lem quickly shot the snake, and I nearly became nauseated when I saw it thrashing around in the grass. I even thought for a few minutes about giving up bird hunting for good."[14]

In another dramatic account, Carter was clearing brush near a pond with Mrs. Carter, who was pregnant at the time, when he was alerted to her horrific screams. "Between her and the pond was a large water moccasin, crawling directly toward her, either angry or confused. He was less than five feet from her when I saw him. There was no limb or other club around, so I had to resort to my rifle. My first shot broke its back, and the vicious snake began to thrash around at her feet, apparently still lunging toward her. It was pure luck that my second shot blew its head off. Rosalynn collapsed in my arms when I reached her. We'll never forget that snake writhing in its death throes almost under her."[15]

Such recollections made *An Outdoor Journal* an interesting read. The book was the first post-presidential book about fishing since Herbert Hoover's *Fishing for Fun*, published in 1963. It is reminiscent of Theodore Roosevelt's numerous (and lively) hunting and fishing memoirs, and even more so by Carter's lifelong respect and obvious concern for America's great outdoors.

After a four-year hiatus, Carter returned with a new book in 1992. *Turning Point: A Candidate, a State, and a Nation Come of Age*, would be a political memoir concentrating on his first run for public office in 1962. It recalls Carter's campaign for Georgia's 14th Senatorial District, and how he confronted political machinery and a domineering political boss. Carter ran a small, almost non-existent campaign, and wrote about personally nailing campaign posters on telephone poles while driving around country back roads. Carter initially lost the election, but proved voter fraud, and after filing an appeal was declared senator-elect.

Turning Point remains an interesting coming-of-age memoir regarding Southern politics and the beginning of the Civil Rights Movement. In the introduction, Carter frankly wrote "this book looks at Southern politics in microcosm, with glimpses of a more panoramic scene that encompasses the past lives of our state and nation, often at their worst."[16] Surprisingly absent from the book were any recollections of personal fear Carter possibly felt for himself, his family, or their property, during the campaign and its aftermath.

The year 1993 saw publication of *Talking Peace: A Vision for the Next Generation*. Written for a teenage audience, failed to sell as well as previous books. Carter became the first living president to see a collection of his poetry published in his lifetime when Times Books released *Always a Reckoning and Other Poems* in 1995.

In an appearance on C-Span's *Booknotes*, Carter explained how difficult it was in getting publishers to consider it:

> About four years ago, I contacted a few publishers about a book of poems and they said, "No. No way." They said they didn't think they wanted to publish a poetry book by me, and they said that my poems that I submitted were not suitable for a book, so I backed away for a while. As a matter of fact, I didn't exactly back away. I took a poem out of a current issue of *The New Yorker Magazine*, which to me was completely garbled. So I cut the poem out and sent it to the publisher of Random House's Times Books and told him that if *The New Yorker* could publish a poem like this, I saw no reason why they couldn't publish my poetry book.[17]

Carter began by submitting poems to different periodicals around the country, including the established quarterlies, as well as the small independent monthlies, all devoted to poetry. Some were published, and Carter asked nothing else be noted except the poem and his name, and soon word got out. He eventually submitted some to a publisher, and was offered a minuscule advance. Publishing a book of poetry is typically a gamble for both the publisher and poet. Financial rewards in the poetry market are few and rare, even if you were once president of the United States. *Always a Reckoning* became the first book of presidential poetry since John Quincy Adams' *Poems of Religion and Society* was published in 1848.

Along with his unusual book of poetry, 1995 also saw publication of a children's book. Times Books also published *The Little Baby Snoogle-Fleejer*, a twenty-two page easy reader with illustrations by daughter Amy. Carter first told the fairy tale, which dates back to thirty years, to his children when they were children. It tells of a handicapped boy, Jeremy, who cannot walk. At the beach one day, his friends spot a sea monster and run away, leaving Jeremy alone. The monster approaches Jeremy, and turns out to be friendly. The two become friends, and Snoogle-Fleejer brings Jeremy gold coins that it finds on the ocean floor, enabling Jeremy's mother to have a badly needed operation.

Carter would follow up with *Living Faith* in 1996. The book was a memoir concerning Carter's religious faith and values. The original outline for the book was to collect a year's worth of Sunday school lessons Carter taught before becoming president. His publisher suggested he write about how his religious faith had shaped his life and his lifestyle instead. Because of this, *Living Faith* is a memoir while also a lesson from Bible School. The book included the revelation that writing *Everything to Gain* with Rosalynn had put a strain on their marriage. "It soon became impossible for us to communicate directly, so we exchanged increasingly unpleasant comments through our word processors. In addition, we had different writing methods. I write quite rapidly, while Rosalynn labors over each paragraph. She always considered my writing as a rough draft, while I accused her of acting as thought every portion of her text had been delivered on stone tablets on Mount Sinai."[18]

The following year, Carter published yet another spiritual book, *Sources of Strength: Meditations on Scripture for a Living Faith*. The close proximity of the two books was not coincidental. "*Sources of Strength* is a companion to *Living Faith*," Carter wrote in the opening lines of the preface, "when I began writing the earlier book, I intended it to be like this one, a collection of some of the favorite Bible lessons I have taught. Now, a year later, I have returned to my original plan."[19] *Sources of Strength* was a collection of fifty-two Bible lessons, or "meditations" as Carter referred to them.

In 1998 Carter published *The Virtues of Aging*, a book that explored the benefits of growing old. The book, which Carter dedicated to his mother, Lillian, who "demonstrated the virtues of aging," picks up much like *Everything to Gain* (1987) does, after he and Rosalynn had written their memoirs but still did not know what to do with their remaining years. Carter also wrote about his success as an author, as well as Rosalynn's:

> Another quite different adventure on which we have embarked is writing books. I wrote my first one in 1975, something of an autobiography and an explanation of my political philosophy as I began my presidential campaign. Later ... the book became a best seller, and a million copies were rushed into print. Since then, I have written eleven other books, including a presidential memoir, histories, an outdoor journal, a collection of my poems, and an account of my experiences in mediating disputes. Rosalyn's autobiography was number one on the *New York Times* best-seller list. She has since written one on care giving, and her third book, on mental health, has just been published. I'm working on a novel of the Revolutionary War. We now edit each other's

work but will never write one again as coauthors, after an earlier effort almost broke up our marriage. Except for this trying experience, our writing has drawn us together. We share the responsibilities of negotiating advances, meeting deadlines, working with editors, and going on book tours after our work arrives in bookstores.[20]

The book ends with the observation, "You are old when regrets take the place of dreams."[21]

In 2001, Carter returned to writing memoir. *An Hour of Daylight: Memories of a Rural Boyhood*, would be his first exercise since 1992's *Turning Point*. *Daylight* deals exclusively with his childhood in the South. It includes chapters on sharecropping, working on a peanut farm, and the Great Depression. Carter also confronts the long concluded but ever-present Civil War and the impact it had on him and his ancestors. He recalls how his mother was the only one in her family to ever defend Lincoln, and relates how his great-great-grandfather lost the family fortunes because of the war, thus establishing the farm life he would remember as a young boy. "He died during the war, in 1864, and in his will he left to his twelve children forty-three slaves, 2,212 acres of land, and other property and cash, or $22,000 for each. Neither he nor his heirs realized at the times that the slaves would soon be free, and that the Confederate money would be worthless. His children ended up with small farms, and they and their descendants retained a deep-seated belief that only the land had any real and lasting value."[22]

An Hour Before Daylight concludes with Carter graduating high school, and joining the Navy. It is at about here that his first autobiography, *Why Not the Best*, begins. In the closing pages of *Daylight*, Carter wrestles with his memories of a happy childhood, at the same time being well aware of the racial divisions that involved his black neighbors.

Later the same year, another book, this time a small memoir, appeared, titled *Christmas in Plains: Memories*. A holiday-themed volume, *Christmas in Plains* is filled with some of Carter's most memorable Christmases. Despite the title, not all took place in Plains, Georgia. For instance, one recalls a holiday spent in an apartment on a military base, and even a submarine.

Carter also documents the four Christmases spent during his presidency, from 1977 to 1980. Of interest are his recollections from 1979. The Iranian Hostage crisis was only a month old, and Carter felt obligated to remain close to Washington. In lieu of returning to Plains, the president, his wife, and daughter Amy spent the holiday at Camp David. In a moment of generosity and holiday spirit, Carter personally invited all of the remaining White House staff to visit them on Christmas Day.

By now, Carter was generating most of his post-presidential income as an author. He had wisely avoided the pitfalls of penning too many politically influenced memoirs, as some of his predecessors had. The new millennium was shaping up nicely and included a multi-book deal from publisher Simon & Schuster.

Carter's published offerings from 2002 were atypical, compared to his other books. In October, The Brookings Institute published *To Assure Pride and Confidence in the Electoral Process*, which was co-authored by former president Gerald R. Ford, Robert H. Michel, and Lloyd N. Cutler. The book was a review of the 2000 presidential election, with suggestions on how to avoid problems in future elections.

In early December, Crown Publishers released *The Personal Beliefs of Jimmy Carter*. The volume was a combination of Carter's earlier spiritual offerings, *Living Faith* and *Sources of Strength*. Apparently the publisher believed the two books would sell better as one volume. *Personal Beliefs* sold well, considering the original books were still in print and the new edition contained no new information. Also in December, Simon & Schuster published *The Nobel Peace Prize Lecture*. In 2002, Carter was awarded the Nobel Peace Prize for his efforts to promote peace and end conflict throughout the world, and delivered the address on December 10, 2002, in Oslo, Norway. Simon & Schuster rushed the book out to bookstores on December 31.

In 2003, Carter published *The Hornet's Nest: A Novel of the Revolutionary War*. The book remains unique because no president had ever published a work of fiction before. The novel's focus is on Ethan and Epsey Pratt, two Northerners who move to Georgia. There they befriend their neighbors and a young Indian. The book is divided into three parts, spanning 1763 to 1785, thus allowing the Revolutionary War to come full circle. Actual historical figures intertwine with the novel, such as Button Gwinnet and Lachlan McIntosh, as well as actual places. Carter had begun working on the novel seven years earlier, while writing three other books. Reviews were mixed, while Simon & Schuster confidently described *The Hornet's Nest* as being "in the tradition of such major classics as *The Last of the Mohicans*."

Simon & Schuster would publish *Sharing Good Times* in 2004. In the introduction, Carter wrote:

> In the past, I have written about history, political science, religion, the technique of negotiation, outdoor experiences, a novel about The Revolutionary War, a book of poetry, and a presidential memoir, all fairly serious subjects. This book is about the more challenging, relaxing, and enjoyable experiences that I have known, both at work and at play. I have described personal hobbies, excursions to exotic places, political campaigns, volunteer work, and simply relaxed days and nights with little to do except exchange memories and ideas with family and friends across the years and across generations.[23]

Despite his best intentions, the book appeared to have been thrown together. He seems to have exhausted his best recollections, leaving the reader with family sporting events, vacations, even bird watching. After eighteen books, sixteen of which were published since leaving the White House, it was easy to repeat things previously published.

After 1996 and 1997's *Living Faith* and *Sources of Strength*, Carter would return with yet another spiritual effort in 2004. *Our Endangered Values: America's Moral Crisis* contained controversial subjects worthy of debate. Topics included the conflict between science and religion, divorce, homosexuality, abortion, and the death penalty. Carter knew the road he was taking was a rocky one, and acknowledged this in the book's introduction, writing "As a private citizen, I will deliberately mix religion and politics in this book."[24]

Our Endangered Values did well at bookstores, and received overall good reviews. It revealed that Carter still practiced what he preached, and was able to articulate controversial topics in an orderly and highly readable manner. The book would eventually reach number one on the *New York Times* bestseller list.

Palestine: Peace Not Apartheid, appeared in 2006. The cover of the book's dust jacket featured a photograph of the West Bank Barrier that Israel had recently erected to isolate Palestine. Carter was an outspoken opponent of the wall, which harkened back to the Berlin Wall and East Germany. Though written in a much different tone than *The Blood of Abraham* (1985), it dealt with the on-going problem of bringing peace to Israel while simultaneously establishing a Palestinian State within its occupied territories. After brokering the 1978 Camp David Peace Accords, Carter had become disappointed with the state of affairs between Israel and Palestine. By voicing his frustration, the book quickly became controversial, a fact Carter was well aware of when written. Carter would later acknowledge that he had become "bitterly disappointed by the actual current state of affairs in Israel and Palestine."[25] Despite being accused of harboring anti–Semitic views, Carter defended his position in writing it.

A new post-presidential memoir was published in 2007. *Beyond the White House: Waging Peace, Fighting Disease, Building Hope* picks up with Carter returning to Plains after completing his presidential term. Carter was fifty-six at the time, and felt he had another twenty-five years left to contribute.

Beyond the White House tells of the establishment of The Carter Center, a think tank which worked out of the Jimmy Carter Presidential Library. Aside from his efforts in the Middle East peace process, Carter details the

Center's role in peace negotiations in Haiti, Sudan, Bosnia, and Nigeria, to name a few. Carter also tells of his 1994 visit to Cuba, and meeting with Fidel Castro. The book depicts Carter doing what he loves most, helping others to improve their own lives. Instead of wallowing in post-election defeat or taking a seat on corporate boards, Carter proved to be the most constructive former president since Herbert Hoover.

In 2008 Carter published his first biography. *A Remarkable Mother* is his account of the life of his mother, Lillian Gordy Carter, otherwise known as 'Miss Lillian." Mrs. Carter, who died in 1983, contributed much of her life to social aid, even volunteering for the Peace Corps at the age of 68. She was a great inspiration to her son. Lillian Carter was also an author, and wrote *Away from Home: Letters to My Family*, which was published in 1977. The book was out of print for many years, but reissued by Simon & Schuster in 2008 to coincide with the release of *A Remarkable Mother*.

Carter would release a third book concerning the Middle East in 2009. *We Can Have Peace in the Holy Land; A Plan That Will Work* dealt with past peace efforts and why they failed.

Carter was also the first president to take advantage of the audiobook format. Around 2007, publishers began offering Carter the opportunity to read from his recent books. Carter also would release several audio-book-only readings not available in printed format. These include such titles as *Leading a Worthy Life, Measuring Our Success*, and *Bringing Peace to a Changing World*. All of these titles are part of Carter's "Sunday Morning in Plains, Bible Study" series.

A presidential diary was published in 2010. *White House Diary* originated by an offhand comment made by Richard Nixon, who Carter met during a governor's conference in 1971. Nixon asked Mrs. Carter whether she kept a diary, and when told she did not, he warned her that she would someday regret it.

In the *Diary's* preface, Carter describes his methods of recording entries:

> During my four years in the White House, I kept a personal diary by dictating my thoughts and observations several times each day. Some days I kept notes and dictated later. When time permitted, my secretary, Susan Clough, would type the notes and file the pages in large binders.
>
> Readers should remember that I seldom exercised any restraint on what I dictated, because I did not contemplate the more personal entries ever being made public. When my opinions of people changed, for instance, I did not go back and amend the entries.[26]

Carter's *White House Diary* stands out among presidential diaries. Entries were not restricted to things presidential, and personal admissions are plentiful. As an example, Carter enjoyed running and desired to keep doing it as president. Apparently Carter would sometimes secretly exercise outside of the confines of the White House, such as told in an entry made shortly after Thanksgiving, 1979: "I went out to run along the canal and told the Secret Service to meet us at Fletcher's boat landing about two and a half miles from town. I ran past Fletcher's in freezing cold weather one and a half more miles and came back. The cars were caught in traffic and not there. I stood there about ten minutes while I fumed, then ran back into town. I was really furious, and my hands almost froze because we were dressed lightly and didn't have gloves. Part of the problem was caused by [my orders to] the Secret Service to keep my running a secret."[27]

The thought of the President of the United States, standing alone on a Washington, D.C., street corner waiting for the Secret Service, is almost unimaginable, but it happened to Carter. He also reveals he stayed upbeat after his re-election defeat and focused on life after the White House. This included packing up for the move back to Plains. Still, little things aggravated him, such as the disappearance of two treasured fishing poles.

White House Diary consisted of Carter's basic diary entries made from 1977 to 1981. *Keeping Faith*, Carter's 1982 memoir, was framed by these entries, and as a result the two books read like companion volumes. Included in the *Diary* was a six-page "Aftermath," which offered recollections of writing *Keeping Faith* as well as the publishing contract negotiations. Shortly after leaving office, Carter purchased a Lanier word processor, which was considered state of the art in 1981. Carter writes, "The machine I purchased, which cost about ten thousand dollars, was a relatively rudimentary word processor; at the time, however, it represented the cutting edge of technology. I remember that I had to return the carriage at the end of each line, and there was no carry-over from one page to the next."[28]

Carter and his literary agents would meet with representatives from Morrow publishing, as well as Bantam. Carter remembers they wanted:

> a highly personal book, expressing my impression of the White House, the presidency, people with whom I met, the ordeal of making difficult decisions. Books written previously by Ford, Johnson, Nixon, even Truman, have been highly impersonal in nature, primarily a recapitulation of the daily schedule or written by a committee. I told them I was going to spend about a year writing the book and five or six months making sure the book was a commercial success, it would be personal, and I would write it myself. I think this is the main message they needed to hear.[29]

Bantam offered a $900,000 advance, of which half would be paid on delivery of the book, as well as paperback edition, Book of the Month Club offer, and a special edition volume. Another publisher promised a $1 million advance but with future receipts, book club sales, and paperback sales credited against the advance. Carter choose Bantam because "if the book is a success, then Bantam is much more generous."[30]

Contract negotiations were completed March 7, 1981. Carter now had to write and deliver the manuscript. *Keeping Faith* was released October 1, 1982.

In 2011 Carter published *Through the Year with Jimmy Carter; 366 Daily Meditations from the 39th President*. For the first time since collaborating with Rosalynn (*Everything to Gain*) Carter would work with a co-author, in this case Steve Halliday. It would be Carter's third religious publication and his first with a new publisher, Zondervan. Like 1997's *Sources of Strength*, both contained lessons and essays drawn from the Bible.

No stranger to the publishing industry, Carter would remark in the introduction "Many centuries ago a wise author warned, "Of making many books there is no end" (Ecclesiastes 12:12). While I'm not sure how many books *he* wrote, I'm pretty sure that, unless I've lost count, *Through the Year with Jimmy Carter* is my twenty-sixth. That's a lot of books!"[31]

In 2014, Carter published *A Call to Action: Women, Religion, Violence, and Power*. The book addressed the abuse collected upon women, which have subrogated them to "second class citizens," throughout history. Carter confronted issues attributed to the writings of the Koran, as well as the Bible.

Carter would release yet another autobiographical volume in 2015. *A Full Life: Reflections at Ninety* contained select moments in Carter's life that he now looked back upon. While many stories mentioned in it had been previously published, Carter adds the wisdom that one acquires with age. With the June release of *A Full Life*, Carter maintained a book tour, which included signing events. In early August 2015, however, Carter revealed that an MRI revealed the presence of cancer. About a week later, a further statement reveled that the cancer had spread to other areas of his body, including his brain. Despite this, Carter chose to continue his scheduled book tour, and delayed surgery until after it was completed.

In 2018, at the age of ninety-three, *Faith: A Journey for All* was released. In the book Carter recalled how his belief in God shaped his life.

Like John Quincy Adams, Theodore Roosevelt, and Herbert Hoover, writing took up a good part of Carter's post-presidency, without overwhelming it. Whether or not Carter ever writes another book, his thirty-two published contributions of autobiographies, politics, poetry, spiritually, social concerns, the great outdoors, biography, and finally fiction, are impressive among themselves, never mind the fact that he once occupied the Oval Office.

Ronald Reagan

> Am glad I only have one life to write about because it's really a chore.[1]
>
> —Ronald Reagan

Reagan's first brush with authorship came in 1965. With his movie career behind him, Reagan attempted to run for governor of California. Used to help introduce voters to his political views, *Where's the Rest of Me? The Ronald Reagan Story* was co-written with Richard G. Hubler, a veteran author of "tell-all" books and published by Duell, Sloan and Pearce of New York.

Reagan's recollections of childhood were told in a folksy manner to the point of him having "rare Huck Finn–Tom Sawyer idylls," while growing up in Illinois.[2] As for his motion picture career and election as president of the Screen Actor's Guild, Reagan later adopted strong anti-union beliefs, which he claimed had been infiltrated with Communists. Biographer Lou Cannon claimed aides believed the book would hurt voters. "By the standards of political memoirs, (Reagan) was unusually frank, so much so that his adversaries thought the book would prove an embarrassment."[3] Biographer Edmund Morris also seemed to agree, noting, "Even that text, eloquent and frank to begin with, shows signs of creeping collaboration (he co-wrote it with Richard G. Hubler), and its overall didactic tone both cloys and annoys."[4]

Morris also compared Reagan's "eccentric personal memoir" to the writings of Theodore Roosevelt[5]:

> Like Theodore Roosevelt's *Autobiography* of 1913, it was a confused mix of sharp but selective personal recollections and long stretches of presentist political philosophy, unreadable by anybody of sound mind. Originally these stretches had bulked even longer, and the publisher, Duell, Sloan & Pearce, had brought in Richard G. Hubler to clarify and shorten Dutch's sprawling manuscript. Hubler (a former editorial colleague of Philip Dunne on *The Screen Writer*) left the personal passages largely alone, but elsewhere cut so ruthlessly that lacunae had to be bridged by ellipses.[6]

In the end, the book was "a minefield of potentially embarrassing quotes. Even the anti–Communist passages were so bellicose as to guarantee opposition from the new anti-war movement."[7]

Released on April 23, 1965, the book was apparently selling well enough to surprise Reagan with a royalty check four years later. After completing the book, co-author Richard G. Hubler was placed under contract by Walt Disney Productions to write an authorized biography of Mr. Disney. Hubler worked on the manuscript from 1967 to 1968, and upon completion was paid off by Disney Productions, with the manuscript never being published.

Historian Gary Wills would sum up *Where's the Rest of Me?* with the observation, "The book is not a Hollywood memoir but a political confession."[8]

Lou Cannon, who authored 1991's *The Role of a Lifetime*, would go on to publish a second volume on Reagan in 2003. In *Governor Reagan, His Rise to Power*, Cannon was still wrestling with exactly how much of *Where's the Rest of Me?* was written by Reagan and how much had been written by Hubler. "Although several of the incidents described in the autobiography are inaccurate or unverifiable, as we shall see, Reagan thought of the book as his true-life story. When I interviewed him in 1968 for my first book, Reagan often repeated passages of *Where's the Rest of Me?* nearly verbatim in response to my questions."[9] In the end, Cannon discovered Reagan "found it easier to tell stories than to write a book."[10]

Aide Peggy Noonan would make a poignant observation involving the book and two of Reagan's children, Patti and Ron Jr. In his biography, *Dutch*, Edmund Morris noted Reagan and first wife Jane Wyman had a child who only lived a few hours. Neither Patti nor Ron Jr. was aware of this until having read *Dutch*. Yet Reagan wrote about it in *Where's the Rest of Me?* twenty-six years earlier. "Because you forget what's in the books written about a famous father," Noonan wrote, adding, "This is the nature of modern fame. You talk to your family in books, and they may not read them, or remember them, or absorb the facts put forth in a way that incorporates the information into their emotional experience of who Dad was, or who Mom was."[11]

In January 1981, Reagan was sworn in as president. In May of that year, a book appeared with the title *Rendezvous with Destiny*. A souvenir of Reagan's successful presidential campaign, *Rendezvous* contained addresses and speeches given by Reagan, dating back as early as 1964. Osmond Publishers of Salt Lake City, Utah, published it. George Osmond, who operated the publishing company, was an older (and non-performing) brother of the popular Osmond Brothers musical group of the 1970s.

After serving two terms as president, Reagan would release a memoir in 1990. *An American Life: The Autobiography*, covered Reagan's early life, his political career in California, as well as his presidency. It was written with the help of Robert Lindsey, who had ghostwritten several other best sellers with celebrities such as Marlon Brando. Edmund Morris would dismiss it as "a ghostwritten work, undertaken at the behest of Mrs. Reagan, and may be safely described as the most boring book of its kind since Herbert Hoover's *Challenge to Liberty*."[12]

An American Life opens with the humble line, "If I'd gotten the job at

Montgomery Ward, I suppose I would have never left Illinois."[13] Reagan's recollections as a Hollywood actor are brief, and treated like a cameo. He describes his years as California's governor as being difficult and ulcer producing. As for his first experience in national politics, Reagan claims he was never interested in being vice president, despite Gerald Ford's people offering it to him. As for his two terms as president, much of *American Life* was culled from Reagan's personal White House diaries. Like Jimmy Carter, Reagan would later publish his own White House diaries.

Biographer Marc Eliot pointed out that much of Reagan's screen career was left out of *An American Life*, just as in *Where's the Rest of Me?* Eliot wrote that "less than 20 percent, about a fifth, deals with Reagan's Hollywood years, despite the fact that his film and TV career lasted nearly three decades."[14]

An American Life would be the last real literary effort from Reagan. Reagan was diagnosed with Alzheimer's disease in 1994, and the books that followed contained material that had been written prior to his illness.

Reagan's next book was really a collection of speeches and radio addresses written during the 1970s. *Reagan in His Own Hand* was published in 2001 and compiled and edited by Kiron K. Skinner, Annelise Anderson, and Martin Anderson. The credentials shared among the three include an assistant professor of history, research fellows, a senior fellowship, and a special assistant to a former president. The book came about when Skinner discovered several boxes of handwritten drafts of radio broadcasts, speeches and correspondence by Reagan in the Reagan Presidential Library.

Reagan: A Life in Letters, followed in 2003, also edited by Skinner, Anderson and Anderson. It is, as the title reads, a collection of letters written by Reagan, dating from 1922 to his "farewell letter" of November 5, 1994, in which he announced he was in the early stages of Alzheimer's disease. The book's introduction notes:

> President Reagan wrote wherever he was and whenever he had time to write. He wrote letters in the Oval Office, in his study at the White House, at Camp David, on the helicopter ride to Camp David, and on long trips on *Air Force One*.[15]
>
> Free Press would publish *Reagan: A Life in Letters*. It should be noted that wife Nancy Reagan was instrumental in releasing the material used in the previous two books. Reagan was most likely experiencing the late stages of Alzheimer's by then. Mrs. Reagan believed the letters and speeches collected reflected her husband's true nature and said, "I just want people to know who Ronnie is."[16]

Reagan died in 2004, and did not live to see some of his best, if not historical, writing see publication. Published in 2007, *The Reagan Diaries* were edited by Douglas Brinkley. Reagan now joined John Quincy Adams and predecessor Jimmy Carter as notable diarists. Brinkley noted, "Unlike so many new diarists who trail off after the first few weeks, he took his task seriously, and in eight years he never neglected a daily entry, except when he was in the hospital."[17]

Brinkley recalled the first time seeing the diaries:

> When I first saw the White House diaries at the Ronald Reagan Presidential Library in Simi Valley, California, I was astounded. Lined up on a research table, all five volumes resemble a handsome half-set on an encyclopedia. For a moment, I just looked at them. In physical appearance, the diaries are hardcover books, 8 1/2 by 11, bound in maroon and brown leather with a presidential seal embossed on the center of the front and the name RONALD WILSON REAGAN in gold lettering at the bottom right.
>
> Within the pages themselves, you see immediately that Reagan had neat, rounded handwriting, done in ink that is variously blue or black. It is a welcoming script, easy to read. Cross-outs are rare. Economical to the core, Reagan filled every page to the very bottom.[18]

After leaving office, Reagan would sometimes bring out the diaries after dinner and reread them. In a 1991 letter, Reagan admitted this and was considering publishing them. "Believe it or not, I'm rereading my diaries because my memory needs help. When I left the governorship I was amazed at my lack of recall of all that had happened. When I became president I decided to keep a record of each day's happenings. I'm not sure they would outdo the book I've already done but I'm continually amazed at how many things I've forgotten."[19]

Among the hundreds of entries made in *The Reagan Diaries*, Reagan's entry of an occurrence in the Lincoln bedroom is perhaps the most chilling. "I think the ghost of Abe Lincoln is stirring around upstairs where we live. Rex sets up a holler & goes around barking down the great hall for all the world as if he's barking at someone. Finally I accompanied him all the way to Lincoln's bedroom. There he balked at going into the room."[20]

As editor, Brinkley had to heavily edit entries to keep the book within one volume. In 2009 an expanded edition was published which included more material.

The second book of Reagan's writing published after his death was *The Notes: Ronald Reagan's Private Collection of Stories and Wisdom*. Also edited by Douglas Brinkley, the 2011 offering was a small volume containing notes, quotes, and one-liners made on a collection of index cards, which were discovered among the holdings of the Reagan Presidential Library. Called "the Rosetta stone" of the Reagan Library collection, it is believed to date back to the time Reagan was working for General Electric Theater.

With the release of *The Notes*, the published efforts of Ronald Reagan came to a close.

In Edmund Morris's 1999 Reagan biography *Dutch*, Morris disclosed the discovery of a grouping of early writings from Reagan dating back to 1925, when he was in high school. Morris noted, "It is sad, but not surprising, that the youthful literary effusions of Ronald Reagan remain unpublished. Mr. Reagan never pretended to be a writer, nor had he the least holographic vanity."[21] As Reagan's authorized biographer, Morris was permitted to rummage through materials stored at the Reagan Presidential Library. Morris lamented finding the pieces in their present state, despite their significance. "Had Mr. Reagan never risen to world power, the few browning manuscripts of his late teens and early twenties—essays, fantasies, and some patently autobiographical short stories—would doubtless crumble unread. Archivists at the Reagan Presidential Library, who store so meticulously every last lunch voucher of the White House Interagency Low Income Opportunity Advisory Board, seem unaware of their significance. The present reviewer found them in a tin trunk of items considered unworthy of display or preservation."[22]

As of this writing, these manuscripts remain unpublished in book form. There always remains the possibility that they may someday be properly edited and collected with proper consideration. Until then, Morris's account will have to do.

George H.W. Bush

By the time he won the presidency, George Herbert Walker Bush had accumulated a career in politics that had not been seen for some time. Previously, Bush had served in the House of Representatives, ambassador to the United Nations, special envoy to China, director of the CIA, RNC chairman, and vice president under Reagan.

Bush's first book would be the typical campaign-style autobiography published by countless of his predecessors. *Looking Forward* was co-written with journalist Victor Gold, who previously served as a consultant on Bush's presidential campaigns of 1980 and 1984. Published in 1987, *Looking Forward* was the lightweight autobiography one would come to expect written during a national campaign, and was aimed at getting Bush out of the shadows of Ronald Reagan's legacy. No sitting vice president had succeeded to the presidency in his own right since Martin Van Buren in 1837, and this was not lost on Bush or his handlers.

One of the most interesting revelations to come out of the book was Bush's offhand comment that he had originally considered writing a book as early as 1977. Apparently his plans were derailed once Reagan chose him as his running mate in 1980. Bush and Gold constructed the book to act as the quick autobiography needed for the campaign, which was a challenge considering the various and wide ranging positions and appointments Bush previously served. Bush would casually note this in the introduction. "The origin of this book in fact predates the Reagan administration by several years. The story it tells precedes it by more than five decades. Strictly speaking, this isn't a "Washington book." It's also a book about Texas, Maine, the Bonin Islands, and China."[1]

Co-author Victor Gold would be attacked in several Bush-related biographies. Author Russ Baker would dismiss Gold as a "longtime Washington PR man," and claimed *Looking Forward* was "full of self-serving inaccuracies."[2] Biographer Herbert S. Parmet would describe Gold as a "former deputy press secretary for Barry Goldwater and speechwriter for Vice President Spiro Agnew, [and] was pretty savvy. He had no great love for Ronald Reagan, and certainly was pushing for a Bush nomination."[3]

Bush would eventually donate the book's royalties to the M.D. Anderson Hospital and Tumor Institute, as well as the United Negro College Fund.[4]

After his presidential term ended in 1993, Bush published *A World Transformed*, which was co-written with General Brent Scowcroft in 1998. While readers were assuming Bush would quickly publish his presidential memoirs, he would not. "What follows is not a memoir or history of the Bush Administration, or even of its foreign policy. We prefer to leave history to the historians."[5] Bush would stand by this statement for the rest of his life. While he may write books regarding issues and events that transpired during his presidency, he would not author a memoir. That was for the historians to do.

Instead, *A World Transformed* focused on international events such as the end of the Cold War, Tiananmen Square, the Gulf War, and the collapse of the Soviet Union. The book closes with a Christmas day 1991 entry. Gorbachev had just resigned and the USSR was now dissolved. After a final phone call from Gorbachev, Bush recorded his thoughts into a small tape recorder, as was his custom, and remembered "It was the voice of a good friend; it was the voice of a man to whom history will give enormous credit."[6]

The following year, Bush published *All the Best: My Life in Letters and Other Writings*. Like the previous book, it did not initially strike the reader as the typical autobiography or memoir. Bush addressed the subject in the book's preface. "This book is not meant to be an autobiography. It is not a historical document of my life. But hopefully you, the reader, will have a look at what's on the mind of an eighteen-year-old kid who goes into the Navy and then at nineteen is flying a torpedo bomber off an aircraft carrier in World War II; what runs through the mind of a person living in China, halfway around the world from friends and family; what a President is thinking when he has to send someone else's son or daughter into combat."[7]

All the Best fulfilled Bush's best intentions. As RNC chairman, Bush witnessed President Nixon's presidency disintegrate. For Bush it was personal and devastating, claiming, "my heart went totally out to him even though I felt betrayed by his lie of the day before. The man is amoral.... He became President of the United States and a damn good one in many ways, but now it has all caught up with him."[8]

With Gerald Ford expected to assume office any day, Bush's name was floated as a potential vice presidential nominee. Bush felt his role as RNC chairman would taint his nomination, and prepared to be passed over once again, yet retained his sense of humor. "I am convinced that it won't happen and almost that it shouldn't because the Vice President [Ford] needs something separate, apart and clean. And unfairly or not I may have tracked it in and kind of spread it around the living room carpet—not by design and hopefully not by character, but rather by an association. It's a weird, weird world."[9]

Despite having two post-presidency books under his belt, publishers still desired an actual memoir. Unlike his predecessors, Bush had little interest in penning his recollections. He repeatedly said that anyone who wished to find out what George H.W. Bush was about only needed to visit his Presidential Library in College Station, Texas.

In 2009, author Russ Baker claimed Bush could never pen a proper autobiography because of certain elements in his past. Baker claimed Bush was possibly an agent for the CIA long before serving as director in 1975. When Bush's Navy fighter was shot down in 1943, Baker claimed Bush's crew was actually working for naval intelligence, and theoretically spies. The less Bush wrote the better. When it came to Bush's lack of authorship, Baker observed that:

> Perhaps this problem with story discrepancies, a problem that would resurface time and again in Poppy's life, so often it became a virtual theme, explains why Poppy [George] Bush never penned a comprehensive autobiography. There were too many secrets, too many different stories to keep straight.[10]
>
> When combined, *Looking Forward*, *A World Transformed*, and *All the Best* paint a suitable portrait of George H.W. Bush. An underlying common thread in all three is Bush's admitted reluctance to get too emotional in the retelling of the history he witnessed or to get caught up in. Like other presidents, Bush kept a White House diary, composed mainly of thoughts dictated into a tape recorder. In *A World Transformed*, Bush's diary is acknowledged, but never intended to be a source of information. "The President's diary is a different matter. On an episodic basis he kept record of his thoughts, which was never meant to be (and is not) either all-inclusive or an official record of his life. Portions have been included in the book, but these do not represent a larger work meant for publication—or for scholars.[11]

In these three sentences, the door was closed. It was safe to assume that the publication of Bush's White House diary, despite the success of his two most recent predecessors, was nil.

In 2008, however, Bush's *China Diary* appeared. The diary was written and kept by Bush while serving as a de facto United States ambassador from October 1974 until December 1975. The diary, published as *The China Diary of George H.W. Bush: The Making of a Global President*, was published with Bush's authorization, and edited by Jeffery A. Engel, a professor at Texas A&M University. In the book's preface, Bush acknowledged it was Engel who first considered publishing it. "When professor Jeffrey Engel first approached me about publishing the diary, I really had no hesitations. I had not looked at it in years and did not recall what it said. My one great fear was that perhaps I had dwelled a little too much on the great hot dog bun crisis of 1975, instead of more substantive issues. But I readily put all such misgivings aside and gave Professor Engel complete editorial control."[12]

Bush's preface is revealing in that he almost had to be nudged into allowing it to be published, and only after giving Engel complete editorial control. It seems clear that he wanted nothing further to do with it. It is very possible that *Chinese Diary* was Bush's most important book. It serves as a unique record of China, and Chinese life and customs, in the days before its transformation from a land of isolation to the international community and global economy of today. In the conclusion Engel writes how the diary showed "what Bush planned to do with [power] if ever entrusted with it. It helps us better understand his later policies when he was in fact granted that power. But most fundamentally, it shows Bush's thinking, and indeed his style, well before the Oval Office."[13]

In 2012, Bush was diagnosed with Vascular Parkinsonism, a form of Parkinson's disease, which affects the lower half of the body. This affliction, which struck him at the age of eighty-eight, appeared to silence any speculation left that he would publish anything further.

In 2015, Random House published *Destiny and Power: The American Odyssey of George Herbert Walker Bush*, a biography written by Pulitzer Prize winner Jon Meacham. Meacham had been granted unparalleled access to Bush's diaries, and had extensively interviewed the former president since 2006. For many readers, *Destiny and Power* became the "unwritten autobiography" that Bush never wrote. Meacham emphasized that while he was exposed to a wealth of Bush's personal and private material, in the end the book was his own. Meacham also revealed plans to eventually edit and publish the Bush diaries in coming years.

In the end, Bush did what men like Andrew Jackson and Franklin Pierce wanted, which was have someone competent write their story for them. He also chose to do what Lyndon B. Johnson preferred, and let his Presidential Library speak for him.

In the end, Bush had no desire to write any further, and had no problem turning his back on something that had become a modern-day industry ever since Harry S. Truman wrote his memoirs.

Bill Clinton

> I think it's a good story, and I've had a good time telling it.
> —Bill Clinton[1]

> I would never claim to read his memoir, except perhaps as a sleep aid.
> —Paul Greenberg[2]

As a youth growing up in Arkansas, and even while attending college at Oxford and Yale universities, William Jefferson Clinton possessed a fondness for American history. Between jobs such as teaching law, and being the youngest governor in the history of Arkansas, he never got around to writing. Future wife (and lawyer) Hillary Rodham Clinton even beat him to the punch by having an article published in the prestigious *Harvard Educational Review*, long before Bill put anything substantial to paper.

Putting People First: How We Can All Change America would be Clinton's freshman effort into the world of authorship and campaign literature. Co-authored with running mate Al Gore, it introduced the Arkansas governor and Tennessee senator to national politics and described their agenda in detail. Clinton was a novice author, and Gore had previously published *Earth in the Balance* only weeks before Clinton chose him as his running mate.

In 1996, Random House published *Between Hope and History: Meeting America's Challenges for the 21st Century*. The book was conveniently released in time for the upcoming Democratic National Convention, where, as the incumbent, Clinton would be nominated for a second term.

Between Hope and History read like a summary of his first four years in office, while addressing the work still left for a second term. "I did this book because I wanted to get a simple, straightforward, fairly brief account out to the American people in 1996, for anyone who wanted to read it, about what we had tried to do, what we were going to do if I got another term," Clinton explained.³ He also acknowledged the assistance of a ghostwriter, William E. Nothdurft, who had become an invaluable resource. "I couldn't have done the book without him, because I was in the middle of not only being president, but running for president."⁴ Nothdurft, a writer who had been active in Democratic Party causes, quickly impressed the president. "He seemed to understand what it was we were about, what our administration was trying to do."⁵

Unfortunately, Clinton found that as a sitting president running for reelection, he had little time to devote to the book once it was released. Clinton later lamented the fact in an interview for C-Span:

> This book didn't sell well because I didn't promote it. First of all, I thought we probably should have made a paperback book and had fewer copies out. But I know how hard Hillary worked to sell her book. Books sell when people go around and go on book tours and talk about them and do interviews; sit in bookstores and sign copies for hours. And I think I was in a bookstore when my book was out, and that's because I just happened to be in Chautauqua, New York, one day preparing for the debates, and there was a pretty bookstore there. I went in and shook hands with people and talked to them. And I think I signed twelve copies in ten minutes—or five minutes or something. But you have to sell a book, and I think I feel bad for the publishers.⁶

The book leaned heavily on the approaching millennium, and at times resembles Franklin D. Roosevelt's 1934 effort, *On Our Way*, which was also published while in office. There is nothing personal or autobiographical in it; save for Clinton's explanation of how he arrived at the title. He had apparently met Nobel Prize–winning poet Seamus Heaney in Ireland the previous year, and Heaney wrote one of his poems out in longhand for the president. It contained the phrase "between hope and history." Clinton framed the paper, and hung it in his White House study for inspiration.

Shortly after leaving office in 2001, literary agent Robert Barnett announced that Clinton had signed a contract with Knopf to publish his memoirs. Barnett had also served as Hillary Clinton's agent for her upcoming book, *Living History*, and was said to have secured a $20 million advance for the couple, $12 million for the former president's book alone. Clinton signed his contract with Knopf in August, with a release scheduled sometime for early 2003. Both Bill and Hillary cited Katharine Graham's memoir, *Personal History*, as a template for what they hoped to produce in the end. In her book, *Clinton in Exile*, author Carol Felsenthal wrote although Clinton "was then seen as a disgraced president," it "did not depress the size of the advance. His tarnished image might have pushed the advance up, in hopes that he would reveal what he was thinking when he had sex with an intern in the White House."⁷ In an early interview with *Newsweek*, Clinton hinted that the memoir would not be mean-spirited, and would not be "about settling scores but setting the record straight."[8] He also wanted to "explain to people who I am and what I tried to do in public life—the good things we did and the mistakes I made. And I want to make it come alive."[9]

Much of what would later become *My Life* started as an oral history, captured on tape with Pulitzer Prize-winning author Taylor Branch, first while still in the White House, and later at the Clintons' home in Chappaqua, New York. These tapes would amount to seventy-nine hours' worth of material while Clinton was still in the White House. Much of these taping sessions were eventually released in a book by Branch in 2009, appropriately titled *The Clinton Tapes: Wrestling History with the President*. Well-written and intimate, Branch's book conveys the comfortable atmosphere upon which Clinton related his thoughts, opinions, and much of what occurred behind closed doors. A good deal of what was transcribed in these sessions was later used to help jog Clinton's memory once he seriously began work on his memoir after leaving office.

As president, Clinton was ignorant of personal computers, instead choosing to write his manuscript out in longhand on yellow pads and working much like Truman and Eisenhower had fifty years earlier. While he did not secure the services of a full-fledged ghostwriter, Clinton had speechwriter Ted Widmer assist him in structuring what would become his book. Early in 2003, Clinton invited Branch to his Chappaqua home to evaluate what he had written so far. In his book, Branch recalls staying up all through the night to read the seven hundred-page manuscript in one sitting. By the end, he was frustrated to discover the manuscript only covered up until Clinton's 1992 presidential campaign. When Branch asked Clinton where the rest of the book was, Clinton innocently replied that he was working on the next chapter. Branch immediately confronted Clinton, reminding him of the book's deadline and publication. "Mr. President, they have announced your book for Father's Day in June. This is the end of February. You can't write your whole presidency in a month or two. That's impossible. Well, he would try. He worked all night in the barn, in fact, and he would get back out there after a nap. I stared in disbelief. He looked dead serious."[10]

As a seasoned author, Branch knew what Clinton wanted to do would be impossible, and suggested either he demand more time, or focus on a two volume memoir. This struck fear in Clinton. "He said the publisher wouldn't let him. He had a deadline, and they would sue him. No, they won't, I said. They could make more money on two books. And to hell if they did sue. You are President of the United States. Say what you want and let the business people adjust."[11]

It was then that Clinton led Branch into a room where an aide was transcribing Clinton's latest handwritten draft into legible type. Even more impressive was the shelf containing bound volumes of the transcripts from their White House recordings. Clinton, Branch had discovered, was resigned to writing as much of the book as he could in the shortest amount of time possible.

Clinton had been bookish most of his adult life, and sought out the memoirs of past presidents to compare with. His hands-down favorite was Ulysses S. Grant's *Personal Memoirs*. While Grant raced to finish his book in a deadly battle with cancer, Clinton had to fight off lucrative speaking engagements. These engagements usually involved traveling, sapping his energy and distracting him. A typical week's worth of writing would then involve only two days. Yet, there were those who knew Clinton personally that said writing the book was perhaps the best thing to happen to him. Family friend Irena Medavoy recalled, "He has a very strong survival instinct and I think the book was cathartic for him. I think the book saved his life at that point. It gave him such focus, such direction."[12]

Despite his bouts of enthusiasm, Clinton could not meet the publisher's original deadline, and Hillary's book was published first. Finally, in June 2004, Clinton's memoir was published. Simply titled *My Life*, the book totaled 957 pages. In the book's prologue, Clinton revealed a list of life goals, made when he was young and out of law school. The list included his desire to "be a good man, have a good marriage and children, have good friends, make a successful political life, and write a great book."[13]

Unfortunately, this would not be it. *My Life* would bear the brunt of poor reviews. *Newsweek's* Jonathan Alter claimed the book was bad enough to honestly believe Clinton's claims of having written most of it himself, adding, "If it had been a lot better, I would have been awfully suspicious about whether he wrote it or not."[14] Alter went on to say the book suffered from a "kind of all-over-the-map, up-until-four-AM Clinton thing," which could possibly reflect Clinton's desire to meet the publisher's umpteenth deadline.[15] It resembled a "laundry-list," and was just Clinton "sitting there with his legal pads."[16]

Even a few of Clinton's friends admitted how they were unable to sit down with the book. Donna Shalala is typical of his friends in saying she "loved" the first part and then trailed off when talking about the rest. A surprising number of people didn't read it; they read the reviews and just couldn't muster the enthusiasm. Leon Panetta says he "brushed" through it, that he read enough "to get a feel for it." While the first half perhaps merits an "A," the rest, says Panetta, is a failure. When he got to the presidency, the deadline noose was tightening and he "just kind of ran through his schedules." One friend called it "a brain dump."[17]

My Life garnered much publicity when first published, partly because of the public's fascination in finally reading Clinton's account of his affair with White House intern Monica Lewinsky. Clinton writes that he was "disgusted with myself for doing it, and in the Spring, when I saw her again, I told her it was wrong for me, wrong for my family, and wrong for her, and I couldn't do it anymore."[18] While he describes the legal maneuvering in great detail, Clinton did not delve into the physical accounts of the relationship. Instead, he sums the entire episode up in one brief paragraph, noting, "What I had done with Monica Lewinsky was immoral and foolish. I was deeply ashamed of it and didn't want it to come out. In the deposition, I was trying to protect my family and myself from my selfish stupidity."[19]

Clinton was disappointed that he could not include everyone who deserved a mention in the book and included an apology in the acknowledgments section, adding that editor Robert Gottlieb "convinced me to take out countless names of people who helped me along the way, because the general reader couldn't keep up with them. If you're one of them, I hope you'll forgive him, and me."[20]

My Life would have probably read better as a two-volume memoir, as author Taylor Branch personally suggested to Clinton. In doing so, perhaps it could have captured what Clinton enjoyed and strived for when reading Katharine Graham's *Personal History*.

With his book now published, Clinton went about rewarding those who had toiled over the manuscript alongside him. Taylor Branch, whose extensive collection of tapes helped to shape much of the book, wrote of one such encounter:

> In July, the president invited me to celebrate the publication of his book at their home in Washington. I found him alone in the dining room, signing copies of *My Life* on the dining room table. He asked me to sit down, and spoke to me quite sternly. "I have something for you," he said, "and you'll really hurt my feelings if you don't take it." He handed me an envelope with a check for $50,000. I was speechless. Clinton continued like a runaway train. "Now, I'm giving out bonuses to everybody who was involved in the book, and there couldn't have been a book without you. I couldn't get you to ghost-write for me. You've turned down money, but I want you to have this. I'm the same person I was when you and I were in Texas together and neither of us had a pot to piss in. And you've spent all this time writing about Martin Luther King, and sometimes I wish I had done that myself. But you *still* don't have a pot to piss in. I've never had money, and now I do, and frankly the only reason I want some is to share it with people who are my friends and are doing good."[21]

With *My Life* on many of the best seller lists, Clinton went on a lengthy book signing tour. Because his popularity extended overseas as well, the former president also included stops in Europe and the United Kingdom. By the end of August, however, Clinton noticed he tired easily, and could no longer perform book signings while standing up, which had been his custom. While at his home in Chappaqua, New York, Clinton experienced tightness in his chest and shortness of breath. After performing tests, doctors found blocked arteries, and scheduled surgery for a quadruple bypass on September 6, 2004. Because of this surgery and the following recuperation, the remaining dates of Clinton's book signing tour and any plans for extending the tour were cancelled.

As a reader and great lover of history, Clinton flirted with the possibility of writing historical non-fiction. At a book party in 2006, Clinton approached writer Jay Winik. *April 1865: The Month That Saved America* had recently been published, and Clinton had enjoyed it. Clinton enjoyed reading anything about Lincoln and conversation turned to Joshua Wolf Shenk's book, *Lincoln's Melancholy*. Clinton enjoyed Shenk's book as well, claiming, "I wanted to write that book, but he beat me to the punch. I was going to write it next year. I love Lincoln—for all of his problems he grows larger with history."[22]

Another Lincoln-related story was when Clinton attended a memorial service for historian Arthur Schlesinger, Jr., in February of 2007. Clinton recalled that Schlesinger, who was editing a series of presidential biographies for Times Books, approached Clinton about writing one about Lincoln. Clinton, who was under contract to write his own memoir at the time, had to decline.

In 2007, Clinton published what would be his third book, *Giving: How Each of Us Can Change the World*. "I wrote this book to encourage you to give whatever you can, because everyone can give something. And there's so much to be done, down the street and around the world. It's never too late or too early to start."[23] *Giving* assigned no blame, and instead focused on what the individual could do to make the world a better place. Like former presidents Carter and Hoover, Clinton felt it was his place to use the office of ex-president to address worldwide issues such as poverty. He gave credit where credit was due, even when it came to multinational corporations that had shouldered much of the blame when it came to the world's social, environmental, and economic ills.

In 2009, Hillary Clinton, now a United States senator, was named secretary of state under President Obama. With his wife now traveling the world, Clinton found himself alone once again, and undertook a new book project. A catastrophic economic recession had enveloped the country during President George W. Bush's second term, and the nation had yet to climb out of it. This resulted in Clinton publishing *Back to Work: Why We Need Smart Government for a Strong Economy*, in 2011.

Back to Work was filled with ideas and suggestions of how the United States could get back in the "Future Business" once again. It stressed the need to re-educate the country, impose tax relief, and provided ways for the government to lead the private sector out of the present economic nightmare. He strongly advocated an America that was no longer dependent on foreign energy sources as a way out, and encouraged an infrastructure made up of Green technology. As with *Giving*, Clinton did not dish out blame, instead emphasizing unity.

Back to Work received mixed reviews. The *Washington Post* wrote, "*Back to Work* contains sensible ideas that have been floating around think thanks, policy conferences, and White House brainstorming sessions for years."[24] The *New York Times*, however, noted that "there is no Roosevelt Moment," in the book.[25] Perhaps *The Telegraph* said it best with, "Love him or hate him, he hasn't lost his touch."[26]

Clinton would co-author a novel with author James Patterson in 2018. *The President Is Missing* was a thriller and published under a collaboration of Knopf and Little & Brown. The book made Clinton the second president to publish a work of fiction, as Jimmy Carter did in 2004 with *The Hornet's Nest*.

George W. Bush

> I did not realize how enjoyable it would be.[1]
> —George W. Bush

Bush's first book, *A Charge to Keep*, was published in 1999, while governor of Texas. In the book's foreword, Bush admits he was "not inclined" to write a book at the time.[2] He was, however, throwing his hat into the ring for the presidency, and recalled a valuable political lesson, "and that was to never allow others to define me. When I discovered that a number of other people were writing books about me, I decided to tell my story from my own perspective. Plus, in our family, even the dog has written a book."[3] (Bush's remark stems from his parents' cocker spaniel, Millie, who "co-authored" a book with Barbara Bush in 1990.) Bush was quick to point out his book was in no way a detailed autobiography. "It is not in chronological order and does not cover everything I have ever done. That would be far too boring. The book chronicles some of the events that have shaped my life and some of my major decisions and actions as governor of Texas. It is intended to give the reader a sense of my values, my philosophy, and how I approach and make decisions."[4]

In *A Charge to Keep*, Bush acknowledged his faults, particularly drinking, which he quit at the age of forty because it "began to compete with my energy."[5] Bush hoped that speaking in a frank manner would "help purge [politics] of its relentless quest for scandal and sensation. I worry that when gossip spread on the Internet is repeated on the front page of respected newspapers, we are undermining our American Democracy."[6]

A Charge to Keep was the typical campaign-style entry into the world of publishing that future presidents would routinely tout as their first book. It was said that Karen Hughes, who was working as Bush's director of communications, was responsible for much of the finished book. Bush acknowledged this in the book's foreword by noting, "She persuaded me to write the book and did much of the work."[7]

There were claims that Hughes had replaced Mickey Herskowitz, who wrote for the *Houston Chronicle*, and was a close friend of the Bush family. Herskowitz was originally contracted to ghostwrite the book, biographer Russ Baker claimed, and *A Charge to Keep* had originally been the idea of Herskowitz's agent. After being approved by Karl Rove, Herskowitz and Bush agreed on a 50/50 split of the book's future proceeds. Herskowitz remembers Bush "worried whether there would be enough content for such a book," and wondered, "what had he accomplished that was worth talking about?"[8] Herskowitz also claimed that Bush campaign lawyers had become concerned with the manuscript, which led to an unexpected early morning raid at his home, where all his notes were removed. As for Herskowitz's sudden departure, "Hughes intimated that Herskowitz was hitting the bottle—a claim Herskowitz said was unfounded. Later, the campaign put out the word that Herskowitz had been removed for missing a deadline. Hughes subsequently finished the book herself; it received largely negative reviews for its self-serving qualities and lack of spontaneity or introspection."[9]

Biographer David Frum noted Bush admitted not having much to do with the book: "He referred to his campaign book, *A Charge to Keep*, as 'the book I wrote.' He caught himself with a chuckle. 'Well, they say I wrote it.'"[10] Yet another biographer claimed Bush depreciated it by calling it a "novel," and admitting that, "some of it [was] fiction, some of it nonfiction."[11]

The book would have its share of controversy regarding Bush's service in the National Guard during the 1960s, which could have gotten him out of serving in Vietnam, as well as a meeting with the Reverend Billy Graham, which was said to have been fictionalized. *A Charge to Keep* was published by William Morrow. Later editions include the subtitle *My Journey to the White House.*

After Bush was declared the victor in the 2000 presidential election, he apparently began reading up on past presidents. Author Jacob Weisberg noted that Bush "spent his pre-inaugural break reading *John Quincy Adams: A Public Life, a Private Life,* by Paul C. Nagel, to see what might be in the comparison. But the shoe didn't fit; he had virtually nothing in common with the dour, meditative writer-statesman at the level of policy or personality."[12] Weisberg also wrote, "Bush is not a historical ignoramus. Contrary to what many believe, he does have an appetite for books, which has grown larger during his White House years."[13]

In 2010, one year after he left the White House following two terms as president, Bush published *Decision Points*. In the book's introduction, Bush recalled that he began to consider writing his memoirs in the final year of his presidency. Karl Rove, his senior advisor, had Bush meet with numerous historians who told him he had an obligation to write. "Nearly all the historians suggested that I read *Memoirs* by President Ulysses S. Grant, which I did. The book captures his distinctive voice. I could see why his work has endured. Like Grant, I decided not to write an exhaustive account of my life or presidency. Instead I have told the story of my time in the White House by focusing on the most important part of the job: making decisions. Each chapter is based on a major decision or a series of related decisions. As a result, the book flows thematically, not in a day-to-day chronology."[14]

By formatting the book on fourteen decision points, Bush followed an example used by Richard Nixon in his book, *Six Crises*. Bush's fourteen chapters include his decision to quit drinking, his run for the presidency, the wars in Afghanistan and Iraq, and Hurricane Katrina. He also recalls the events of September 11, 2001, which he named the "Day of Fire."

Bush also acknowledged the book was written with help. "When I considered writing this book I knew the task would be a challenge. I did not realize how enjoyable it would be. The main reason is that I worked with Chris Michel. At the end of my administration Chris was my chief speechwriter. He knew how I talked and saw much of the history we made. His broad range of talents, from research to editing, made the book project move smoothly."[15]

By acknowledging Michel as his ghostwriter, it puts into perspective the busy transformation Bush must have made after leaving office. How someone could entertain publishers, secure a contract, produce, polish, and publish a 481-page manuscript, while also establishing their Presidential Library, all by November 2010, is extraordinary. Bush would officially release *Decision*

Points at groundbreaking ceremonies for the library November 16, 2010. It should be noted Bush supposedly began work on the book two days after leaving office.

Decision Points opened at the number one spot on the *New York Times* best seller list upon release. It received a variety of mixed reviews. Michael Kinsley of the *New York Times* observed, "It would be nice to say that Bush grew in office—like Henry V, the wastrel youth and son of a famous father to whom he was often compared. But judging by this book it did not happen."[16]

In 2014, Bush followed up with *41: A Portrait of My Father*. The book, honoring his father, was both a mixture of biography and memoir. By then, their father-son presidencies were commonly referred to as "41" and "43." Bush claimed to have gotten the idea of a book about his father from Dorie McCullough Lawson, the daughter of Pulitzer Prize–winning historian David McCullough. David McCullough, who authored a notable biography of John Adams, had observed that history was at a loss because John Quincy Adams never left a "serious account" of his father. This was all Bush needed, and he soon began working on a manuscript.

At times *Portrait* read like a typical Bush biography, the difference being his observations as a son, and the times he was a part of it. Throughout the book Bush celebrates his father as a compassionate and caring individual. As an example, he recalls Bush going to Andrews Air Force Base to see outgoing president (and fellow Texan) Lyndon B. Johnson leave Washington, shortly after Richard Nixon's 1969 inauguration. Bush was the only Republican Congressman to show up, and Johnson was genuinely touched by his appearance.

He also speculated why his father never authored a presidential memoir after leaving office: "Dad also spent some time writing. He decided to coauthor a book about his foreign policy with Brent Scowcroft. The decision to write a joint book was revealing. No President had ever split his byline with an aide. But Dad wanted to share credit with his friend. He also wanted to avoid a memoir that was focused on himself. I suspect that the disappointment about his defeat played a role as well. At that point, he may not have been able to summon up the energy to write a book that had an unhappy ending. He never did write a presidential memoir."[17]

Like John Adams, George H.W. Bush was able to relish seeing his son become president in his own right. Bush recalls that the first time a new president walks in the Oval Office is memorable, but his own was even more memorable by the appearance of his father. "A few minutes later the door swung open and he walked in. We spent a few minutes together just soaking in the moment. Over the next eight years, I would have many memorable meetings in the Oval Office. None would compare to standing in the office with my father on my first day."[18]

Like Ronald Reagan, George H.W. Bush would drop out of the public eye due to health issues.

Despite his disability, Bush remembers his father making the best out of life. "Sitting in his wheelchair, he realized that his socks were among the most visible parts of his wardrobe. So he started wearing brightly colored socks. His favorites are red, white, and blues. Even though it is a struggle for him to climb in and out of his wheelchair, he accepts invitations to public events. After all, he is the President who signed the Americans with Disabilities Act."[19]

Portrait remains unique as a biography about a president, authored by a president, who also happened to be his son. In one stroke of a pen, Bush became a member of a small group of presidents who authored books about fellow presidents, as well as those who ventured into the world of biography.

Shortly after leaving office Bush acquired an interest in art, particularly painting. After a computer hack exposed his secret hobby, Bush became comfortable with showing his art. For a while it appeared any interest in writing had waned. In 2017 Bush published *Portraits of Courage: A Commander in Chief's Tribute to American Warriors*. The book contained sixty-six original portraits painted by Bush, along with commentary. A 2017 exhibition at the Bush Presidential Library coincided with the book's release.

In *Portraits*, painting replaced writing. Like other former presidents, Bush found writing to be a chore while art became an enjoyable escape. In the book, Bush recalls Pulitzer Prize–winning author John Lewis Gaddis recommended reading Winston Churchill's essay "Painting as a Passion." In publishing *Portraits*, Bush broke new ground by become the first to author a book concerning art.

Barack Obama

> I confess to wincing every so often at a poorly chosen word, a mangled sentence, an expression of emotion that seems indulgent or overly practiced.[1]
> —Barack Obama

As a youth, Barack Obama was well read, and familiar with a great deal of literature concerning African American history. In 1979, at the age of eight-

Barack Obama visiting a Washington, D.C., bookstore with daughters Sasha (center) and Malia in 2014. As a young grassroots organizer and author, Obama made himself available for bookstore appearances long before entering politics (Official White House photograph by Pete Souza).

een, Obama attended Occidental College, near Pasadena, California. While there, he took creative writing courses, and considered pursuing a career in writing. He also published two of his poems in the campus literary magazine, *Feast*. By 1983, Obama was attending Columbia University, and contributed an article on the nuclear freeze movement in the student newspaper, *Sundial*.

That same summer, he took a job at Business International Corporation, where he "edited a reference guide on overseas markets, called *Financing Foreign Operations*, and wrote a newsletter called *Business International Money Report*."[2] Supervisors would later recall Obama as being "intelligent and mature, with good writing skills," but he "did not stand out in any material way."[3] Lou Celi, a vice president at B.I. remembers Obama being "interested in pursuing a career in editing and writing," but "not [in] fiction, he wanted to be in journalism. He came from the right school and had a background in international relations; he was eager to get into writing and editing, and he didn't require a lot of money. We hired him at entry level."[4] Although Obama possessed a talent for writing about economic matters, he also held "a young idealist's disdain" for much of the way the markets operated.[5] Apparently this "disdain" was strong enough for him to quit the job after a year, and tell his co-workers that he was going to become a community organizer. Whether or not anything Obama wrote or edited while at Business International was published with a by-line is not known.

In 1988, Obama enrolled in Harvard University, where he met his future wife, Michelle Robinson, and was elected editor, then president, of the *Harvard Law Review*. After graduating with a law degree, Obama turned down the offer of a clerkship on the U.S. Court of Appeals, "which would have led to a powerful clerkship the following year on the U.S. Supreme Court, where Obama would have been drafting major, even historic opinions, before age 30."[6]

Obama was elected to the Illinois General Assembly in 1997, and elected to the United States Senate in 2004. Shortly before his election to the Senate, Obama's first book, a memoir, was published. Titled *Dreams from My Father: A Story of Race and Inheritance*, it documented his search for identity as the son of a black African father and white American mother, and his travels to Kenya, Hawaii, Kansas, and finally Illinois. *Dreams* also recalls the seeds Obama planted as a community organizer that would take him to the U.S. Senate and eventually the White House. Ever the optimist, Obama would admit he wasn't sure what a community did, but proceeded anyway. "In 1983, I decided to become a community organizer. There wasn't much to the idea; I didn't know anyone making a living that way. When classmates in college asked me just what a community organizer did, I couldn't answer them directly."[7]

Author David Remnick noted that at first the publishers did not consider *Dreams* an important book. Peter Osnos and his colleagues at Times Books did not have high commercial ambitions for *Dreams from My Father*. "We had mid-list hopes for Obama," Osnos said. "Most galleys were done plain then, but we did a nice advance reader's edition, which indicates a certain interest. We were going for the multicultural thing."[8]

Despite receiving positive reviews in major newspapers, the book still garnered little publicity. Yet the first-time author dove headfirst into a humbling book tour. "As part of a modest book tour, Obama gave readings for small crowds at bookstores including his local, Fifty-seventh Street books, in Hyde Park. At Eso Won Books, an African-American bookstore in Los Angeles, just nine people came to see him, and Obama simply sat everyone in a circle and, after reading for a few minutes, shared details of his life and, ever the community organizer, asked people, "Tell me your name and what you do."[9]

Times Books originally shipped "about twelve thousand copies of

Dreams from My Father and sold nine thousand."[10] Between 1995 and 2003, the book fell out of print. With Obama's newfound popularity during his 2004 Senate run, however, Three Rivers Press reprinted the book. There, it quickly found a larger audience, and brought the candidate a fresh wave of publicity. As a result, Obama included a new Preface to the edition.

> Almost a decade has passed since this book was first published. As I mentioned in the original introduction, the opportunity to write the book came while I was in law school, the result of my election as the first African-American president of the *Harvard Law Review*.
>
> Like most first-time authors, I was filled with hope and despair upon the book's publication, hope that the book might succeed beyond my youthful dreams, despair that I had failed to say anything worth saying. The reality fell somewhere in between. The reviews were mildly favorable. People actually showed up at the readings my publisher arranged. The sales were underwhelming. And, after a few months, I went on with the business of my life, certain that my career as an author would be short-lived, but glad to have survived the process with my dignity more or less intact.[11]

Despite any temptation to edit or revise it, Obama stood by the original edition. "Whatever the label that attaches itself to this book—autobiography, memoir, family history, or something else—what I've tried to do is write an honest account of a particular province of my life."[12]

The book's origins began in February of 1990, when literary agent Jane Dystel read an article about Obama in the *New York Times*. Dystel contacted Obama at Harvard and suggested he draft a book proposal, and then shopped it around. Dystel would sell the book to Poseidon Press, a small imprint of Simon & Schuster. The contract included an advance reported to be over one hundred thousand dollars with Obama receiving half at signing. The November 28, 1990, contract named the yet-unfinished manuscript as "Journeys in Black and White."[13]

In 1993, however, Simon & Schuster shut down Poseidon, and attempted to find the orphaned manuscript a new home with another one of its many in-house imprints. After Obama missed numerous deadlines, Simon & Schuster dumped the project, and re-sold it to Random House. David Remnick notes, "Times Books paid Simon & Schuster forty thousand dollars for the book—a very good deal, it turned out, for Random House," because "Simon & Schuster ended up losing the rest of the advance it had paid."[14] Henry Ferris, an editor at Times Books, worked closely with Obama in editing the lengthy manuscript into acceptable book form.

Once published, *Time* magazine declared *Dreams from My Father* as possibly being "the best-written memoir ever produced by an American politician."[15] Before long there were claims that the book had been ghostwritten. Jack Cashill, the former host of a radio talk show and a writer, first brought these claims to light. Cashill named Bill Ayers, who worked with Obama on his senatorial campaign, as ghostwriter. Ayers was also a published author, and when comparisons of his writings were made to Obama's book, some claimed the similarities were great.

Ayers also brought potentially damaging baggage along with him as a former member of the 1960s radical group The Weather Underground. Author Christopher Anderson would later quote insiders stating, "Ayers was brought in to help Obama finish his memoir."[16] Anderson's book described how Obama was introduced to Ayers through their neighbors, and that "neither Michelle nor Barack seemed particularly troubled to discover that William Ayers" had been one "of the 1960s most famous radicals."[17] Anderson also writes that Obama toiled over the book, and worked until the early-morning hours in what Michelle dubbed "the Hole," his tiny, cluttered office tucked discreetly behind their kitchen."[18]

Ayers' association with Obama would fuel controversy with the book. Cashill would claim: "Only in America could an American-hating terrorist conspire with an unskilled writer of uncertain origins on an untruthful memoir and succeed in getting the man elected president."[19] Political commentator Rush Limbaugh also entered the fray saying of Obama, "There's no evidence that he has any kind of writing talent. We haven't seen anything he wrote at Harvard Law."[20] Such accusations quickly led to claims of racism. In his Obama biography *The Bridge*, author David Remnick noted how "the denial of literacy, the denial of authorship—had a particularly ugly pedigree."[21]

Over time, *Dreams* would establish itself as an important book worthy of praise. Remnick would specifically claim the book's importance because "it was written when Obama was young and unguarded."[22] Remnick also notes, "*Dreams from My Father* was not intended as a campaign biography, but ended up acting as one."[23]

In *A Bound Man*, biographer Shelby Steele would write that among the "small but interesting genre of interracial memoirs, this book will have a lasting place. Instead of the politician's usual guardedness, the book is almost naïve in its degree of selfdisclosure. There are pretentious passages and longueurs, but there are also places where he writes as if the reader is almost beside the point, as if he is marching through certain emotional details for his own private purposes. The book will not be toted up as a political accomplishment, but it is an accomplishment nonetheless."[24]

In 2006, Obama published his second book, *The Audacity of Hope*. In the book's prologue, Obama expressed the need to pull together or risk failure. "That's the topic of this book: how we might begin the process of changing our politics and our civic life. This isn't to say that I know how exactly to do it. I don't. Although I discuss in each chapter a number of our most pressing policy challenges, and suggest in broad strokes the path I believe we should follow, my treatment of the issues is often partial and incomplete. I offer no unifying theory of American government, nor do these pages provide a manifesto for action, complete with charts and graphs, timetables and ten-point plans."[25]

Like *Dreams from My Father*, *Audacity* was written with an openness that was consistent with Obama's personality. "I am a prisoner of my own biography: I can't help but view the American experience through the lens of a black man of mixed heritage," he writes, and also confesses how the Democratic Party "can be smug, detached, and dogmatic at times."[26] He ends with the observation that "some of [my] views will get me in trouble," and that he will be "bound to disappoint some" of the American electorate who will read this book.[27]

Among the junior senator's memorable reflections of Washington political life was his first time in the White House, and finding it far from what he originally expected. "The inside of the White House doesn't have the luminous quality you might expect from TV or film; it seems well kept but worn, a big old house that one imagines might be a bit drafty on cold winter nights."[28] He evens finds President George W. Bush, who years later would prove to be his predecessor, as "a likeable man, shrewd and disciplined but with the same straightforward manner that had helped him win two elections; you could easily imagine him owning the local car dealership down the street, coaching Little League, and grilling in his backyard—the kind of guy who would make for good company so long as the conversation revolved around sports and kids."[29]

Audacity could also be unpleasant at times, if not blunt:

> They are out there, I think to myself, those ordinary citizens who have grown up in the midst of all the political and cultural battles, but who have found a way—in their own lives, at least—to make peace with their neighbors, and themselves. I imagine the white Southerner who growing up heard his dad talk about niggers this and niggers that but who has struck up a friendship with the black guys at the office and is trying to teach his own son different. Or the former Black Panther who decided to go into real estate, bought a few buildings in the neighborhood, and is just as tired of the drug dealers in front of these buildings as he is of the bankers who won't give him a loan to expand his business.
> They are out there, waiting for Republicans and Democrats to catch up with them.[30]

Upon its release, *Audacity* rose to the top of the best seller list, where it remained for thirty weeks. Both *Dreams from My Father* and *The Audacity of Hope* would win Grammy Awards for their 2006 and 2008 audio versions. It was observed that Obama "could lovingly mimic even the female voices in his family saga and slipped easily into the accents of the black church. But his act was never based on looking like an act."[31]

While *Dreams of My Father* and *The Audacity of Hope* would later prove their value when Obama ran for president, he would not publish the campaign-style autobiography/manifesto like many of his predecessors. Instead, Three Rivers Press would publish *Change We Can Believe In*. While not authored by Obama, it featured a foreword written by him, and contained eight speeches from the presidential campaign. The 2008 book was subtitled *Barack Obama's Plan to Renew America's Promise*. It remains the only officially authorized campaign publication.

Obama would win the presidency in 2008, and served two terms.

Of Thee I Sing: A Letter to My Daughters appeared in 2010. The book, aimed at a juvenile audience, was taken from a letter written to his daughters, about thirteen Americans who helped change American history. Noted children's illustrator Loren Long, whose drawings follow the storyline of the letter, illustrated the book. It was published by Alfred A. Knopf. Proceeds were donated to a scholarship fund for children of disabled veterans. It reached number fifteen on the best seller list.

Obama has yet to publish a presidential memoir since leaving the presidency. In March 2017 it was announced both Barack and Michelle Obama had signed a deal with Crown Publishing (Penguin Random House). Under the reported $65 million deal, the couple would author one book each. The former president's book is expected to be his much-anticipated memoir.

Donald J. Trump

I may not be Stephen King, but I can appreciate what he does.[1]
—Donald Trump

When Donald Trump was inaugurated in 2017, he became the first president since Eisenhower who had not previously held elected office. Before Trump, a career in the military had been the primary occupation of presidents Jackson, Harrison, Taylor, Grant, and Eisenhower. Trump, however, was a businessman with emphasis on real estate, gambling, and entertainment.

Trump's father, Fred, was a successful New York City real estate developer by the time Donald joined the family business. Through well-crafted publicity,

Donald became well known, and secured his first book deal with Random House in 1987. When *Trump: The Art of the Deal* was published, books concerning business executives were much in demand. Chrysler CEO Lee Iacocca's autobiography *Iacocca*, published in 1984, became a best seller, even though biographer Michael D'Antonio noted that such books "were of limited value to the public record and rarely offered much insight."[2]

The Art of the Deal was co-written with professional writer Tony Schwartz. Schwartz would later regret working with Trump, and became one of his critics. According to biographer Harry Hurt, the origins of the book were said to come from a *Playboy* interview Trump sat for with Schwartz. When Schwartz complained the interview was not going well, Trump admitted he was saving good material for the Random House book. Schwartz then suggested Trump abandon the autobiography format and focus on Trump's deal making. Trump liked the idea, and hired Schwartz to co-author the book.[3]

To help sales, Trump spent over $90,000 to run full-page ads in the *New York Times* and *Washington Post*, claiming America needed to desperately correct its foreign policy. Many assumed Trump was preparing for a political run, although he denied it. In the end, the ads would "spur press attention worth far more than $90,000 to someone about to publish a book."[4]

The Art of the Deal begins with Trump claiming why he wrote it. "I don't do it for the money. I've got enough, much more than I'll ever need. I do it to do it. Deals are my art form. Other people paint beautifully on canvas or write wonderful poetry. I like making deals, preferably big deals. That's how I get my kicks."[5] Included was a week-long diary of deal making, complete with endless phone calls and numerous meetings. In a chapter concerning his childhood, Trump claims to have given a teacher a black eye in the second grade, and punching his music teacher because he disagreed with him. Trump believed this showed "clear evidence that even early on I had a tendency to stand up and make my opinions known in a very forceful way."[6]

Trump would later look back on the book with great affection, and claim it was a defining moment in his career. "I've had many best-selling books of all time—that's really what started this whole thing, I think, *Trump: The Art of the Deal*. Now in all fairness, it became a number-one best seller for many, many months, and the reason is because of what I had done before. So I was well known before I did the *Art of the Deal*, but it was a big breakthrough."[7]

The book, however, had its share of critics. In his biography, *Lost Tycoon*, author Harry Hurt wrote:

> If Donald's book claimed any distinction in the field of American business literature, it was as a classic in self-serving myth creation. While the reading public naturally

expected any autobiographer to write with an unexpurgable measure of personal bias, it also expected him or her to tell his or her side of the story as fully and truthfully as possible. No one expected Donald to give away trade secrets or make public his tax returns. But no one was prepared for the shameless lies, half-truths, omissions, distortions, exaggerations, image burnishings, and lily gildings.[8]

Hurt goes on to add that the book became successful because it was published at a fortunate time. Junk Bond financier Michael Milken had yet to be indicted, and *Wall Street*, starring Michael Douglas as Gordon Gekko (a ruthless corporate raider), would be released a month later.

Biographer John O'Donnell recalled when *The Art of the Deal* was first published, the book was expected to be prominently displayed at Trump properties such as casinos and hotels. At the time O'Donnell was working at Trump Plaza and was given the task of handling an oversupply of the book with strict orders of no returns. "Even so, the books did not sell fast enough, and months later, we were still searching for ways to unload them. We gave them away at customer parties. We sent dozens at a time to New York for Donald to sign, and then we mailed those to our preferred players as gifts. Then someone hit on the idea of placing copies in all the guest rooms on New Year's Eve 1987 with our normal chocolate turndown service."[9]

Sales of the book would total nearly one million copies in hardcover, and wherever Trump appeared for a book signing, crowds were sure to form. Despite claims to donate his share of royalties to charity, insiders claimed Trump kept most of it.

Trump: Surviving at the Top would follow in 1990. Like his previous book, Trump acknowledged another co-author, in this case Charles Leerhsen. *Surviving* starts off with Trump's reluctance to write the first book, let alone author another. "When my good friend Si Newhouse, the owner of Random House, suggested that I write my first book, I was wary. The last thing I needed was to do a book about myself that went nowhere. Si was confident that when my picture appeared on the covers of magazines he owned, they became top sellers. Si is a very persistent man, and I was flattered by his interest. "Okay," I finally said, "let's do it."[10]

On the business side, much of the book delves into Trump's purchases of Atlantic City casinos, four-star hotels, and an airline venture. Trump claims he never imbibed in alcohol, drugs (even coffee) or gambling. His views on gambling were revealed from a business perspective: "You don't have to be a gambler to be a success in the casino business; in fact, you're barred from gambling by law. What is absolutely necessary, however, is that you like and understand gamblers, from the slot-machine players, who are your bread and butter, to the high rollers, who can make a difference of millions of dollars in your bottom line in the course of one weekend. Frankly, the idea of risking hard-earned money on the toss of the dice or spin of a wheel seems slightly ludicrous to me personally."[11]

Trump's weeklong diary from *The Art of the Deal* also reappears. It consumes twenty-five pages of phone calls, meetings, dinners, as well as celebrity name dropping, all involved with making money, cutting deals, and solving various financial dilemmas. The photo section is filled with celebrity photo opportunities, Trump-owned properties and business associates, but not one family photo.

Trump's third book with Random House appeared in 1997. *Trump: The Art of the Comeback* was co-authored with Kate Bohner. In the book's introduction, Trump confesses the 1990s were not kind to him. "It's usually fun being The Donald, but in the early 1990's, trust me, it wasn't. My journey is a hard one to believe. I was many billions in the red, $975 million of that debt I'd personally guaranteed. The banks were crawling all over me."[12]

As with his two previous efforts, *The Art of the Comeback* is filled with Trump's recollections of riding a mega-million dollar rollercoaster through good times and bad. Trump sprinkles financial advice throughout the book, advising readers to avoid Wall Street and instead pursue real estate. The book also has its share of embarrassments. A photograph with first lady Hillary Clinton includes the caption that she "has handled pressure incredibly well."[13] He also writes of his mistrust of the media, which would become legendary as president. "People of the media are often recklessly devious and deceptive. Recent polls have shown that the general public is wise to the act. Journalism—if you even want to call it that these days—is widely considered one of the most untrustworthy professions in the United States."[14]

Trump also confides his reluctance to enter politics. "People have always asked me if I'll ever be involved in politics. It seems every so often there's some unfounded rumor that I'm considering seeking office—sometimes even the presidency! The problem is, I think I'm too honest, and perhaps too controversial, to be a politician. I always say it like it is, and I'm not sure a politician can do that, although I might just be able to get away with it because people tend to like me. Honesty causes controversy, and therefore, despite all the polls that say I should run, I would probably not be a very successful politician."[15]

By 2000, however, Trump had second thoughts and did everything but officially throw his hat into the ring. This explained the publication of *The America We Deserve* by Renaissance Press. Co-authored by Dave Shiflett, Trump wastes no words in the book's introduction. "Let's cut to the chase. Yes, I am considering a run for the presidency of the United States. The reason has nothing to do with vanity, as some have suggested, or merely to block the advancement of other candidates. I will run if I become convinced I can win. Two things are certain at this point, however: I believe nonpoliticians represent the wave of the future and if elected I would make the kind of president America needs in the new millennium."[16]

The America We Deserve is Trump's campaign platform for his ill-fated (and short lived) Reform Party presidential run. Trump entered the race in October 1999, published the book in January 2000, and ended the campaign in February. The chapters are headed under subjects such as business, schools, safe streets, social security and healthcare. *The America We Deserve* is interesting when compared to the same ideals discussed in Trump's future campaign-oriented books, such as *Time to Get Tough* (2011) and *Crippled America* (2015), both of which will be discussed later.

Trump: Think Like a Billionaire (2004) promised to address everything one needed to know about success, real estate, and life. In this book, which found Trump back at Random House with co-author Meredith McIver, Trump offered rudimentary advice such as how to rent an apartment, how to read a classified ad or listing, how to buy a house as well as sell one, how to get the best mortgage, and how to landscape. Trump also discloses he never took a vacation because he enjoyed his work too much, that the most successful people have short attention spans, and one should never sleep more than needed.

Another book, *How to Get Rich*, was also published in 2004 with Meredith McIver. It was subtitled "Big Deals from the Star of *The Apprentice*," and rode the wave of success Trump was enjoying with his television show.

Yet another Trump offering would see publication in 2004. *Trump: The Way to the Top. The Best Business Advice I Ever Received* at first appeared to be another business-related book authored by Donald Trump. Trump's photograph is featured on the cover, along with his name in noticeably large font. A look inside reveals it is a collection of business advice, wisdom, and anecdotes from various CEOs, chairmen, and other business executives. Trump's only contribution is a four-page introduction. Crown Business, an imprint of Trump's longtime publisher, Random House, published the book. Trump and Bill Adler Books also held the copyright. Despite Trump's brief introduction, *Way to the Top* remains listed as a Trump-authored book by major Internet booksellers.

Another Trump offering would be published through Crown Business in 2005. *The Best Golf Advice I Ever Received* featured advice from numerous golf pros. Golf would remain the closest thing to a hobby for Trump. Like Grover Cleveland, Theodore Roosevelt, Herbert Hoover and Jimmy Carter, Trump had a reason to write about the great outdoors, even if it meant playing golf.

In 2006, Thomas Nelson published *The Best Real Estate Advice I Ever Received*. Subtitled *101 Top Experts Share Their Strategies,* Trump noted, "I am friends with some of these contributors and some I've never met, although I've admired them from afar."[17] Among the contributors were Donald Trump, Jr., and former wife Ivanka. The aforementioned three "*Best Advice*" books were among Trump's weakest. They are compilations of brief snippets from numerous authors, and aside from a preface or foreword, have little to do with Trump. They resemble something designed to keep Trump's name in bookstores while he was busy doing other projects such as television, getting remarried, filing a bankruptcy, and establishing Trump University.

In 2006, Trump co-authored *Why We Want You to Be Rich* with Robert T. Kiyosaki. Kiyosaki had previously been successful with his book *Rich Dad, Poor Dad*. Both were speaking at a lecture sponsored by the Learning Annex (the Annex will reappear in several Trump books) when Trump introduced himself. "You're the number one personal-finance author, and I'm the number one business author," Trump observed. "We should do a book together. What do you think?"[18] Published by Rich Press, the book's subtitle was *Two Men, One Message*. Trump and Kiyosaki contributed alternating chapters, while both working with additional co-authors. Hence, the book had four authors.

Think Big and Kick Ass came out the following year. Co-written with Bill Zanker, the book blatantly plastered advertising on the front cover, offering two tickets to a "Wealth Expo" at the Learning Center (valued $358). In the book Trump acknowledges his love for deal making. "For me it is even better than sex, and I love sex. But when you hit, when the deals are going your way, it is the greatest feeling! You hear lots of people say a good deal is when both sides win. That is a bunch of crap. In a great deal you win—not the other side."[19]

Think Big and Kick Ass resembled an infomercial for "The Learning Annex Wealth Expo" mentioned on the front cover. A good portion of the book's end matter concerns Learning Annex testimonials and information. Co-author Bill Zanker, who founded the Learning Annex, lets his talents as a motivational speaker flourish in his acknowledgment page. "What an honor to write a book with my own personal hero, Donald Trump. It has been so exciting! When I visit Donald in his office, I get goose bumps. Even though I have visited him often, it is always extraordinary and I learn something new every time. The day before I am going to meet him, I can hardly sleep, I get so excited. Thank you Donald for taking me into your life."[20]

Trump 101 was released in 2007. Co-authored with Meredith McIver, the book was apparently meant to coincide with the opening of Trump University, hence the title's reference to a university textbook. The book's copyright was in the name of Trump University, and an advertisement for the university is evident in the endpapers.

Never Give Up, again co-written with Meredith McIver, came out in 2008. Throughout his career, Trump has boasted of going to court to protect his reputation. In *Never Give Up*, he recollects suing author Tim O'Brien over material published in his book *Trump Nation*. "He had outright lies in his book, and he intended to damage me personally and my business. His reporting was reprehensible, and as a writer he is not very talented. I decided not to look the other way and toss it off as jealousy, malice, or greed. Instead, I sued him and the publisher for a lot of money. The writer got the attention he was obviously looking for, but his publisher got something they weren't looking for. They obviously didn't know they were dealing with a guy who would eventually write *Never Give Up*—and actually mean it."[21]

O'Brien's "reprehensible" reporting concerned an underestimation of Trump's net worth. The lawsuit went to court in 2016, where a judge dismissed it.

Think Like a Champion, which was published in 2009, came with the subtitle *An Informal Education in Business and Life*. Co-authored once again with Meredith McIver, the book contained topics Trump would later probably regret. Consider his enthusiasm for President Obama, whom he would later criticize.

> What [Obama] has done is amazing. The fact that he accomplished what he has—in one year and against great odds—is truly phenomenal. If someone had asked me if a black man or woman could become president, I would have said yes, but not yet. Barack Obama proved that determination combined with opportunity and intelligence can make things happen—and in an exceptional way.
>
> His comments have led me to believe that he understands how the economy works on a comprehensive level. He has also surrounded himself with competent people, and that's the mark of a strong leader. I have confidence he will do his best, and we have someone who is serious about resolving the problems we have and will be facing in the future.
>
> The world is excited about Barack Obama and the new United States. Let's keep it that way.[22]

Trump also criticizes the Republican Party, claiming "[George W.] Bush had been so incompetent that any Republican would have a hard time unless they could bring back Eisenhower."[23]

In 2011 Trump reunited with entrepreneur Robert T. Kiyosaki to co-author *Midas Touch: Why Some Entrepreneurs Get Rich, and Why Most Don't*. As with 2004's *Why We Want You to Get Rich*, the book is written in individual alternating chapters.

Regnery Publishing would publish *Time to Get Tough: Making America #1 Again*, also in 2011. Like *The America We Deserve*, the book is a campaign manifesto for a campaign that never happened. Unlike his lavish comments for President Obama in *Think Like a Champion,* Trump criticizes Obama and his policies for most of the book, while offering his own alternatives. Unlike *America We Deserve*, in which Trump announced that he was running for office on page one, the reader must wade through 178 pages of *Time to Get Tough* before Trump announces why he would *not* run in 2012:

> Most people have never heard of a very stupid law—called equal time—that prevents someone with a major television show from running for political office. So Obama is allowed to go on television every day and can fly around the country any time he wants at taxpayer expense, but I'm not allowed to do *The Apprentice* and run for office at the same time. You tell me, is that right? Were it not for that ridiculous law I would probably be running for office right now and having a good time doing it—because America has tremendous potential, unbelievable potential, and it is being wasted.[24]

Trump also acknowledges the contract NBC was offering for *The Apprentice* was too good to refuse. As he said back in *The Art of the Deal*, "The dollar always talks in the end."[25]

After a hectic run of eleven published books between 2004 and 2011, Trump was quiet for two years. After one short-lived presidential campaign, and another aborted one, he was finally ready to make a traditional run for office as a Republican.

Crippled America: How to Make America Great Again (2015) was Trump's campaign manifesto for his 2016 presidential campaign. Published by Simon & Schuster, it would be his third campaign manifesto. The book was Trump's first without benefit of a co-author, although it was rumored in publishing circles that Trump was given use of a ghostwriter in his contract. It should be noted that Trump thanked Bill Zanker and Meredith McIver "for their enthusiasm and assistance throughout the writing of this book."[26] Zanker and McIver co-authored several Trump books between them. Eight months later the publisher would offer a revised paperback edition renamed *Great Again: How to Fix Our Crippled America*. Subjects included Trump's hatred of the media, as well as the Affordable Care Act. He also pushes for a border wall along Mexico, and disputes global warming. Regarding his financial ties and net worth, which had become a campaign issue, Trump included a three-page outline.

The majority of Trump's books encompass the world of business, as well as his dealings in such. They tend to mix autobiography with financial instruction, the exception being his three campaign-oriented offerings. All of Trump's books have been co-authored and can appear repetitive at times.

This has been a common complaint found in book reviews and can almost be expected when one considers Trump mostly wrote about the subject of business, and primarily his own.

It is safe to say Trump's efforts greatly differ from any other office holder. George Washington, after all, never wrote how to get rich managing his Mount Vernon plantation. Nor did Abraham Lincoln ever expand upon his years as a successful corporate attorney for railroad monopolies. Author Robert Slater explained why books mattered to Trump in his biography *No Such Thing as Over-Exposure: Inside the Life and Celebrity of Donald Trump.* "No one talks more about himself than Donald Trump; and no one writes about himself more than he does. He has written book after book on what it's like to be Donald Trump. The book world was, indeed, in his word, "seductive" and he loved seeing his name and his books in bookstores. "It's a cool thing. It's one of the very cool feelings." When asked why he wrote these books, he said it was because "they sell like hotcakes" and because "I get a great kick at looking at my name on top of all the lists and telling everyone else to go fuck themselves."[27]

In 2018, author Michael Wolff published *Fire and Fury*, his controversial biography about the Trump White House. The book quickly became a best seller, partly due to Trump's public displeasure over its publication. Trump called the book "phony" and claimed it contained lies and misrepresentations. A legal attempt to block the book's release was unsuccessful. In the book, Wolff dismissed Trump's reputation as an author, writing, "Trump was not a writer, he's a character."[28]

A Brief History of Publishing the Presidents
Booksellers, Copyrights, Royalties, Ghostwriters and Literary Agents

In 1972, author John Tebbel published his superior history of United States book publishing. Published by R.R. Bowker, *A History of Book Publishing in the United States* would encompass four hefty volumes, and required a span of nine years between volumes one and four. Tebbel's history covers the crude beginnings of author's copyright in America, as well as how booksellers (and not publishers), conducted business.

As an example, Tebbel writes, "Massachusetts had a statute, passed by the General Court in 1673, which is often called the first American copyright; it protected publishers, not writers. It had been correctly identified as a "booksellers' copyright," inasmuch as the protection it offered was merely against the reprinting and not the sale of a book by another publisher. The author had no ownership of his own work, nor did he for another 110 years, when the first American copyright law was passed."[1]

Tebbel also points out that Massachusetts' law was unique, and was not enacted in any other colony. By not having to worry about the author, printers had only each other to look out for, and there was often even a comradery involved. "Agreements of protection, when they were made, might be between printers operating in different colonies, thus virtually eliminating the possibility of competition. Again, a publisher might be dealing with several printers at once in the publication of a book, or an author might make a similar arrangement in order to further distribute his work."[2]

In the case of George Washington, whose *Journal* was published in 1754, Washington himself had no rights whatsoever. Since the *Journal* was in actuality a military report, it legally became a government document once delivered to his superior. Hence, Washington could only fret and plead for extra time to correct his grammatical errors once he discovered the intention to publish it.

During the American Revolution, attempts were made to secure proper copyrights, particularly on the behalf of the author, but it was not until January 1783 that the first copyright law in the United States was enacted. This was done largely in part through the efforts of Noah Webster. Webster, who became known as the "father of American copyright," campaigned tirelessly by arguing his case. An addition copyright law was enacted in 1790, which gave American authors "the sole Liberty of printing, publishing, and vending" any book of their creation not previously printed, for a term of fourteen years.[3] Once copyright was registered, the author was given the privilege of extending the copyright an additional fourteen years.

Regarding the relationship of the publisher and author, Tebbel writes that copyright laws were often muddled by private contracts made between the two:

> It was the bookseller, rather than the printer or the author, who often undertook the risk of publication. As a publisher, the bookseller usually paid the author an outright sum for his book, or sometimes gave him a share of the profits. An author who insisted on keeping ownership of his property for himself had to make his own arrangements with the printer or bookseller as publisher, ordering a specific edition of a certain number of copies, and retaining the right of publication for a specific period of time. It was not until the second quarter of the nineteenth century [1850] that the royalty system was introduced, making the author in effect a partner of the publisher.[4]

Such was the case of Thomas Jefferson's *Notes on the State of Virginia*, which was privately published by Jefferson in 1785. This private printing was completed in France, which had its own copyright laws, and cost Jefferson considerable heartache. "It was naïve of Jefferson to think that such a valuable literary commodity, unprotected by any copyright, could long escape publication—and it did not. Within a year's time, a poor French translation had been issued, and Jefferson was faced with the prospect of that being translated back into English."[5]

Because of this, Jefferson's finest book, and the first major literary work of any president, was endlessly reprinted and translated without his approval. While *Notes on the State of Virginia* would make Jefferson famous, it did nothing to his pocketbook. Printing one's work outside of America had its own risks. "It encouraged some publishers to evade copyright restrictions in the case of native authors, and to be reluctant to share profits with them. Some, too, saw little profit in setting laboriously from a handwritten manuscript when it was so easy to reprint a foreign book, on which they could also be assured they would not have to pay royalty," Tebbel writes.[6]

For someone having what was then regarded as the finest library in Virginia, it is ironic knowing that *buying* books attributed to the pressing debt that Jefferson carried to his deathbed, while *writing* books brought him nothing at all.

At the time, many books authored by presidents were sold through "subscription." Most booksellers were only located in cities, leaving a good deal of the country with no place to buy a book. "After 1825, 'subscription publishing' meant producing books sold directly to people through book agents rather than by bookstores or any other part of the retail trade."[7]

In his book *Many Are the Hearts*, author Richard Goldhurst described the benefits and pitfalls of subscription publishing:

> Subscription distribution offered publishers a guaranteed return for their books, but, in turn, it demanded a large initial investment. This method of selling books, popular in the nineteenth century, has largely gone out of favor, and is associated today with encyclopedias. Sixteen agents divided up the country into markets, and hired canvassers who sold the book door-to-door. While subscribers were not obligated to make payment until delivery, the majority, having signed a contract, paid the money then and there. Thus many of the publisher's costs were met before the book went to press.[8]

Consider James Madison. After Madison's death in 1836, Jared Sparks, a Boston historian, attempted to find a publisher for Madison's writings. In a letter to Dolley Madison, Sparks noted the slow manner that subscription sales worked. Madison himself probably scared off more than a few prospective publishers by appropriating the princely sum of $12,000 toward "future book sales" in his will. This vain prediction caused the Madison family to "have an exaggerated idea of the profit they expected to make from them."[9] Madison's writings would eventually be published in 1840, and the remainder purchased by the Library of Congress. John Quincy Adams, who produced a considerable body of work prior to his presidency, suffered much as Jefferson did, and frequently discovered his manuscripts translated into foreign tongues without his prior knowledge.

Shortly before the Civil War, publishers routinely began paying authors royalties. Even Abraham Lincoln never saw a cent from royalty payments despite multiple reprints of his popular 1860 Cooper Union Address. Instead, Lincoln was paid in copies from the publisher. The speech, however, proved politically beneficial to Lincoln, and was instrumental in helping him capture the Republican Party's nomination. The first presidents who benefited from actual royalty payments were most likely Van Buren and Buchanan, whose books were published in 1866 and 1867.

With the appearance of Ulysses S. Grant's *Personal Memoirs* in 1885, everything changed. Grant, who never strived to author anything, had finally succumbed to writing his story through the persistence of Mark Twain. Twain nursed Grant's manuscript through its long and difficult progression, even serving as Grant's publisher and agent. Because of Twain's involvement Grant was able to secure a good deal and saw amazing royalties. In 1886, Grant's widow was presented with a royalty check of $200,000, and "probably the largest sum ever given to an author at one time up to that point."[10] *Personal Memoirs* also took home royalties from the sales of foreign editions, which is something Thomas Jefferson could have only dreamed of.

Twain's publishing house, Charles L. Webster, sold the book mainly through subscription, which was still a popular alternative at the time. Twain, however, soon discovered the book being marketed outside of his jurisdiction:

> Webster had taken every precaution to prevent the book from being sold in any other way except by subscription. Each volume carried a private mark by which it could be traced to the general agent through the canvassers he supplied, and every canvasser was under contract not to furnish the book to the trade, with heavy penalties for breaking it. Nevertheless, several books with titles nearly like the genuine volume had appeared by publication day, in spite of every precaution, John Wanamaker of Philadelphia was advertising in May 1886 that he would sell the *Memoirs* for $5.50, or $1.50 under the regular price.[11]

Twain sued Wanamaker, arguing his agents were bound to subscription sales only. Wanamaker then disclosed the purchase of a large number of books, in which he "obliterated" the canvasser's identification mark, thus establishing his territory, and claiming he had the legal right to sell them. The court favored Wanamaker, leaving "no doubt that he was successful in breaking down the exclusivity of subscription selling."[12]

After Grant's best seller, the literary stock of a former president rose considerably. Whether it was Benjamin Harrison's *Views of an Ex-President*, or Grover Cleveland's *Fishing and Shooting Sketches*, their books found their audiences easier, and with considerably better publishing terms than their predecessors.

Perhaps no president knew his way around a publishing house better than Theodore Roosevelt. Roosevelt was a throwback to the days of Thomas Jefferson and John Quincy Adams, and had published a considerable amount of work before entering the White House. During the time in which Roosevelt's political career rose from an assemblyman to the presidency, he had already authored several books. Among these were his *Naval War of 1812*, and *The Winning of the West*. These were published by G.P. Putnam's Sons, a publishing house of which Roosevelt had become a "silent partner" by way of monetary investment.

Well into his first term, and under somewhat odd circumstances, Roosevelt's participation became known:

In 1904, a suit brought on by Mrs. Elizabeth Sanderson, a rich book collector from Newark, against Putnam disclosed for the first time the surprising news that President Theodore Roosevelt had been a partner. At the time, it was learned that the total sale of four limited editions of Roosevelt's works had reached nearly a million dollars. The President said he had been given only his regular royalty on these four special editions, but the minimum price fixed for an autographed edition was $3,300 a set and as high as $4,000 was actually paid. One edition of fifty sets was to be sold for as much as $2,200 a set, while the cheapest sets went for $385. The total sale of the four editions came to $775,250, from which the president's straight 20 percent royalty would give him $165,050.[13]

Putnam was quick to point out Roosevelt's involvement in the company had ended years ago, but the American public was amazed at the figures their president was pulling down for the printed word. While most authors would have left such business practices to an accomplished agent, Roosevelt went through his entire life, and dozens of books, without one. Roosevelt had such pull that he once brought in a completed manuscript to a publisher on a Monday morning, demanding to know how soon he could have bound copies, and was told Saturday afternoon. Sure enough, the "400 page book was composed, proofread, printed and bound in five days."[14]

With Harry S. Truman came book signings, as well as personal involvement regarding the publicity of his published works. Truman took great pleasure in promoting his books, giving press conferences over them, and signing copies in his office and bookstores. Because of this, Truman brought the art of book selling into the twentieth century. Soon, it would be a normal practice to meet a former president at a big-chain bookstore, sitting behind a desk with a stack of books piled before him. After writing his first book, Truman was shocked to discover the staggering amount of capital gains tax he had to pay, and complained to Congress. Because of this, former presidents were allowed tax-incentives for personal office space and staff. Truman also despised professional ghostwriters, and fired his share of them, preferring instead to work on his manuscripts as much as possible.

With Truman, ex-presidents were getting book advances valued in the hundreds of thousands. Truman himself was said to have received $600,000 for his memoirs, and by the time Richard M. Nixon was writing his, the price had risen to $2.5 million. Bonuses such as expense accounts, staff, and office space often sweetened the deal.

Authoring a book prior to seeking the presidency also would prove to be a great asset, such as John F. Kennedy's *Why England Slept* and especially *Profiles in Courage*, which won a Pulitzer Prize. Books (not to mention an occasional Pulitzer) also proved to be a valuable campaign tool, and it is now tradition for a candidate to author a campaign autobiography, along with their platform.

Since the 1950s, the question of whether books authored by a president were actually written by them has repeatedly arisen. Kennedy's charges of not being the sole author of *Profiles* would become a campaign issue in 1960, and the claims of using a ghostwriter would haunt him long after. Because of this, many give due credit upfront, often in the book's acknowledgments. Such persons may be identified as research assistants, historians, editors, or editorial assistants.

Readers should be suspicious of any lengthy memoir written, printed, and distributed within the span of two years after leaving office. Publishers like to strike when the iron is hot and have the resources to do so, yet one cannot be less than amazed at the speed that some books arrive at bookstores.

In 1996, former first lady Hillary Clinton published *It Takes a Village*. At the time, Clinton was rumored to be considering a run for the presidency, and many considered the book pre-campaign literature. During her book tour, the subject of using a ghostwriter repeatedly came up, forcing Clinton to acknowledge the assistance of Barbara Feinman, a Georgetown University professor of journalism. In his book, *Write a Book Without Lifting a Finger*, author (and ghostwriting agency president) Mahesh Grossman confirmed Clinton's use of a ghostwriter. "Her [Feinman's] contract with Hillary Clinton called for a payment of $120,000 and that she be mentioned in the acknowledgements section of the book. However, First Lady Clinton reneged. Feinman was only paid $90,000 and given no credit in the book."[15] This led Feinman to openly criticize Clinton's book, which eventually forced Clinton to acknowledge Feinman's assistance. In the end, Clinton stood by her claims that the book was hers and hers alone, while Feinman toned down her complaints, saying she worked on the book as an editor and research assistant. Although Feinman was snubbed by Clinton's refusal to acknowledge her input, she realized it was better she remained in the background, like a ghostwriter should.

Former President Carter is believed to be the exception to this rule, and claims to author his own books. Carter has also successfully crossed over into fiction and poetry. Among recent presidents, only Richard M. Nixon came close to Carter's published efforts. It is also the norm for a president to begin receiving solicited offers from publishers as his term of office draws to a close.

Naturally, this is done with the assistance of an agent. In 2001, literary agent Arthur M. Klebanoff published *The Agent: Personalities, Politics and Publishing*. Klebanoff, who worked with former presidents Nixon, Ford, and Carter on behalf of Easton Press, also represented Nixon individually. Klebanoff writes, "A rarely known fact was that Nixon had written more nonfiction *New York Times* best sellers than any author of his generation. Of course, the New York publishing community was largely liberal and had a relatively hard time dealing with his literary success. And likewise, Nixon generally had contempt for the publishing community."[16]

Klebanoff was approached by John Taylor, Nixon's chief of staff, and asked whether he would be interested in representing Nixon. Taylor had warned Klebanoff to expect fifteen minutes at best with Nixon to sell himself, along with his ideas for Nixon's literary career. It was 1988, and by then Nixon had published several books, so Klebanoff decided to start with Nixon's current catalog. "My experience with Easton (Press) had taught me the value of uniform editions. My thought was to create 'Nixon Library' uniform trade paperback editions of the prior books with new introductions by Nixon and to require the publisher of the new memoir to reissue these books as well. Using the rights skills I had sharpened for Easton, I would clear the rights from the original publishers as a courtesy. Since these already had agents of record, I would have to look for my commission from the new tide. In effect, this would create a valuable backlist project out of moribund books."[17]

Klebanoff's fifteen minutes turned into two hours, and included an exchange between Nixon and Taylor, in which they discussed how to fire Nixon's current agent, with Klebanoff still in the room. When Klebanoff had come aboard, Simon & Schuster was offering Nixon $750,000 for two books. This offer was eventually raised to $1 million for one book, then $1.5, along with the Nixon Library securing the rights to all of Nixon's past books. Nixon remained at Simon & Schuster, and the book, *In the Arena*, sold well, although Klebanoff admitted that he "did have to deal throughout the project with Nixon idiosyncrasies."[18]

The appearance of C-Span's *Booknotes* television program in 1989 took book tours a step further. Presidents were now able to sit and speak of their books at leisure on national TV, while gaining additional sales and exposure. This was particularly noted by Bill Clinton, who observed that in the end, "you [the author] have to sell a book."[19]

At this writing, it appears safe to say that both pre- and post-presidential literature is in no danger of disappearing from bookshelves. For once a freshly turned-out president departs Washington and returns home, the publishing world waits with baited breath for any stirrings of their memoirs.

Perhaps John Eisenhower got it right when he lamented on writing being "almost the only dignified occupation" worth pursuing after leaving the White House.

First Editions, Limited Editions and Other Collectibles

Among the numerous books authored by the presidents, there exist a multitude of editions in various forms and formats, as well as a staggering array of pricing. Such editions are subject to the year published, not to mention publisher, and other factors that include the book presented not simply as a physical artifact, but as a work of printed art, with gilded fore-edges and hand-rubbed raised leather bindings. In other words, welcome to the complicated world of book collecting.

Consider Thomas Jefferson's *Notes on the State of Virginia*. Jefferson completed the manuscript by the time he left for France in 1784, and intended to publish it in America. He submitted it to several Philadelphia printers, but was shocked at the prices quoted for the work. Therefore, he took it with him and had it first published in France. Originally published in 1785, the initial press run was for two hundred copies. One of these copies fell into the hands of a French bookseller, and soon a poorly translated French edition appeared. This distressed Jefferson to the point of permitting London publisher John Stockdale to publish an authorized edition in 1787. Most bibliophiles (or book collectors) acknowledge Stockdale's edition as being *the* first edition. Those two hundred copies first struck off by Jefferson in France, however, can also be termed as the *true* first, should you ever encounter one. Stockdale's copy is considered superior because it the first *authorized* edition, and thus commands anywhere from $9,000 to $63,000 per copy. Yet another avenue purists often pursue is known as "following the flag." When following the flag, one acknowledges the author's birthright, which supersedes all other editions. Jefferson was born in Virginia, which means the first *American* appearance of *Notes* is considered the first edition. In this case it would be the edition published by Prichard & Hall of Philadelphia in 1788. Such copies can be found in the $8,000 range.

Of course, *Notes on the State of Virginia* has never been out of print, and continues to be published to this day. Therefore, a plethora of editions exist, in hardbound and paperback, by an endless stream of publishers.

When it comes to modern day collectibles, Theodore Roosevelt, who authored numerous books, had a hand in the cookie jar. Roosevelt authorized several "special editions" of his work purely for profit. These include *Hunting Trips of a Ranchman*, which was published in a "limited, exceedingly elegant quarto-sized edition priced at an unheard of $15," in 1885.[1] This edition, also known as the Medora Edition, was farmed out by G.P. Putnam's Sons to the Knickerbocker Press, and very fine copies can be found for over $2,000. In 1904, Roosevelt's involvement with publisher George Putnam became known through a lawsuit filed from a wealthy book collector. It acknowledged that Roosevelt (who was still in office) received anywhere from $3,000 to $4,000 for a set of autographed limited editions. Roosevelt would pursue the emerging limited edition market by authorizing such multi-volume works as *The Works of Theodore Roosevelt* and *The Writings of Theodore Roosevelt*. What was ironic was that everything contained in these editions were previously published and still widely available in print.

Even a family relative, W. Emlen Roosevelt, joined in the fray by privately publishing the legal transcript of Roosevelt's 1913 libel suit. *Roosevelt vs. Newett, a Transcript of Testimony taken and Depositions read at Marquette, Michigan*, was published in 1914, with the satisfaction of hopefully forever squashing rumors of Roosevelt's alleged "drunkenness." The book's preface noted, "We have all been greatly incensed, from time to time in recent years, by reports that Theodore Roosevelt was a drinking man. We, who knew the unusual purity and wholesomeness of his life, felt especial anger at this rumor, both because of its persistence and of its cruel falsity. I have had this book printed because I knew we all wanted to have a complete copy of the official record, which contradicts the libel."[2]

Although since reprinted, original copies of the 1914 privately printed edition are scarce and remain among the oddities of works associated with Roosevelt.

In all fairness, it should be noted that Roosevelt was most likely naturally drawn to publishing his books in limited edition formats, because after all, he was a book lover. Roosevelt was even known to have carried a "portable library" with him wherever he traveled. Jefferson also loved books, and reveled in the knowledge that his library at Monticello was probably the best private collection of books in Virginia, if not America.

Surely the most unique book ever published by a president was Herbert and Lou Hoover's 1912 translation of Georgius Argicola's *De Re Metallica*. Hoover was introduced to the 1556 original through his background as a mining engineer, but it was surely his love of historical literature that induced him to tackle a proper translation. When the *Mining Magazine* published their edition of the work in 1912, they cut no corners and afforded Hoover the honor of a vellum edition, with faithful reproductions of 289 original woodcuts. Published by Albert Frost and Sons of Rugby, England, the edition mimics the original, and was limited to 3,000 signed copies. These were quickly bought up by both book collectors and historians, and today command prices ranging anywhere from $700 to $2,000. Although Hoover's translation still remains in print, the Frost and Sons edition remains the most beautifully elaborate book ever to have been written by a president.

In 1935, Farrar & Rinehart of New York published Franklin D. Roosevelt's "mystery novel" *The President's Mystery Story*. What makes the book unusual was that Roosevelt never actually contributed anything, save for a bare-bones outline. A team of hired writers handled the writing, each contributing a chapter, which did not help. Editions can be easily found ranging from $10 to $100, depending on the existence of a dust jacket. A second edition was published in 1967, under the title *The President's Mystery Plot*, which included a final chapter. These are looked upon as a curiosity, and are of little value.

Harry S. Truman became the first president to truly push the envelope when it came to signed copies. He willingly submitted himself to sit through massive book signings of his memoirs, thus establishing the pattern for his successors. Truman's 1955 double volume memoir, published by Doubleday, was even subject to a "Kansas City Edition" of 20,615 signed copies of volume one, and 11,000 signed copies of volume two. Truman, who enjoyed writing about his presidency, was said to have enjoyed the entire ordeal, never once complaining of writer's cramp.

John F. Kennedy's *Profiles in Courage* can be collected in several editions since its original appearance in 1956. An Inaugural Edition was published in 1961 and a Memorial Edition in 1964. Twentieth and Fiftieth Anniversary Editions also exist. Each edition typically included a new preface.

Despite a long political history, Richard M. Nixon never was able to escape his share of vicious satire, and this includes all things literary. Consider *The Poetry of Richard M. Nixon*, which appeared in 1974. This slim, staple-bound unpainted card stock edition resembles privately published poetry chapbooks frequently found by underground poets. Compiled by Jack S. Margolis, the text (or "poetry") was taken from excerpts of the actual Watergate transcripts, which were secretly recorded by Nixon in the Oval Office. Margolis ingeniously gave Nixon's words a proper poetic structure, rendering previously unreadable transcripts into poems.

As an example, here is "Together":

> We are all
> In it
> Together.
> We take
> A few shots
> And
> It will be over.
> Don't worry.
> I wouldn't
> Want to be
> On the other side
> Right now.[3]

Copies of *The Poetry of Richard M. Nixon* can be found in the $10–$40 range.

During the early 1970s, while Nixon was president, there was a resurgence in the limited edition book market. Publisher George Macy, who in 1929 founded the Limited Editions Club, originated this genre. The Limited Editions Club published classic works of literature, typically fiction, in fine bindings and on quality archival paper. The books often included illustrations by renowned artists, which were exclusively commissioned by the publisher, with prefaces explaining the history of each book. To wrap things up, the entire production was typically encased in its own matching slipcase.

The Limited Editions Club later produced a more affordable offshoot, known as The Heritage Press. Heritage Press offerings mimicked LEC books, but with much larger press runs. In 1956 George Macy died, and Heritage Press was sold to the Danbury Mint, who published books under the Easton Press imprint. The Easton Press also maintains reprint rights to many LEC titles.

Easton Press included acclaimed works of non-fiction, among them American history. Its "Library of the Presidents" series included a mix of biographies and autobiographies written by or about those who had occupied the office. Of particular significance were memoirs written and signed by presidents Nixon, Carter, Ford, and later, George H.W. Bush. The publisher's website featured each copy of the library at $64.70, with one signed volume for every ten volumes purchased.

Also available were limited editions published by the Franklin Library. As a branch of the Franklin Mint, Franklin Library published books from 1973 to 2000. In his four-volume work, *A History of Book Publishing in the United States*, author John Tebbel recalls a typical Franklin Press offering:

> Most of the quality in these volumes was concentrated not on their typography, which was often dull, but in the bindings, which were in full genuine leather and tooled in historical patterns. Front cover, back cover, and spine were worked in 22-karat gold, and the spines were "hubbed" with raised horizontal ridges, in the traditional manner.

Endsheets were of moiré fabric, and a ribbon marker was inserted in each book. High-quality paper, edged in gold, was used. While the books were univocally designed, they did not represent the most modern typography, as the Limited Editions Club had done and was doing again. Franklin's limited editions, like those of Limited Editions, were sold only by subscription.[4]

At the time Easton Press originated their Library of the Presidents, Former President Nixon was alive. In his book *The Agent*, Arthur M. Klebanoff recalls landing Easton as a client, as well as having to deal with the individual personalities of Nixon, Ford and Carter. As the only surviving presidents, each was expected to sign 15,000 copies of their book. Klebanoff secured a deal that each would receive exactly what the others would get financially. Carter agreed on the basis that his book be released first, which was no big deal to either Ford or Nixon. When the time came to sign the contract, however, Nixon refused. Klebanoff presumed that "Nixon hated any activity that presented him parallel to Carter and Ford," and the only reason Nixon originally agreed was that he believed Ford and Carter chose not to participate.[5] Nixon eventually agreed, on the provision that his book be released last. This gave him more time to sign sheets, and allow Easton to better figure the total amount of subscribers when he did. Klebanoff recalled the delicate handling of the entire project, which proved to be very successful:

> As a reward for signing the three living former presidents, I was invited to secure the rights to publish biographies of each of the other presidents. Working on the forty volumes helped me develop a relationship with the Easton team. The subscriber base for *Library of the Presidents* exceeded Easton's highest expectations. The program ultimately had revenues more than $25 million and is successfully offered today. There were moments of tension with Ford, Nixon, and Carter. Carter at first balked, then calmed down, when the 15,000 sheets arrived in his office for autographing (15,000 sheets is quite a pile). Ford at one point refused to approve a new set of marketing materials, as his staff pointed out that Nixon and Carter had one photograph more in the spreads than did Ford. We added a Ford photo. Nixon waited until the last minute to deliver his sheets. With the program more than two years old, two dozen-plus presidential biographies shipped and more than 10,000 subscribers, Easton began to get very nervous about whether they would get a flood of refund requests if the Nixon book was not forthcoming.[6]

Easton and Klebanoff would later approach Ronald Reagan, but Reagan remained committed to his own publisher, Simon & Schuster. When Reagan's memoir was released, Simon & Schuster offered several different editions of the book, both deluxe and signed. They were not accustomed, however, to Easton's successful merchandising, and the campaign failed. Klebanoff was then able to pounce on their misfortune, and make the best of it: "The most expensive included a signed leather-bound book and a set of Reagan recorded speeches in a wood presentation box with the presidential seal. Simon & Schuster's own direct marketing efforts for the deluxe editions was not successful.

They had more than 1,000 of these boxes, manufactured at a cost of one hundred dollars each, in their warehouse. Internally, the boxes were referred to as "the coffins." I arranged for Easton to buy the boxes, the signed books, and the audios, and sell them successfully for $250 to their subscribers, so that at least some of the Library of the Presidents subscribers could enjoy Reagan, too."[7]

Overall, book collectors tend to shy away from Franklin and Easton Press editions. Book collecting manuals also have little to say about them: "These publishers put out fairly nice editions, usually bound in leather, frequently signed by the author. However, no one outside the companies is exactly sure how 'limited' these editions are—estimates are usually in the several thousand-copy range. These are nice books; they sell them new for about $35, and 99 percent of them will still be worth $35 ten or fifteen years from now. They're nice on the shelf, they're good to read, but most of them are not real collectible books."[8]

Another collecting manual appears to agree. "Franklin, Limited Editions Club, and Easton books are expensive to buy new, and they look and feel expensive—not to mention distinctive. All of which means that you're unlikely to find them at yard sales for 50 cents each. Indeed, that's true of limited editions in general—they look different and, more important, are initially distributed to people who either keep them or who sell high-level books professionally. If you want them, fine, but you're unlikely to get a bargain."[9]

Richard Nixon would go on to conduct additional business with Easton Press in the form of *The Richard M. Nixon Library*, a six-volume matched set of selected books, each signed and in a limited edition of 1,500.

In the end, Easton Press's Library of the Presidents series turned out to be a scattered mixture of autobiographies and biographies. Previously published memoirs such as Coolidge's *Autobiography* and Hoover's *Memoirs* are absent, and represented by biographies instead. Lyndon B. Johnson's *Vantage Point* is also ignored. As for the prolific Thomas Jefferson, his *Notes on the State of Virginia* does not appear, and instead is represented by biographies as well as two volumes, titled *Writings*. Grant's *Memoirs* is included, as well as a biography by William McFeely. Similar treatment is given to Eisenhower and Truman.

Another strange offering, this time from Flatsigned Press, was *The Watergate Tapes*. The *Watergate Tapes* collection featured a gold embossed leather bound book, as well as four audiocassettes, which were housed in a felt-lined cherrywood presentation box. The offering was limited to 94 sets, with the book signed by Nixon. Nixon, however, had passed away by the time *The Watergate Tapes* was being offered, and the sole reason the publishers were able to offer it as being "posthumously" signed was due to the fact that an unnamed publisher (such as Easton) had extra or "remainder" sheets on hand, which had been previously signed by Nixon, but were never used. Flatsigned Press simply purchased the signed sheets, and thus "built" the Watergate book around them. This apparently explains the oddly numbered limited edition of ninety-four copies. Despite being presented in audiocassette format, the set was offered at $699.

Nixon would also choose to re-publish his books in formatted editions. This permitted readers (and collectors) to have all of his published works in a uniform format of folio size and bindings. Jimmy Carter would also do this in 1996, with the University of Arkansas. As an added feature, these typically included new prefaces written by the author.

Aside from Easton Press, several limited edition books from Gerald Ford can be found published under Lord John Press. In the early 1980s, Lord John Press published the text of three separate speeches given by Ford. These slim volumes were printed in limited runs, and signed by Ford. The three speeches include *A Vision for America*, a speech delivered at the Republican National Convention in Detroit, Michigan. The 1980 address was limited to 500 copies. A second volume, *Global Stability*, was given in Quebec, Canada, in 1981, and limited to 400 copies. The third and last address, the [Winston] *Churchill Lecture*, was delivered in London, England, in November 1980. The press run was limited to 350 copies.

For collectors desiring something more historical, Flatsigned Press offered limited edition leather bound copies of the *Warren Commission Report*, with a wood presentation box, at just under $1,300. At first glance, the volume has the appearance of a Bible.

Jimmy Carter, who continues to author books more than thirty years after leaving the White House, dominates the field when it comes to signed copies. Though several of his books are available from Easton Press, Carter continued to promote new releases with tours and book signings. Signed books from Carter are so frequent, that a used bookseller once humorously remarked that an unsigned copy of a Jimmy Carter book might actually be worth more than a signed one.

Recently published presidential memoirs still receive the signed limited edition treatment, complete with matching slipcase. The old rules still apply, with press runs limited to 1,500 copies. The occasional oddity still appears, such as a 1956 first edition copy of John F. Kennedy's *Profiles in Courage*, signed by none other than Barack Obama. Flatsigned Press, the bookseller offering the volume, guarantees it to be unique, and claims Obama signed it shortly before his election to the presidency. The asking price is $25,000.

Offerings such as these seem to establish that the current collector market can be robust, if not imaginative.

Chronological List of Publications Authored by U.S. Presidents

Date indicates year of publication
* Denotes a manuscript published posthumously

George Washington
The Journal of Major George Washington (1754)
The Diaries of George Washington (1748–1799)* (1861)

John Adams
Thoughts on Government (1776)
A Defence of the Constitutions of Government of the United States of America (1787)
Autobiography* (1802–07)

Thomas Jefferson
A Summary View of the Rights of British America (1774)
Notes on the State of Virginia (1785)
A Manual of Parliamentary Practice for the Senate of the United States (1801)
Anas* (1809)
Autobiography* (1821)

James Madison
The Federalist (1788)
Autobiography* (1832)
Notes of the Debates in the Federal Convention* (1787)

James Monroe
A View of the Conduct of the Executive in the Foreign Affairs of the United States Connected with the Mission to the French Republic During the Years 1794, 5 & 6 (1797)
The People the Sovereigns, Being a Comparison of the Government of the

United States with Those of the Republics Which Have Existed Before, with the Causes of Their Decadence Plus Fall* (1829)

Autobiography* (1830) (published 1959)

John Quincy Adams

Letters of Publicola (1791)

Letters on Silesia (1804)

Lectures on Rhetoric and Oratory, Delivered to the Classes of Senior and Junior Sophisters in Harvard University (1810)

Report of the Secretary of State Upon Weights and Measures (1821)

The Duplicate Letters, the Fisheries, and the Mississippi, Documents Relating to Transactions at the Negotiations of Ghent (1822)

Dermot MacMorrogh or the Conquest of Ireland: A Historical Tale of the 12th Century in Four Cantos (1832)

Poems of Religion and Society* (published 1848)

Letters of John Quincy Adams, to His Son, on the Bible and Its Teachings* (1813) (Published 1848)

Letters on the Masonic Institution* (Published 1847)

The Lives of James Madison and James Monroe* (Published 1850)

Documents Relating to New England Federalism, 1800–1815* (1829) (Published 1877)

Diary of John Quincy Adams* (1779–1847) (Published 1956)

German to English Translations: *The Origin and Principles of the American Revolution Compared with the Origin of the French Revolution* (Friedrich von Gentz) (1800)

Oberon. Translated from the German of Christoph Martin Wieland* (1800) (Published 1940)

Martin Van Buren

Mr. Van Buren's Opinions (1835)

Inquiry into the Origin and Course of Political Parties in the United States* (1854–58) (Published 1867)

Autobiography* (1854–58) (Published 1920)

James K. Polk

Diary* (Published 1929)

James Buchanan

Mr. Buchanan's Administration on the Eve of the Rebellion (1866)

Abraham Lincoln

Political Debates Between Hon. Abraham Lincoln and Hon. Stephen A. Douglas in the Celebrated Campaign of 1858 in Illinois (1860)

Speech of Hon. Abraham Lincoln in New York, in Vindication of the Policy of the Framers of the Constitution and the Principles of the Republican Party Delivered in the Cooper Institute, February 27, 1860 (1860)

Ulysses S. Grant
   Personal Memoirs of U.S. Grant* (1885)

Rutherford B. Hayes
   Diary and Letters* (Published 1922–1926)
   Diary* (1875–1881) (Published 1964)

Benjamin Harrison
   This Country of Ours (1897)
   Views of an Ex-President (1901)

Grover Cleveland
   Presidential Problems (1904)
   Fishing and Shooting Sketches (1906)

Theodore Roosevelt
   The Summer Birds of the Adirondacks (with H.D. Minot) (1874)
   The Naval War of 1812 (1882)
   Hunting Trips of a Ranchman (1885)
   Thomas Hart Benton (1886)
   Ranch Life (1888)
   Essays on Practical Politics (1888)
   Gouverneur Morris (1888)
   The Winning of the West (1889–1896)
   Vol. I. *From the Alleghenies to the Mississippi, 1769–1776*
   Vol. II. *From the Alleghenies to the Mississippi, 1777–1783*
   Vol. III. *The Founding of the Trans-Alleghany Commonwealths, 1784–1790*
   Vol. IV. *Louisiana and the Northwest, 1791–1807*
   New York (1891)
   The Wilderness Hunter (1893)
   American Big Game (with George Bird Grinnel) (1893)
   Hero Tales from American History (with Henry Cabot Lodge) (1895)
   Hunting in Many Lands (with George Bird Grinnel) (1895)
   The Hunting-Trail (1896)
   Some American Game (1897)
   Trail and Campfire (with George Bird Grinnel) (1897)
   American Ideals and Other Essays (1897)
   The Rough Riders (1899)

The Strenuous Life and Other Essays (1900)
Oliver Cromwell (1900)
The Naval Operations of the War between Great Britain and the United States, 1812–1815 (1901)
The Deer Family (with T.S. van Dyke, D.G. Elliot, and A.J. Stone) (1902)
Outdoor Pastimes of an American Hunter (1905)
Good Hunting (1907)
The Works of Theodore Roosevelt: Seventeen Volume Set (1907)
Outlook Editorials (1909)
African and European Addresses (1910)
African Game Trails (1910)
The New Nationalism (1910)
American Problems (1910)
The Conservation of Womanhood and Childhood (1912)
Realizable Goals (1912)
History as Literature and Other Essays (1913)
An Autobiography (1913)
Progressive Principles (1913)
Through the Brazilian Wilderness (1914)
African Game Animals (with Edmund Heller) (1914)
America and the World War (1915)
A Book-Lover's Holidays in the Open (1916)
America and the World War: Fear God and Take Your Own Part (1916)
The Foes of Our Own Household (1917)
Social Justice and Popular Rule (1917)
National Strength and International Duty (1917)
The Great Adventure (1918)
Letters to His Children (1919)
The Complete Writings of Theodore Roosevelt: "Elkhorn Edition" 28 Volume Set* (1920)
The Summer Birds of the Adirondacks in Franklin County, N.Y. with Notes on Some of the Birds of Oyster Bay (with H.D. Minot)* (1925)
Diaries of Boyhood and Youth* (1928)
Letters and Speeches* (2004)

William Howard Taft

Four Aspects of Civic Duty (1906)
Popular Government: Its Essence, Its Permanence, and Its Perils (1913)
The Anti-Trust Act and the Supreme Court (1914)
Ethnics in Service (1915)

The Presidency: Its Duties, Its Powers Its Opportunities and Its Limitations (1916)
The Chief Magistrate and His Powers (1916)
Service with Fighting Men: An Account of the Work of the Young Men's Christian Associations in the World War (1922)
Liberty Under Law: An Interpretation of the Principles of Our Constitutional Government (1922)

Woodrow Wilson
Congressional Government (1885)
The State: Elements of Historical and Practical Politics (1889)
Division and Reunion, 1829-1889 (1893)
An Old Master and Other Political Essays (1893)
Mere Literature and Other Essays (1896)
George Washington (1896)
When a Man Comes to Himself (1901)
A History of the American People: Volumes I-V (1902)
The New Freedom: A Call for the Emancipation of the Generous Energies of a People (1913)
The Road Away from Revolution (1923)

Calvin Coolidge
Have Faith in Massachusetts (1914)
The Autobiography of Calvin Coolidge (1929)

Herbert Hoover
Principles of Mining (1909)
List of Books [compiled for use in translating *De Re Metallic*] (1911)
De Re Metallic by Georgius Agricola (translation with Lou Hoover) (1912)
Waste in Industry: The Committee on Elimination of Waste in Industry (1921)
American Individualism (1922)
The New Day (1928)
A Remedy for Disappearing Game Fishes (1930)
A Boyhood in Iowa (1931)
Hoover After Dinner (1934)
The *Challenge to Liberty* (1934)
Addresses Upon the American Road, 1933-1938 (1938)
American Ideals versus the New Deal (1936)
America's Way Forward (1938)
Shall We Send Our Youth to War? (1939)
Further Addresses Upon the American Road, 1938-1940 (1940)
Addresses Upon the American Road, 1940-1941 (1941)

America's First Crusade (1941)
The Hoover-Gibson Plan for Making Lasting Peace (with Hugh Gibson) (1942)
New Approaches to Lasting Peace (with Hugh Gibson) (1942)
The Problems of Lasting Peace (with Hugh Gibson) (1942)
Further New Approaches to Lasting Peace (with Hugh Gibson) (1943)
The Basis of Lasting Peace (with Hugh Gibson) (1944)
Addresses Upon the American Road, World War II, 1941–1945 (1946)
Addresses Upon the American Road, 1945–1948 (1949)
Addresses Upon the American Road, 1948–1950 (1951)
The Memoirs of Herbert Hoover:
- *Volume I: Years of Adventure, 1874–1920* (1951)
- *Volume II: The Cabinet and the Presidency, 1920–1933* (1952)
- *Volume III: The Great Depression, 1929–1941* (1952)

40 Key Questions About Our Foreign Policy (1952)
Addresses Upon the American Road, 1950–1955 (1955)
The Ordeal of Woodrow Wilson (1958)
An American Epic, Vol. I. The Relief of Belgium and Northern France, 1914–1930 (1959)
An American Epic, Vol. II. Famine in Forty-five Nations: Organization Behind the Front Line, 1914–1923 (1961)
An American Epic, Vol. III. Famine in Forty-Five Nations: The Battle on the Front Line, 1914–1923 (1961)
On Growing Up (1962)
Fishing for Fun, and to Wash Your Soul (1963)
An American Epic, Vol. IV. The Guns Cease Killing and the Saving of Life from Famine Begins, 1939–1963 (1964)
Freedom Betrayed: Herbert Hoover's Secret History of the Second World War and Its Aftermath* (2011)

Franklin D. Roosevelt
Looking Forward (1933)
On Our Way (1934)

Harry S. Truman
Memoirs: Year of Decisions (1955)
Memoirs: Years of Trial and Hope (1956)
Mr. Citizen (1960)
Truman Speaks (1960)
Where the Buck Stops* (1989)
Off the Record* (1980)

Dwight D. Eisenhower
Report by the Supreme Commander to the Combined Chiefs of State on the Operations in Europe of the Allied Expeditionary Force. 6 June 1944 to 8 May 1945 (1946)
Crusade in Europe (1948)
Peace with Justice: Selected Addresses (1961)
The White House Years:
- *Mandate for Change: 1953–1956* (1963)
- *Waging Peace: 1956–1961* (1965)

At Ease: Stories I Tell to Friends (1967)
In Review: Pictures I've Kept (1969)
he Eisenhower Diaries* (1981)

John F. Kennedy
Why England Slept (1940)
As We Remember Joe (1945)
Profiles in Courage (1956)
A Nation of Immigrants (1958)
The Strategy of Peace (1960)
To Turn the Tide (1962)
The Burden and the Glory* (1964)

Lyndon B. Johnson
This America (1966)
The Vantage Point (1971)

Richard M. Nixon
The Challenges We Face (1960)
Six Crises (1962)
RN: Memoirs of Richard Nixon (1978)
The Real War (1980)
Leaders (1982)
Real Peace (1984)
No More Vietnams (1985)
1999: Victory Without War (1988)
In the Arena (1990)
Seize the Moment (1992)
Beyond Peace (1994)
Richard Nixon: Speeches, Writings and Documents* (2008)

Gerald R. Ford
The Warren Commission Report (1964)
Portrait of the Assassin (with John R. Stiles) (1965)

A Time to Heal (1979)
Grand Rapids: The City That Works (with John Coriveau) (1998)
To Assure Pride and Confidence in the Electoral Process (with Jimmy Carter) (2002)
A Presidential Legacy and the Warren Commission Report* (2007)

Jimmy Carter
Why Not the Best? (1977)
A Government as Good as Its People (1977)
Keeping Faith: Memories of a President (1982)
Negotiation: The Alternative to Hostility (1984)
The Blood of Abraham: Insights into the Middle East (1985)
Everything to Gain: Making the Most of the Rest of Your Life (1987) (with Rosalynn Carter)
An Outdoor Journal: Adventures and Reflections (1988)
Turning Point: A Candidate, a State and a Nation Come of Age (1992)
Talking Peace: A Vision for the Next Generation (1993)
Always a Reckoning, and Other Poems (1995)
Little Baby Snoogle-Fleejer (1995)
Living Faith (1996)
Sources of Strength: Meditations on Scripture for a Living Faith (1997)
The Virtues of Aging (1998)
An Hour Before Daylight: Memories of a Rural Boyhood (2001)
Christmas in Plains: Memories (2001)
The Personal Beliefs of Jimmy Carter (2002)
To Assure Pride and Confidence in the Electoral Process (with Gerald Ford) (2002)
The Nobel Price Peace Lecture (2002)
The Hornet's Nest: A Novel of the Revolutionary War (2003)
Sharing Good Times (2004)
Our Endangered Values: America's Moral Crisis (2005)
Palestine: Peace Not Apartheid (2006)
Beyond the White House: Waging Peace, Fighting Disease, Building Hope (2007)
A Remarkable Mother (2008)
We Can Have Peace in the Holy Land: A Plan That Will Work (2009)
White House Diary (2010)
Throughout the Year with Jimmy Carter: 366 Daily Meditations from the 39th President (2011)
A Call to Action: Women, Religion, Violence, and Power (2014)

A Full Life: Reflections at Ninety (2015)
Faith: A Journey for All (2018)

Ronald Reagan
Where the Rest of Me? (1965)
Rendezvous with Destiny (1981)
An American Life (1990)
Reagan in His Own Hand (2001)
Reagan: A Life in Letters (2003)
The Reagan Diaries* (2007)
The Notes* (2011)

George H.W. Bush
Looking Forward: An Autobiography (1987)
A World Transformed (1998)
All the Best: My Life in Letters and Other Writings (1999)
The China Diary of George H.W. Bush: The Making of a Global President (2008)

Bill Clinton
Putting People First (1992) (with Al Gore)
Between Hope and History (1996)
My Life (2004)
Giving (2007)
Back to Work (2011)
The President Is Missing (2018) (with James Patterson)

George W. Bush
A Charge to Keep (1999)
Decision Points (2010)
41: A Portrait of My Father (2014)
Portraits of Courage (2017)

Barack Obama
Dreams from My Father (1995)
The Audacity of Hope (2006)
Of Thee I Sing (2010)

Donald J. Trump
Trump: The Art of the Deal (1987)
Surviving at the Top (1990)
Trump: The Art of the Comeback (1997)
The America We Deserve (2000)

Think Like a Billionaire (2004)
Why We Want You to Be Rich (2004)
The Way to the Top: The Best Business Advice I Ever Received (2004)
The Best Golf Advice I Ever Received (2005)
The Best Real Estate Advice I Ever Received (2006)
Trump 101: The Way to Success (2007)
Think Big and Kick Ass in Business and Life (2007)
Never Give Up (2008)
Time to Get Tough: Make America Great Again (2011)
Midas Touch (2011)
Crippled America: How to Make America Great Again (2015)

Notes

Flyleaf quote: John S. D. Eisenhower, *Strictly Personal. a Memoir.* (Doubleday & Company, 1974) 303.

Diaries, Letters, and Papers

1. John Adams, Edited by L. H. Butterfield, *Diary & Autobiography of John Adams, Vol. I.*, (The Belknap Press, 1962), lxv.
2. *Ibid.*, lxiv.
3. *Ibid.*, lxvi.

George Washington

1. George Washington to George Washington Parke Curtis, December 19, 1796.
2. Ron Chernow, *Washington: A Life* (Penguin Press, 2010), 12.
3. *Ibid.*, 13.
4. *Ibid.*
5. A noteworthy account of Washington's journey can be found in Volume I of Douglas Southall Freeman's *George Washington: A Biography*, pages 259-326.
6. Washington, George, *The Journal of Major George Washington* (Xerox, 1966), foreword.
7. *Ibid.*, Advertisement (preface).
8. Chernow, *Washington: A Life*, 37.
9. *Ibid.*, 38.
10. *Ibid.*
11. Douglas Southhall Freeman, *George Washington: A Biography. Volume II, Young Washington* (Charles Scribner's Sons, 1948), 236.
12. *Ibid.*, 237.
13. *Ibid.*
14. *Ibid.* Though Washington apparently subscribed to the volume, there is no record of him ever owning the edition. A critique of the French translation can be found in Vol. I of Freeman's *Washington*, pages 540-545.
15. George Washington to James McHenry, May 29, 1797.
16. Washington, George, edited by John C. Fitzpatrick. *The Diaries of George Washington* (Houghton Mifflin Company, 1925), Vol. I., vii.
17. *Ibid.*
18. *Ibid.*, xi.
19. *Ibid.*, 355.
20. *Ibid.*, 320.
21. George Washington, edited by Dorothy Twohig. *George Washington's Diaries: An Abridgement* (The University Press of Virginia, 1999), ix.
22. An example is number 90: "Being Set at Meat Scratch Not Neither Spit Cough or Blow Your Nose Except There's a Necessity for It."

John Adams

1. John Adams, edited by L. H. Butterfield, *Diary and Autobiography of John Adams* (The Belknap Press, 1962), Vol. I, 168.
2. David McCullough, *John Adams* (Simon & Schuster, 2001), 103.
3. Page Smith, *John Adams, Vol. I* (Greenwood Press, 1963), 247.
4. Adams, Butterfield, *Diary*, Vol. III, 333.
5. Smith. *John Adams*, 247.
6. *Ibid.*, *Vol. II*, 691.
7. McCullough, *John Adams*, 373. John Adams to James Warren.
8. *Ibid.*, 374.
9. Smith. *John Adams, Vol. II*, 691.
10. *Ibid.*, 692.
11. *Ibid.*, 700.
12. Smith. *John Adams*, 1086-1087.
13. *Ibid.*, 1087.
14. *Ibid.*, 1087.
15. Adams, Butterfield. *Diary*, Vol. I., lxxi.
16. *Ibid.*, lxxiv.

Thomas Jefferson

1. Thomas Jefferson to John Adams, June 10, 1815. Thomas Jefferson Papers, Library of Congress.

2. Dumas Malone, *Jefferson: The Virginian* (Little, Brown and Company, 1948), 181–182.
3. Joseph J. Ellis, *American Sphinx: The Character of Thomas Jefferson* (Knopf, 1997), 31.
4. Ellis, *American Sphinx*, 32.
5. Malone, *Jefferson: The Virginian*, 181.
6. *Ibid.*, 230.
7. *Ibid.*
8. Noble E. Cunningham, Jr., *In Pursuit of Reason: The Life of Thomas Jefferson* (Louisiana State University Press, 1987), 76.
9. Cunningham, *In Pursuit of Reason*, 94.
10. *Ibid.*, 94.
11. *Ibid.*, 96.
12. Thomas Jefferson, *Notes on the State of Virginia*, Query V.
13. Adrienne Kock & William Pedan, *The Life and Selected Writings of Thomas Jefferson* (The Modern Library, Random House, 1944), 186.
14. Malone, *Jefferson and the Rights of Man*, 505–506. A "Long Note on the English Edition of Notes on the State of Virginia," was included by Malone in the second volume. Jefferson's arrangements with publisher John Stockdale are given great attention.
15. Malone, *Jefferson and the Ordeal of Liberty* (Little, Brown and Company, 1962), 456. Malone notes, "The Text Appears to Have Remained Unaltered in the Many Later Printings."
16. *Ibid.*
17. *American Bar Association Journal*, October 1955. Vol. 41., 951. Book reviewed was *Learning Parliamentary Procedure* by Alice F. Sturgis. Reviewer quoted is David F. Maxwell.
18. Thomas Jefferson, *Autobiography*, 3.
19. Kock, Peden, *The Life and Selected Writings of Thomas Jefferson*, 290.
20. *Ibid.*
21. C-Span, National Book Festival, September 2, 2017.

James Madison

1. Irving Brant, *The Fourth President: A Life of James Madison* (Bobbs-Merrill, 1970), 197. The title was first used in a public address by Charles J. Ingersoll in 1827.
2. Jacob E. Cooke, *The Federalist. Edited with Introduction and Notes* (Wesleyan University Press, 1961), xiv. Volume I was published March 22, 1788, with Volume II on May 28.
3. *Ibid.*, xv.
4. *Ibid.*
5. *Ibid.*, xvi.
6. *Ibid.*, xvii.
7. Brant, *The Fourth President*, 201.

8. An alliterate title frequently given is *A Brief System of Logick*. Biographer Irving Brant disputed conclusions that Madison filled out the notebook while attending college. See, *The Fourth President*, 7–9.
9. Brant, *The Fourth President*, 7.
10. Irving Brant, *James Madison: The Virginia Revolutionist* (Bobbs-Merrill, 1941), 60.
11. *Ibid.*, 59.

James Monroe

1. C. P. Cresson, *James Monroe* (Archon Books, 1971), 155.
2. *Ibid.*, 173.
3. Harlow Giles Unger, *The Last Founding Father: James Monroe and a Nation's Call to Greatness* (Da Capo Press, 2009), 135.
4. Cresson, *James Monroe*, 173.
5. Harry Ammon, *James Monroe: The Quest for National Identity* (McGraw-Hill, 1971), 561.
6. *Ibid.*, 562.
7. *Ibid.*
8. *Ibid.*
9. *Ibid.*
10. *Ibid.*
11. John Quincy Adams, edited by Charles Francis Adams, *Memoirs: Vol. VIII* (Philadelphia, 1874), 131. George Hay to JQA, April 6, 1829.
12. Unger, *The Last Founding Father*, 335.
13. James P. Lucier, *The Political Writings of James Monroe* (Regnery Publishing, 2001), 722.
14. *Ibid.*, 721.
15. *Ibid.*, 724.
16. Stuart Gerry Brown, *The Autobiography of James Monroe* (Syracuse University Press, 1959), iv.
17. *Ibid.*, 12–13.
18. Ammon, *James Monroe*, 562.</NOTES>

John Quincy Adams

1. Paul C. Nagel, *John Quincy Adams: A Public Life, a Private Life* (Alfred A. Knopf, 1997), 121.
2. Marie B. Hecht, *John Quincy Adams: A Personal History of an Independent Man* (The Macmillan Company, 1972), 67.
3. Nagel, *John Quincy Adams*, 73.
4. *Ibid.*, 76.
5. *Ibid.*, 119.
6. Hecht, *John Quincy Adams*, 131.
7. Nagel, *John Quincy Adams*, 120.
8. *Ibid.*
9. *Ibid.*
10. *Ibid.*
11. Hecht, *John Quincy Adams*, 184.

12. *Ibid.*
13. *Ibid.*, 185.
14. Nagel, *John Quincy Adams*, 262.
15. *Ibid.*, 263.
16. *Ibid.*
17. *Ibid.*
18. *Ibid.*, 284.
19. *Ibid.*
20. *Ibid.*
21. *Ibid.*, 329.
22. *Ibid.*
23. *Ibid.*
24. *Ibid.*, 338, 341.
25. Hecht, John Quincy Adams, 519.
26. *Ibid.*
27. *Ibid.*, 404.
28. John Quincy Adams, edited by David Grayson Allen, *Diary of John Quincy Adams Vol. I* (The Belknap Press, 1981), xli.
29. *Ibid.*, xxx-xxxi.
30. *Ibid.*, xxxi.
31. Nagel, *John Quincy Adams*, 418.

Three Generals

1. *Poor Richard's Almanack*, 1738.
2. Andrew Burnstein, *The Passions of Andrew Jackson* (Knopf, 2003), 226.
3. *Ibid.* Attributed to historian David Ramsay.
4. Jon Meacham, *American Lion: Andrew Jackson in the White House* (Random House, 2008), 18.
5. *Ibid.*, 18, 29
6. *Ibid.*, 165.
7. *Ibid.* Attributed to British author Harriet Mantineau.
8. *Ibid.*, 51.
9. Burnstein, *The Passions of Andrew Jackson*, 214.
10. James Knox Polk, edited by Allan Nevins, *Polk: The Diary of a President, 1845-1849* (Longmans, Green and Co., 1929), 388–389.

Martin Van Buren

1. John Niven, *Martin Van Buren: The Romantic Age of American Politics* (Oxford University Press, 1983), 397.
2. *Ibid.*, 400.
3. *Ibid.*, 598.
4. Ted Widmer. *Martin Van Buren* (Times Books, 2005), 162.
5. Niven, *Martin Van Buren*, 608.
6. *Ibid.*
7. *Ibid.*

8. Widmer, *Martin Van Buren*, 166.
9. Niven, *Martin Van Buren*, 608.
10. *Ibid.*
11. *Ibid.*, 609.
12. *Ibid.*
13. Martin Van Buren, *The Autobiography of Martin Van Buren* (Augustus M. Kelley, 1969), 3.
14. Widmer, *Martin Van Buren*, 166.
15. Widmer, *Martin Van Buren*, 162.

John Tyler and Millard Fillmore

1. Oliver Perry Chitwood, *John Tyler: Champion of the Old South* (American Political Biography Press, 1939), 15–16.
2. *Ibid.*, 18.
3. Robert J. Rayback, *Millard Fillmore: Biography of a President* (American Political Biography Press, 1959), 43.
4. *Ibid.*, 385.
5. *Ibid.*, 386.

James Knox Polk

1. Charles Sellers, *James K. Polk: Jacksonian 1795-1843* (Princeton University Press, 1957), 47.
2. James K. Polk, Nevins, *Polk: The Diary of a President*, v.
3. *Ibid.*, xiii.
4. *Ibid.*
5. *Ibid.*, xvi.
6. *Ibid.*, xvii.
7. *Ibid.*, 46. January 28, 1846.
8. *Ibid.*, xxiii.

Franklin Pierce

1. Roy Franklin Nichols, *Franklin Pierce: Young Hickory of the Granite Hills* (University of Pennsylvania Press, 1958), 19.
2. *Ibid.*, 208-209.
3. *Ibid.*, 212.

James Buchanan

1. Philip Shriver Klein, *President James Buchanan: A Biography* (Pennsylvania State University Press, 1962), 427.
2. *Ibid.*, 408.
3. *Ibid.*, 410.
4. *Ibid.*
5. *Ibid.*, 416.
6. *Ibid.* Black served as secretary of state from December 17, 1860, to March 5, 1861.

7. *Ibid.*, 417.
8. *Ibid.*
9. *Ibid.*, 419.
10. *Ibid.*
11. *Ibid.*
12. *Ibid.*
13. Shunk's notes remain lost.
14. Jean H. Baker, *James Buchanan* (Times Books, 2004), 142.

Abraham Lincoln

1. Abraham Lincoln, edited by Roy P. Basler, *The Collected Works of Abraham Lincoln: Vol. III* (Rutgers University Press, 1953), 360.
2. Abraham Lincoln, edited by David D. Anderson, *The Literary Works of Abraham Lincoln* (Charles E. Merrill, 1970), iv.
3. *Ibid.*, ix.
4. Chris DeRose, *Congressman Lincoln: The Making of America's Greatest President* (Threshold Editions, 2013), 106.
5. *Ibid.*
6. Harold Holzer, *Lincoln at Cooper Union: The Speech That Made Abraham Lincoln President* (Simon & Schuster, 2004), 44–45.
7. Archives.org. The Lincoln Financial Foundation Collection, held in the Lincoln Library, Allen County Public Library, Fort Wayne, Indiana.
8. Holzer, *Lincoln at Cooper Union*, 221.
9. Ronald C. White, *The Eloquent President: A Portrait of Lincoln Through His Words* (Random House, 2005), 132.
10. *Ibid.*, 224–225.
11. *Ibid.*, 225.
12. *Ibid.*, 233–234.
13. *Ibid.*, 234.
14. Abraham Lincoln, edited by Roy P. Basler, *Abraham Lincoln: His Speeches and Writings* Preface by Carl Sandburg (De Capo Press, 1946), xviii.
15. Lincoln, *The Literary Works of Abraham Lincoln*, xi.

Andrew Johnson

1. Paul H. Bergeron, *The Papers of Andrew Johnson: Vol. XVI, May 1869–July 1875* (University of Tennessee Press, 2000), 4. Letter of J. Scott Payne, May 3, 1869.
2. *Ibid.*, see footnote.
3. *Ibid.*, 190–191. Letter of William W. Hicks, May 27, 1870.
4. *Ibid.*, 267. Letter of Joseph S. Fowler, June 16, 1871.
5. *Ibid.*, 287. Letter of Joseph S. Fowler, February 9, 1872.
6. *Ibid.*, xvii.

Ulysses S. Grant

1. Jean Edward Smith, *Grant* (Simon & Schuster, 2001), 628.
2. William S. McFeely, *Grant: A Biography* (W. W. Norton & Company, 1981), 17.
3. *Ibid.*
4. Richard Goldhurst, *Many Are the Hearts: The Agony and the Triumph of Ulysses S. Grant* (Readers Digest press, 1975), xxi.
5. *Ibid.*, 111.
6. *Ibid.*
7. *Ibid.*, 115.
8. Ulysses S. Grant III, *Ulysses S. Grant: Warrior and Statesman* (William Morrow & Company, 1969), 430.
9. Goldhurst, *Many Are the Hearts*, 119–120.
10. Mark Twain, edited by Harriet Elinor Smith, *Autobiography of Mark Twain: Volume I* (University of California Press, 2010), 77–78.
11. *Ibid.*, 78.
12. *Ibid.*
13. *Ibid.*, 78–79.
14. *Ibid.*, 79.
15. *Ibid.*
16. Goldhurst, *Many Are the Hearts*, 120.
17. *Ibid.*, 120–121.
18. *Ibid.*, 80–81.
19. *Ibid.*, 81
20. *Ibid.*, 81–82.
21. *Ibid.*, 130–131.
22. *Ibid.*, 123.
23. Grant, *Warrior and Statesman*, 433.
24. Twain, *Autobiography*, 84.
25. *Ibid.*, 91.
26. *Ibid.*
27. *Ibid.*
28. *Ibid.*
29. William E. Woodward, *Meet General Grant* (Liveright Publishing, 1956), 495.
30. *Ibid.*
31. Julia Dent Grant, edited by John Y. Simon, *The Personal Memoirs of Julia Dent Grant* (Southern Illinois University Press, 1975), 330.
32. *Ibid.*, 330–331.
33. Goldhurst, *Many Are the Hearts*, 194.
34. *Ibid.*, 195.
35. *Ibid.*, 493. Letter of May 3, 1885.
36. Goldhurst, *Many Are the Hearts*, 197.
37. *Ibid.*, 196.
38. McFeely, *Grant*, 497–498.
39. *Ibid.*, 498.

40. *Ibid.*
41. Grant, *Warrior and Statesman*, 442.
42. *Ibid.*, 446. Note of June 28, 1885.
43. Grant, *Warrior and Statesman*, 449.
44. Ulysses S. Grant, *Personal Memoirs of U.S. Grant* (Charles L. Webster & Company, 1894), 7–8.
45. *Ibid.*
46. *Ibid.*
47. C. Stuart Chapman, *Shelby Foote: A Writer's Life* (University Press of Mississippi, 2003), 182.
48. Goldhurst, *Many Are the Hearts*, 260.
49. McFeely, *Grant*, 510–511.
50. Jimmy Carter, *White House Diary* (Farras, Strause, and Giroux, 2010), 523.
51. Dominic Streatfeild, *Cocaine: An Unauthorized Biography* (Thomas Dunne Books, 2001), 124.
52. Lisa Rogak, *Haunted Heart: The Life and Times of Stephen King* (St. Martins Press, 2008), 96.

Rutherford B. Hayes

1. Rutherford B. Hayes, edited by T. Harry Williams, *Hayes: The Diary of a President 1875–1881* (David McKay Company, 1964), 178.
2. *Ibid.*, vii.
3. *Ibid.*, xxviii.
4. *Ibid.*, xxviii.
5. *Ibid.*, 305–306.

James A. Garfield and Chester A. Arthur

1. Hayes, *Hayes: The Diary of a President*, 279.

Benjamin Harrison

1. Harry J. Sievers, *Benjamin Harrison: Hoosier President. Vol. III.* (Bobbs-Merrill Company, 1968), 255.
2. *Ibid.*, 256.

Grover Cleveland

1. Allan Nevins, *Grover Cleveland: A Study in Courage* (Dodd, Mead & Company, 1966), 737.
2. *Ibid.*, 736.
3. *Ibid.*
4. *Ibid.*, 738.
5. Grover Cleveland, *The Writings and Speeches of Grover Cleveland* (Cassell Publishing Company, 1892), xxiii.
6. Nevins, *Grover Cleveland*, 738.

7. Alyn Brosky, *Grover Cleveland: A Study in Character* (Truman Talley Books, 2000), 412.
8. *Ibid.*
9. *Ibid.*
10. Nevins, *Grover Cleveland*, 738.
11. *Ibid.*, 739.
12. Brodsky, *Grover Cleveland*, 443.
13. Henry F. Graff, *Grover Cleveland* (Times Books, 2002), 133.

William McKinley

1. Margaret Leech, *In the Days of McKinley* (Harper, 1960), 61.

Theodore Roosevelt

1. Edward Wagenknecht, *The Seven Worlds of Theodore Roosevelt* (Longmans, Green & Co., 1958), 32.
2. Theodore Roosevelt, edited by H. W. Brands, *The Selected Letters of Theodore Roosevelt* (Cooper Square Press, 2001), ix.
3. Theodore Roosevelt, *The Naval War of 1812* (Modern Library, 1999), ix. From an introduction by John Allen Gable.
4. *Ibid.*, xii.
5. *Ibid.*, xii–xiii.
6. *Ibid.*, xiii.
7. Theodore Roosevelt, *An Autobiography* (The Library of America, 2004), 275.
8. H.W. Brands, *T. R.: The Last Romantic* (BasicBooks, 1997), 187.
9. *Ibid.*
10. *Ibid.*, 188.
11. Elting E. Morison, *The Letters of Theodore Roosevelt: Vol. I.* (Harvard University Press, 1951), 89. Letter to Henry Cabot Lodge, March 8, 1885.
12. *Ibid.*, 95. Letter to Henry Cabot Lodge, March 27, 1886.
13. Brands, *T. R.: The Last Romantic*, 213.
14. *Ibid.*
15. Theodore Roosevelt, *Gouverneur Morris* (Arlington House), preface.
16. Theodore Roosevelt, *Ranch Life and the Hunting-Trail* (St Martin's Press, 1985), 31.
17. David McCullough, *Mornings on Horseback* (Simon & Schuster, 1981), 340.
18. Brands, *Selected Letters*, 52. Letter to Henry Cabot Lodge, February 15, 1887.
19. *Ibid.*, 55. Letter to Jonas Van Duzer, January 15, 1888.
20. *Ibid.*, 55–56. Letter to Francis Parkman, April 23, 1888.
21. Wagenknecht, *The Seven Worlds of Theodore Roosevelt*, 43.
22. Theodore Roosevelt, *The Winning of the*

West (University of Nebraska Press, 1995), ix. From a Foreword by John Milton Cooper, Jr.
23. Morison, *Letters of Theodore Roosevelt*, Vol. I., 210–211. Letter to George Haven Putnam, January 13, 1890.
24. Edmund Morris, *The Rise of Theodore Roosevelt* (Ballantine Books, 1979), 388.
25. Morison, *Letters of Theodore Roosevelt*, Vol. I., 705. Letter to George Haven Putnam, November 1, 1897.
26. Michael Puncke, *Last Stand: George Bird Grinnell, the Battle to Save the Buffalo, and the Birth of the New West* (Smithsonian Books, 2007), 163.
27. *Ibid.*, 164.
28. Morison, *Letters of Theodore Roosevelt*, Vol. II., 1046–1047. Letter to Charles Scribner, August 10, 1899.
29. Brands, *Selected Letters*, 270. Letter to Henry Cabot Lodge, September 23, 1901.
30. R. L. Wilson, *Theodore Roosevelt: Outdoorsman* (Winchester Press, 1971), 185–186.
31. Roosevelt, *The Rough Riders: An Autobiography*, 571.
32. Brands, *TR, the Last Romantic*, 730.
33. McCullough, *Mornings on Horseback*, 366. McCullough pointed out that Roosevelt "Devotes All of Three Sentences to His Mother."
34. Patricia O'Toole, *When Trumpets Call* (Simon & Schuster, 2005), 235.
35. *Ibid.*, 239.
36. *Ibid.*, 244.
37. *Ibid.*, 242.
38. Joseph Bucklin Bishop, *Theodore Roosevelt and His Time: Vol. II* (Charles Scribner's Son's, 1920), 374. Letter to Sir George Otto Trevelyan, February 6, 1915.
39. Wilson, *Theodore Roosevelt, Outdoorsman*, 96.
40. Bishop, *Theodore Roosevelt and His Time, Vol. II*, 361. Letter to Charles Scribner, January 24, 1915.
41. Theodore Roosevelt, *Letters and Speeches* (Library of America, 2004), 729. Letter to Quentin Roosevelt, December 24, 1917.
42. *Readers Encyclopedia of American Literature, Second Edition* (Harper Collins, 2002), 881.
43. Douglas Brinkley, *The Wilderness Warrior: Theodore Roosevelt and the Crusade for America* (Harper Collins, 2009), 267.

William Howard Taft

1. Henry F. Pringle, *The Life and Times of William Howard Taft: Vol. I* (Anchor Books, 1964), 99–100.
2. *Ibid.*, 100.

3. Carl Sferrazzo Anthony, *Nellie Taft: The Unconventional First Lady of the Ragtime Era* (William Morrow, 2005), 70.
4. Lewis L. Gould, *The William Howard Taft Presidency* (University Press of Kansas, 2009), 203
5. Jonathan Lurie, *William Howard Taft: The Travails of a Progressive Conservative* (Cambridge University Press, 2012), 20.

Woodrow Wilson

1. Arthur Walworth, *Woodrow Wilson* (W.W. Norton, 1978), 43
2. *Ibid.*, 22.
3. *Ibid.*
4. *Ibid.*
5. Phyllis Lee Levin, *Edith and Woodrow: The Wilson White House* (Scribner, 2001), 23.
6. *Ibid.*
7. Levin, *Edith and Woodrow*, 23.
8. Walworth, *Woodrow Wilson*, 32.
9. Mario R. Dinunzio, *Woodrow Wilson: Essential Writings & Speeches of the Scholar-President* (New York University Press, 2006), 4.
10. Walworth, *Woodrow Wilson*, 43.
11. Arthur S. Link, *The Papers of Woodrow Wilson: Vol. IV* (Princeton University Press, 1968), 3. Letter of January 24, 1885.
12. Walworth, *Woodrow Wilson*, 42.
13. Kendrick A. Clements, *The Presidency of Woodrow Wilson* (University Press of Kansas, 1992), 3.
14. Dinunzio, *Essential Writings & Speeches*, 232.
15. *Ibid.*
16. Clements, *The Presidency of Woodrow Wilson*, x.
17. John Milton Cooper, Jr., *Woodrow Wilson: A Biography* (Knopf, 2009), 20.
18. Walworth, *Woodrow Wilson*, 49.
19. *Ibid.*
20. Walworth, *Woodrow Wilson*, 63.
21. Weinstein, *Woodrow Wilson: A Medical and Psychological Biography*, 120.
22. *Ibid.*, 121.
23. Cooper, *Woodrow Wilson, a Biography*, 36.
24. Levin, *Edith and Woodrow*, 30.
25. Edwin A. Weinstein, *Woodrow Wilson: A Medical and Psychological Biography*, 138.
26. Cooper, *Woodrow Wilson*, 296.
27. Heckscher, *Woodrow Wilson*, 132.
28. Dinunzio, *Essential Writings & Speeches*, 6.
29. *Ibid.*
30. Woodrow Wilson, *The New Freedom* (Doubleday & Company, 1913), vii–viii.

31. John Wells Davidson, *A Crossroads of Freedom* (Yale University Press, 1956), 4.
32. Gene Smith, *When the Cheering Stopped: The Last Years of Woodrow Wilson* (William Morrow, 1964), 195.
33. Levin, *Edith and Woodrow*, 460.
34. Heckscher, *Woodrow Wilson*, 667.
35. *Ibid.*

Warren G. Harding

1. John W. Dean, *Warren G. Harding* (Times Books, 2004), 30.

Calvin Coolidge

1. William Allen White, *A Puritan in Babylon: The Story of Calvin Coolidge* (Peter Smith, 1973), 422.
2. *Ibid.*
3. *Ibid.*, 422–423.
4. *Ibid.*, 425.
5. *Ibid.*, 440.

Herbert Hoover

1. Richard Norton Smith, *An Uncommon Man: The Triumph of Herbert Hoover* (Simon and Schuster, 1984), 24.
2. David Burner, *Herbert Hoover: A Public Life* (Alfred A. Knopf, 1979), 64.
3. Herbert Hoover, *the Memoirs of Herbert Hoover: Years of Adventure 1874–1920* (The Macmillan Company, 1951), 117.
4. Burner, *Herbert Hoover*, 67.
5. *Ibid.*
6. *Ibid.*
7. *Ibid.*
8. *Ibid.*, 68.
9. Eugene Lyons, *Herbert Hoover: A Biography* (Doubleday & Company, 1964), 70.
10. Hoover, *Memoirs Of*, 118. In *Addresses Upon the American Road, 1950–1955*, Hoover also gives an account of the translation. See "A Discussion of De Re Metallica," pgs. 179–182.
11. *Ibid.*, 119. Hoover notes that as of 1951, a copy sold for as high as $225. As of 2011, an on-line bookseller was offering a copy at $3,000.
12. Lyons, *Herbert Hoover*, 142
13. Lyons, *Herbert Hoover*, 152.
14. Smith, *An Uncommon Man*, 196.
15. Hoover, *The Challenge to Liberty*, 49.
16. Smith, *An Uncommon Man*, 202.
17. Lyons, *Herbert Hoover*, 393.
18. Hoover, *The Memoirs of Herbert Hoover: Years of Adventure*, vi.
19. Lyons, *Herbert Hoover*, 438.
20. Herbert Hoover, *On Growing Up* (William Morrow & Company, 1962), 10.
21. Lyons, *Herbert Hoover*, 433.

Franklin D. Roosevelt

1. Nathan Miller, *FDR: An Intimate History* (Doubleday & Company, 1983), 195.
2. John Gunther, *Roosevelt in Retrospect: A Profile in History* (Harper & Brothers, 1950), 120.
3. Miller, *FDR*, 195–196.
4. Gunther, *Roosevelt in Retrospect*, 120.
5. Miller, *FDR*, 211.
6. Gunther, *Roosevelt in Retrospect*, 121.
7. *Ibid.*

Harry S. Truman

1. Harry S. Truman & Dean Acheson, *Affection & Trust: The Personal Correspondence of Harry S. Truman and Dean Acheson, 1953–1971* (Knopf, 2010), 29. H.S.T. to D.A. August 18, 1953.
2. Truman, Acheson. *Affection & Trust*, 7. H.S.T. to D.A., February 18, 1953.
3. Merle Miller, *Plain Speaking: An Oral Biography of Harry S. Truman* (G. P. Putnam's Sons, 1974), 38.
4. Truman, Acheson. *Affection & Trust*, 29.
5. Miller, *Plain Speaking*, 24.
6. Truman, Acheson. *Affection & Trust*, 63. H.S. T. to D. A. January 11, 1955.
7. Miller, *Plain Speaking*, 25.
8. Harry S. Truman, edited by Robert H. Ferrell, *Off the Record: The Private Papers of Harry S. Truman* (Harper & Row, 1980), 319. H.S.T. to Ken McCormick, July 1, 1955.
9. Truman, 346. See footnote.
10. *Ibid.*, 346–347. H.S.T. to John W. McCormack. January 10, 1957.
11. *Ibid.*, 1.
12. *Ibid.*, 369. H.S.T. to Edward F. McFaddin. September 29, 1958.
13. Truman, Acheson. *Affection & Trust*, 104–105. D.A. to H.S.T. July 18, 1955.
14. Harry S. Truman, edited by Margaret Truman, *Where the Buck Stops: The Personal and Private Writings of Harry S. Truman* (Warner Books, 1989), ix–x.
15. *Ibid.*
16. Harry S. Truman, *Letters Home* (G. P. Putnam's Sons, 1984), 14.

Dwight D. Eisenhower

1. Dwight D. Eisenhower, *At Ease: Stories I Tell to Friends* (Doubleday & Company,1967), 324.
2. *Ibid.*
3. Stephen E. Ambrose, *Eisenhower: Vol. I., 1890-1952* (Simon and Schuster, 1983), 325.
4. Stephen E. Ambrose, *To America: Personal Reflections of an Historian* (Simon & Schuster, 2002), 161.
5. Ambrose, *Eisenhower, Vol. I.*, 474-475. Ambrose also noted that the book was "Still Selling Briskly in the 1980s."
6. Peter Lyon, *Eisenhower: Portrait of a Hero* (Little, Brown & Company, 1974), 833
7. *Ibid.*, 834.
8. John S. D. Eisenhower, *Strictly Personal: A Memoir* (Doubleday & Company, 1974), 311.
9. Dwight D. Eisenhower, *Waging Peace* (Doubleday & Company, 1965), 660.
10. Lyon, *Eisenhower*, 844.
11. Dwight D. Eisenhower, edited by Robert H. Ferrell, *The Eisenhower Diaries* (W.W. Norton & Company, 1981), 385.

John F. Kennedy

1. Thomas C. Reeves, *A Question of Character: A Life of John F. Kennedy* (The Free Press, 1991), 49.
2. Joan and Clay Blair, *The Search for JFK* (Berkley Publishing, 1976), 95.
3. Reeves, *A Question of Character*, 50.
4. Robert Dallek, *An Unfinished Life: John F. Kennedy 1917-1963* (Little, Brown and Company, 2003), 66.
5. John F. Kennedy, *Why England Slept*, acknowledgments page.
6. Ted Schwarz, *Joseph P. Kennedy: The Mogul, the Mob, the Statesman, and the Making of an American Myth* (John Wiley & Sons, 2003), 293.
7. Michael O'Brien, *John F. Kennedy: A Biography* (Thomas Dunne Books, 2005), 176.
8. Blair, *The Search for JFK*, 398.
9. Hank Searle, *The Lost Prince: Young Joe, the Forgotten Kennedy* (New American Library, 1969), 301.
10. Blair, *The Search for JFK*, 398.
11. Andrew and Stephen Schlesinger, *The Letters of Arthur Schlesinger, Jr.* (Random House, 2013), letter of July 4, 1955, 112-113.
12. Theodore C. Sorensen, *Kennedy* (Harper & Row, 1965), 69.
13. *Ibid.*
14. *Ibid.*
15. Dallek, *An Unfinished Life*,199.
16. O'Brien, Michael. *John F. Kennedy*, 433.
17. Jacqueline Kennedy, *Historic Conversations on Life with John F. Kennedy: Interviews with Arthur Schlesinger, Jr., 1964* (Hyperion, 2011), 128.
18. David G Coleman, *The Fourteenth Day: JFK and the Aftermath of the Cuban Missile Crisis* (W. W. Norton & Company, 2012), 19.
19. *Ibid.*, 20.
20. James Tracy Crown, *The Kennedy Literature: A Bibliographical Essay on John F. Kennedy* (New York University Press, 1968), 23-24.
21. *Ibid.*, 147.

Lyndon B. Johnson

1. Doris Kearns, *Lyndon Johnson and the American Dream* (Harper & Row, 1976), 355.
2. George Reedy, *Lyndon B. Johnson: A Memoir* (Andrews and McMell, 1982), 13.
3. Randall B. Woods, *LBJ: Architect of American Ambition* (Free Press, 2006), 66.
4. *Ibid.*
5. Philip Reed Rulon, *The Compassionate Samaritan: The Life of Lyndon Baines Johnson* (Nelson Hall, 1981), 296.
6. Woods, *LBJ*, 880.
7. Kearns, *Lyndon Johnson and the American Dream*, 12.
8. *Ibid.*
9. *Ibid.*, 13.
10. *Ibid.*
11. *Ibid.*, 14.
12. *Ibid.*, 15.
13. Lyndon Baines Johnson, *The Vantage Point: Perspectives of the Presidency, 1963-1969* (Holt, Rinehart and Winston, 1971), ix-x.
14. Robert Dallek, *Flawed Giant: Lyndon Johnson and His Times, 1961-1973* (Oxford University Press, 1998), 608.
15. Kearns, *Lyndon Johnson and the American Dream*, 355.
16. *Ibid.*, 356.
17. *Ibid.*, 357.
18. *Ibid.*,15.
19. *Ibid.*, 18.
20. *Ibid.*

Richard M. Nixon

1. Richard M. Nixon, *Six Crisis* (Doubleday and Company, 1962), xii.
2. Stephen E. Ambrose, *Nixon: The Education of a Politician 1913-1962* (Simon & Schuster, 1987), 637.

3. Nixon, *Six Crisis*, xii.
4. Ambrose, *Nixon*, 638.
5. Nixon, *Six Crises*, xii.
6. Ambrose, *Nixon*, 640.
7. Richard Nixon, *RN: The Memoirs of Richard Nixon* (Grosset & Dunlap, 1978), 564.
8. Stephen Ambrose, *Nixon: The Triumph of a Politician, 1962–1972* (Simon & Schuster, 1989), 33.
9. Jonathan Aitken, *Nixon: A Life* (Regnery Publishing, 1993), 336.
10. *Ibid.*, 337.
11. Richard Reeves, *President Nixon: Alone in the White House* (Simon & Schuster, 2001), 139–140.
12. Conrad Black. *Richard Nixon: A Life in Full* (PublicAffairs, 2007), 531.
13. Stephen E. Ambrose, *Nixon: Ruin and Recovery, 1973–1990* (Simon & Schuster, 1991), 549.
14. *Ibid.*, 560.
15. Richard M. Nixon, *In the Arena* (Simon & Schuster, 1990), 44.
16. Black, *Nixon: A Life in Full*, 1043.
17. Ambrose, *Nixon: Ruin and Recovery*, 572.
18. Daniel Frick, *Reinventing Richard Nixon, A Cultural History of an American Obsession* (University Press of Kansas, 2008), 179.
19. Aitken, *Nixon: A Life*, 565.
20. Monica Crowley, *Nixon in Winter* (Random House, 1998), 286.
21. Monica Crowley, *Nixon Off the Record* (Random House, 1996), 56.
22. Brian Lamb, *Booknotes* (Times Books, 1997), 320.
23. Kenneth Franklin Kurz, *Nixon's Enemies* (Lowell House, 1998) 308.
24. Lamb, *Booknotes*, 321.

Gerald R. Ford

1. Gerald D. McKnight, *Breach of Trust: How the Warren Commission Failed the Nation and Why* (University Press of Kansas, 2005), 295.
2. *Ibid.*, 295.
3. Bud Vestal, *Jerry Ford Up Close: An Investigative Biography* (Coward, McCann & Geoghegan, 1974), 121.
4. Gerald R. Ford, John R. Stiles, *Portrait of the Assassin* (Simon and Schuster, 1965), 7–8.
5. Henry Hurt, *Reasonable Doubt: An Investigation into the Assassination of John F. Kennedy* (Holt, Rinehart and Winston, 1985), 32.
6. Douglas Brinkley, *Gerald R. Ford* (Times Books, 2007), 25.

7. Gerald R. Ford, *A Presidential Legacy and the Warren Commission* (Flatsigned Press, 2007), xi.
8. *Ibid.*, xxvi.
9. *Ibid.*, xxviii–xxix.
10. Howard P. Willens, *History Will Prove Us Right: Inside the Warren Commission Report on the Assassination of John F. Kennedy* (Overlook Press, 2013), 58.

Jimmy Carter

1. Jimmy Carter, *Keeping Faith: Memoirs of a President* (University of Arkansas Press, 1995), xiii.
2. Kandy Stroud, *How Jimmy Won: The Victory Campaign from Plains to the White House* (William Morrow, 1977), 126.
3. *Ibid.*
4. *Ibid.*
5. Jimmy Carter, *Why Not the Best?* (Broadman Press, 1977), 36.
6. Betty Glad, *Jimmy Carter: In Search of the Great White House* (W. W. Norton, 1980), 286.
7. Jimmy Carter, *Why Not the Best? The First Fifty Years* (University of Arkansas Press, 1996); Introduction by Douglas Brinkley, xvii.
8. Douglas Brinkley, *The Unfinished Presidency: Jimmy Carter's Journey Beyond the White House* (Viking, 1998), 48.
9. Carter, *Keeping Faith*, xiii. Carter's word processor was a Lanier.
10. Jimmy & Rosalynn Carter, *Everything to Gain: Making the Most of the Rest of Your Life* (University of Arkansas Press, 1987, 1995), xi.
11. *Ibid.*
12. *Ibid.*, 14.
13. *Ibid.*, 13.
14. Jimmy Carter, *An Outdoor Journal: Adventures and Reflections* (Bantam Books, 1988), 53.
15. *Ibid.*
16. Jimmy Carter, *Turning Point: A Candidate, a State, and a Nation Come of Age* (Times Books, 1992), xxiii.
17. Lamb, *Booknotes*, 317.
18. Jimmy Carter, *Living Faith* (Times Books, 1996), 73–74.
19. Jimmy Carter, *Sources of Strength; Meditations on Scripture for a Living Faith* (Times Books, 1997), v.
20. Jimmy Carter, *The Virtues of Aging* (The Library of Contemporary Thought, 1998), 72–73.
21. *Ibid.*, 134.
22. Jimmy Carter, *An Hour Before Daylight:*

Memories of a Rural Boyhood (Simon & Schuster, 2001), 19.
23. Jimmy Carter, *Sharing Good Times* (Simon & Schuster, 2004), xi.
24. Jimmy Carter, *Our Endanger Values: America's Moral Crisis* (Simon & Schuster, 2005), 6.
25. Jimmy Carter, *The Blood of Abraham: Insights into the Middle East* (University of Arkansas Press, 2007), 211.
26. Jimmy Carter, *White House Diary* (Farrar, Straus and Giroux, 2010), xiii.
27. *Ibid.*, 374.
28. *Ibid.*, 520.
29. *Ibid.*, 521.
30. *Ibid.*
31. Jimmy Carter, *Through the Year with Jimmy Carter: 366 Daily Meditations from the 39th President* (Zondervan, 2009), introduction.

Ronald Reagan

1. Kiron K. Skinner, Annelise Anderson, Martin Anderson, *Reagan: A Life in Letters*. (Free Press, 2003), 753.
2. Ronald Reagan with Richard G. Hubler, *Where's the Rest of Me? The Ronald Reagan Story.* (Duell, Sloan and Pearce, 1965), 13.
3. Lou Cannon, *President Reagan: The Role of a Lifetime* (Public Affairs, 2000),173.
4. Edmund Morris, *Dutch: A Memoir of Ronald Reagan* (Random House, 1999), 93.
5. *Ibid.*, 335.
6. *Ibid.*
7. *Ibid.*
8. Garry Wills, *Reagan's America: Innocents at Home* (Doubleday & Company, 1987), 288.
9. Lou Cannon, *Governor Reagan, His Rise to Power* (Public Affairs, 2003), 11.
10. *Ibid.*, 10.
11. Peggy Noonan, *When Character Was King: A Story of Ronald Reagan* (Viking, 2001), 158.
12. Morris, *Dutch*, 93.
13. Ronald Reagan, *An American Life: The Autobiography* (Simon and Schuster, 1990), 19.
14. Marc Eliot, *Reagan, the Hollywood Years* (Harmony Books, 2008), 5–6.
15. Skinner, Anderson, Anderson, *Reagan. a Life in Letters*, xv.
16. *Ibid.*, 885.
17. Ronald Reagan. *The Reagan Diaries* (Harper Collins, 2007), ix.
18. *Ibid.*
19. Skinner, Anderson, Anderson, *Reagan, a Life in Letters*, 823. The book Reagan referred to was the recently published *An American Life*.
20. *Ibid.*, 385.
21. Morris, *Dutch*, 92.
22. *Ibid.*, 92–93.

George H.W. Bush

1. George Bush with Victor Gold, *Looking Forward: An Autobiography* (Doubleday, 1987), xi–xii.
2. Russ Baker, *Family of Secrets: The Bush Dynasty, the Powerful Forces That Put It in the White House, and What Their Influence Means for America* (Bloomsbury Press, 2009), 500.
3. Herbert S. Parmet, *George Bush: The Life of a Lone Star Yankee* (Scribner, 1997), 235.
4. Barbara Bush, *A Memoir* (Scribner, 1994), 214.
5. George Bush and Brent Scowcroft, *A World Transformed* (Scribner, 1998), xi.
6. *Ibid.*, 561.
7. George Bush, *All the Best: My Life in Letters and Other Writings* (Scribner, 1999), 21–22.
8. *Ibid.*, 190. August 6, 1974.
9. *Ibid.*, 191–192.
10. Baker, *Family of Secrets*, 18. See "Poppy's Secret," pages 7–21.
11. Bush, Scowcroft, *A World Transformed*, xiii.
12. George H. W Bush, edited by Jeffrey A. Engel, *The China Diary of George H.W. Bush: The Making of a Global President* (Princeton University Press, 2008), xv.
13. *Ibid.*, 462.

Bill Clinton

1. Bill Clinton, *My Life* (Knopf, 2004), 957.
2. Carol Felsenthal, *Clinton in Exile: A President Out of the White House* (William Morrow, 2008), 118.
3. Lamb, *Booknotes*, 340.
4. *Ibid.*, 341.
5. *Ibid.*
6. *Ibid.*, 341–342.
7. Felsenthal. *Clinton in Exile* 68.
8. *Ibid.*, 69.
9. *Ibid.*
10. Taylor Branch, *The Clinton Tapes: Wrestling History with the President* (Simon & Schuster, 2009), 658.
11. *Ibid.*
12. Felsenthal, *Clinton in Exile*, 95.
13. Clinton. *My Life*, 3.
14. Felsenthal, *Clinton in Exile*, 117.
15. *Ibid.*

16. Ibid.
17. Ibid.
18. Clinton, *My Life*, 773–774.
19. Ibid., 774.
20. Ibid., acknowledgments.
21. Branch, *The Clinton Tapes*, 659.
22. Felsenthal, *Clinton in Exile*, 295.
23. Bill Clinton, *Giving: How Each of Us Can Change the World* (Knopf, 2007), xii.
24. Daniel Gross, *Bill Clinton's Back to Work* (The Washington Post), November 4, 2011.
25. Jeff Madrick, *What Bill Clinton Would Do* (The New York Times), December 9, 2011.
26. Mark Vander Weyer. *Back to Work by Bill Clinton* (The Telegraph), November 29, 2011.

George W. Bush

1. George W. Bush, *Decision Points* (Crown, 2010), 478.
2. George W. Bush, *A Charge to Keep* (William Morrow, 1999), ix.
3. Ibid.
4. Ibid.
5. Bush, *A Charge to Keep*, 135.
6. Ibid., 134.
7. Ibid., ix–x.
8. Baker, *Family of Secrets*, 420.
9. Ibid., 422. See pages 419–422 for Baker's complete account of Herskowitz's involvement on *A Charge to Keep*.
10. David Frum, *The Right Man: The Surprise Presidency of George W. Bush* (Random House, 2003), 14.
11. Paul Alexander, *Machiavelli's Shadow. the Rise and Fall of Karl Rove* (Modern Times, 2008), 80.
12. Jacob Weisberg, *The Bush Tragedy* (Random House, 2008), 228.
13. Ibid., 227
14. Bush, *Decision Points*, xi.
15. Ibid., 478.
16. Kinsley, Michael, *Bush on Bush. The New York Times Sunday Book Review* (The New York Times), December 17, 2010.
17. George W. Bush, *41: A Portrait of My Father* (Crown Publishers, 2014), 251.
18. Ibid., 264
19. Ibid., 273.

Barack Obama

1. Barack Obama, *Dreams from My Father: A Story of Race and Inheritance* (Three Rivers, 2004), ix.
2. David Remnick, *The Bridge: The Life and Rise of Barack Obama* (Knopf, 2010), 118.
3. David Maraniss, *Barack Obama: The Story* (Simon & Schuster, 2012), 483.
4. Ibid.
5. Remnick, *The Bridge*, 119.
6. Jonathan Alter, *The Promise: President Obama, Year One* (Simon & Schuster, 2010), 145.
7. Obama, *Dreams for My Father*, 133.
8. Remnick, *The Bridge*, 250.
9. Ibid.
10. Ibid.
11. Obama, *Dreams for My Father*, vii.
12. Ibid., xvii.
13. Remnick, *The Bridge*, 227.
14. Ibid., 228.
15. Aaron Klein with Brenda J. Elliot, *The Manchurian Candidate: Barack Obama's Ties to Communists, Socialists, and Other Anti-American Extremists* (WND, 2010), 14.
16. Ibid., 15.
17. Christopher Anderson, *Barack and Michelle: Portrait of an American Marriage* (William Morrow, 2009), 164.
18. Ibid.
19. Klein, *The Manchurian Candidate*, 16.
20. Remnick, *The Bridge*, 254.
21. Ibid.
22. Ibid., 230, 231.
23. Ibid., 253.
24. Shelby Steele, *A Bound Man, Why We Are Excited About Obama and Why He Can't Win* (Free Press, 2008), 102.
25. Barack Obama, *The Audacity of Hope: Thoughts on Reclaiming the American Dream* (Crown Publishers, 2006), 9.
26. Ibid., 10.
27. Ibid., 11.
28. Ibid., 44.
29. Ibid., 45.
30. Ibid., 41–42.
31. Alter, *The Promise*, 141.

Donald J. Trump

1. Donald Trump, *Think Like a Champion* (Vanguard Press, 2009), 4.
2. Michael D'Antonio, *Never Enough: Donald Trump and the Pursuit of Success* (Thomas Dunne, 2015), 186.
3. Harry Hurt, *Lost Tycoon: The Many Lives of Donald J. Trump* (W.W. Norton, 1993), 162
4. D'Antonio, *Never Enough*, 182.
5. Donald Trump with Tony Schwartz, *Trump: The Art of the Deal* (Random House, 1987), 3.

6. *Ibid.*, 49.
7. D'Antonio, *Never Enough*, 340.
8. Hurt, *Lost Tycoon*, 193.
9. John R. O'Donnell, *Trumped! The Inside Story of the Real Donald Trump: His Cunning Rise and Spectacular Fall* (Simon & Schuster, 1991), 42–43.
10. Donald Trump with Charles Leerhsen, *Trump; Surviving at the Top* (Random House, 1990), ix–x.
11. *Ibid.*, 57.
12. Donald Trump with Kate Bohner, *Trump: The Art of the Comeback* (Random House, 1997), xi.
13. *Ibid.*, xix.
14. *Ibid.*, 176–177.
15. *Ibid.*, 186.
16. Donald Trump with Dave Shiflett, *The America We Deserve* (Renaissance Books, 2000), 15.
17. Donald Trump, *The Best Real Estate Advice I Ever Received* (Thomas Nelson, 2006), xiv
18. Donald Trump and Robert T. Kiyosaki, *Why We Want You to Be Rich* (Rich Press, 2006), 18.
19. Donald Trump, *Think Big and Kick Ass* (Collins, 2007), 48.
20. *Ibid.*, 355.
21. Donald Trump with Meredith McIver, *Trump: Never Give Up* (John Wiley, 2008), 151.
22. Trump, *Think Like a Champion*, 2.
23. *Ibid.*, 1.
24. Donald Trump, *Time to Get Tough* (Regnery Publishing, 2011), 176–177.
25. Trump, *Art of the Deal*, 13.
26. Donald Trump, *Crippled America: How to Make America Great Again* (Threshold, 2015), 171.
27. Robert Slater, *No Such Thing as Over-Exposure: The Inside Life and Celebrity of Donald Trump* (Pearson, 2005), 125.
28. Michael Wolff, *Fire and Fury: Inside the Trump White House* (Henry Holt, 2018), 22.

A Brief History of Publishing the Presidents

1. John Tebbel, *A History of Book Publishing in the United States: Vol. I. the Creation of an Industry, 1630–1865* (R.R. Bowker, 1972), 46.
2. *Ibid.*
3. *Ibid.*, 129.
4. *Ibid.*, 149.
5. Peter S. Onuf, *Jeffersonian Legacies* (University Press of Virginia, 1993), 53.
6. Tebbel, *A History of Book Publishing*, 209.
7. *Ibid.*, 239.
8. Goldhurst, *Many Are the Hearts*, 121–122.
9. John Tebbel, *A History of Book Publishing in the United States: Vol. II. the Expansion of an Industry, 1865–1919* (R. R. Bowker, 1975), 516.
10. *Ibid.*, 526.
11. *Ibid.*, 525.
12. *Ibid.*, 526.
13. *Ibid.*, 221.
14. *Ibid.*, 340. The book in question was *The Foes of Our Own Household*.
15. Mahesh Grossman, *Write a Book Without Lifting a Finger* (Ten Finger Press, 2004), 18–19.
16. Arthur Klebanoff, *The Agent. Personalities, Politics, and Publishing* (Texere, 2001), 135–136.
17. *Ibid.*, 136–137.
18. *Ibid.*, 140. For Klebanoff's association with Nixon, see pages 136–142.
19. Lamb, *Booknotes*, 342.

First Editions, Limited Editions, and other Collectibles

1. McCullough, *Mornings on Horseback*, 316.
2. W. Emlen Roosevelt, *Roosevelt Vs. Newett* (privately printed, 1914), preface.
3. Richard M. Nixon, compiled by Jack S. Margolis, *The Poetry of Richard M. Nixon* (Cliff House Books, 1974).
4. Tebbel, *A History of Book Publishing in the United States: Vol. IV. the Great Change, 1940–1980*, 417.
5. Klebanoff, *The Agent*, 114.
6. *Ibid.*, 115.
7. *Ibid.*, 115–116.
8. Ian C. Ellis, *Book Finds. How to Find, Buy, and Sell Used and Rare Books* (Perigree, 2006), 46.
9. Matthew Budman, *Instant Expert: Collecting Books* (Random House, 2004), 18.

Bibliography

Adams, John Quincy. Ed. David Grayson Allen. *Diary of John Quincy Adams Vol. I & II.* The Belknap Press, Harvard University, 1981.

Aitken, Jonathan. *Nixon: A Life.* Regnery Publishing, 1993.

Alexander, Paul. *Machiavelli's Shadow: The Rise and Fall of Karl Rove.* Modern Times, 2008.

Allen, Craig. *Eisenhower and the Mass Media: Peace Prosperity & Prime-Time TV.* University of North Carolina Press, 1993.

Alter, Jonathan. *The Promise: President Obama, Year One.* Simon & Schuster, 2010.

Alterman, Eric, and Mark Green. *The Book on Bush: How George W. (Mis)Leads America.* Viking, 2004.

Ambrose, Stephen E. *Eisenhower: Vol. I. 1890–1952.* Simon & Schuster, 1983.

Ambrose, Stephen E. *Eisenhower: Vol. II. The President.* Simon & Schuster, 1984.

Ambrose, Stephen E. *Nixon: Ruin and Recovery 1973–1990.* Simon & Schuster, 1991.

Ambrose, Stephen E. *Nixon: The Education of a Politician 1913–1962.* Simon & Schuster, 1987.

Ambrose, Stephen E. *Nixon: The Triumph of a Politician 1962–1972.* Simon & Schuster, 1989.

Ambrose, Stephen E. *To America: Personal Reflection of an Historian.* Simon & Schuster, 2002.

Ammon, Harry. *James Monroe: The Quest for National Identity.* McGraw-Hill, 1971.

Anderson, Christopher. *Barack and Michelle: Portrait of an American Marriage.* William Morrow, 2009.

Anderson, Judith Icke. *William Howard Taft: An Intimate History.* W.W. Norton & Company, 1981.

Anson, Robert S. *Exile: The Unquiet Oblivion of Richard M. Nixon.* Simon & Schuster, 1984.

Anthony, Carl Sferrazzo. *Nellie Taft: The Unconventional First Lady of the Ragtime Era.* William Morrow, 2005.

Baker, Jean H. *James Buchanan.* Times Books, 2004.

Baker, Russ. *Family of Secrets: The Bush Dynasty, the Powerful Forces That Put It in the White House, and What Their Influence Means for America.* Bloomsbury Press, 2009.

Basbanes, Nicholas. *Every Book Its Reader: The Power of the Printed Word to Stir the World.* HarperCollins, 2005.

Bishop, Joseph Bucklin. *Theodore Roosevelt and His Time: Shown in His Own Letters. Vols. I–II.* Charles Scribner's Sons, 1920.

Black, Conrad. *Richard M. Nixon: A Life in Full.* Public Affairs, 2007.

Blair, Joan, and Clay, Jr. *The Search for JFK.* Berkley Publishing Corporation, 1976.

Bourne, Peter G. *Jimmy Carter.* Lisa Drew, 1997.

Branch, Taylor. *The Clinton Tapes: Wrestling History with the President.* Simon & Schuster, 2009.

Brands, H.W. *The Selected Letters of Theodore Roosevelt.* Cooper Square Press, 2001.

Brands, H.W. *T.R: The Last Romantic.* Basic Books, 1997.

Brant, Irving. *The Fourth President: A Life of James Madison.* Bobbs-Merrill Company, 1970.

Brant, Irving. *James Madison: Commander in Chief 1812–1836.* Bobbs-Merrill Company, 1961.

Brant, Irving. *James Madison: Father of the Constitution 1787–1800.* Bobbs-Merrill Company, 1950.

Brant, Irving. *James Madison: The Virginia Revolutionist, 1751–1780.* Bobbs-Merrill Company, 1941.

Brinkley, Douglas. *Gerald R. Ford.* Times Books, 2007.

Brinkley, Douglas. *The Notes: Ronald Reagan's Private Collection of Stories and Wisdom.* HarperCollins, 2011.

Brinkley, Douglas. *The Reagan Diaries.* HarperCollins, 2007.

Brinkley, Douglas. *The Unfinished Presidency: Jimmy Carter's Journey Beyond the White House.* Viking, 1998.

Brinkley, Douglas. *The Wilderness Warrior: Theodore Roosevelt and the Crusade for America.* HarperCollins, 2009.

Brodie, Fawn M. *Richard Nixon: The Shaping of His Character.* W.W. Norton, 1981.

Brodsky, Alyn. *Grover Cleveland: A Study in Character.* Truman Talley Books, 2000.
Brown, Stuart Gerry. *The Autobiography of James Monroe.* Syracuse University Press, 1959.
Budman, Matthew. *Instant Expert: Collecting Books.* Random House, 2004.
Burner, David. *Herbert Hoover: A Public Life.* Alfred A. Knopf, 1979.
Burnstein, Andrew. *The Passions of Andrew Jackson.* Knopf, 2003.
Bush, Barbara. *A Memoir.* Scribner's, 1994.
Bush, George H.W. *All the Best: My Life in Letters and Other Writings.* Scribner's, 1999.
Bush, George H.W., with Brent Scowcroft. *A World Transformed.* Knopf, 1998.
Bush, George H.W., with Victor Gold. *Looking Forward: An Autobiography.* Doubleday, 1987.
Bush, George H.W. Ed. Jeffrey A. Engel. *The China Diary of George H.W. Bush: The Making of a Global President.* Princeton University Press, 2008.
Bush, George W. *A Charge to Keep.* William Morrow, 1999.
Bush, George W. *Decision Points.* Crown Publishers, 2010.
Bush, George W. *41: A Portrait of My Father.* Crown Publishers, 2014.
Bush, George W. *Portraits of Courage: A Commander in Chief's Tribute to American's Warriors.* Crown Publishers, 2017.
Butterfield, L.H., ed. *Diary and Autobiography of John Adams: Volumes I, II & III.* The Belknap Press, Harvard University, 1962.
Cannon, James. *Time and Chance: Gerald Ford's Appointment with History.* HarperCollins, 1994.
Cannon, Lou. *Governor Reagan: His Rise to Power.* Public Affairs, 2003.
Cannon, Lou. *President Reagan: The Role of a Lifetime.* Public Affairs, 2000.
Cappon, Lester J. *The Adams—Jefferson Letters: Vol. I.* University of North Carolina Press, 1959.
Carter, Jimmy. *Always a Reckoning and Other Poems.* Times Books, 1995.
Carter, Jimmy. *Beyond the White House: Waging Peace, Fighting Disease, Building Hope.* Simon & Schuster, 2007.
Carter, Jimmy. *The Blood of Abraham: Insights into the Middle East.* University of Arkansas Press, 2007.
Carter, Jimmy. *A Call to Action: Women, Religion, Violence, and Power.* Simon & Schuster, 2014.
Carter, Jimmy. *Christmas in Plains: Memories.* Simon & Schuster, 2001.
Carter, Jimmy. *A Full Life: Reflections at Ninety.* Simon & Schuster, 2015.
Carter, Jimmy. *A Government as Good as Its People.* Simon & Shuster, 1977.
Carter, Jimmy. *The Hornet's Nest: A Novel of the Revolutionary War.* Simon & Schuster, 2003.
Carter, Jimmy. *An Hour Before Daylight: Memories of a Rural Boyhood.* Simon & Schuster, 2001.
Carter, Jimmy. *Keeping Faith: Memoirs of a President.* University of Arkansas Press, 1995.
Carter, Jimmy. *The Little Baby Snoogle-Fleejer.* Times Books, 1995.
Carter, Jimmy. *Living Faith.* Times Books, 1996.
Carter, Jimmy. *Our Endangered Values: America's Moral Crisis.* Simon & Schuster, 2005
Carter, Jimmy. *An Outdoor Journal: Adventures and Reflections.* Bantam Books, 1988.
Carter, Jimmy. *Palestine: Peace Not Apartheid.* Simon & Schuster, 2006.
Carter, Jimmy. *A Remarkable Mother.* Simon & Schuster, 2008.
Carter, Jimmy. *Sharing Good Times.* Simon & Schuster, 2004.
Carter, Jimmy. *Sources of Strength: Meditations on Scripture for a Living Faith.* Times Books, 1997.
Carter, Jimmy. *Through the Year with Jimmy Carter: 366 Daily Meditations from the 39th President.* Zondervan, 2011.
Carter, Jimmy. *Turning Point: A Candidate, a State, and a Nation Come of Age.* Times Books, 1992.
Carter, Jimmy. *The Virtues of Aging*: The Library of Contemporary Thought, 1998.
Carter, Jimmy. *White House Diary.* Farrar, Strause, and Giroux, 2010.
Carter, Jimmy. *Why Not the Best?* Broadman Press, 1977.
Carter, Jimmy. *Why Not the Best: The First Fifty Years.* University of Arkansas Press, 1996.
Carter, Jimmy, and Gerald R. Ford with Lloyd N. Cutler, Robert H. Michel. *To Assure Pride and Confidence in the Electoral Process.* Brookings Institution Press, 2002.
Carter, Jimmy, and Rosalynn Carter. *Everything to Gain: Making the Most of the Rest of Your Life.* University of Arkansas Press, 2007.
Catton, Bruce. *U.S. Grant and the American Military Tradition.* Little, Brown and Company, 1954.
Chapman, C. Stuart. *Shelby Foote: A Writer's Life.* University Press of Mississippi, 2003.
Chernow, Ron. *Washington: A Life.* The Penguin Press, 2010.
Chitwood, Oliver Perry. *John Tyler: Champion of the Old South.* American Political Biography Press, 1939.
Cleaves, Freeman. *Old Tippecanoe: William Henry Harrison and His Time.* Kennikat Press, 1969.

Clements, Kendrick A. *The Presidency of Woodrow Wilson.* University Press of Kansas, 1992.

Cleveland, Grover. *Fishing and Shooting Sketches.* The Outing Publishing Company, 1906.

Cleveland, Grover. *Presidential Problems.* The Century Company, 1904.

Cleveland, Grover. *The Writings and Speeches of Grover Cleveland.* Carrell Publishing Company, 1892.

Clinton, Bill. *Back to Work: Why We Need Smart Government for a Strong Economy.* Alfred A. Knopf, 2011.

Clinton, Bill. *Between Hope and History: Meeting America's Challenges for the 21st Century.* Times Books, 1996.

Clinton, Bill. *Giving: How Each of Us Can Change the World.* Alfred A. Knopf, 2007.

Clinton, Bill. *My Life.* Alfred A. Knopf, 2004.

Clinton, Bill, and Al Gore. *Putting People First: How We Can Change America.* Times Books, 1992.

Colacello, Bob. *Ronnie & Nancy: Their Path to the White House—1911 to 1980.* Warner Books, 2004.

Coleman, David G. *The Fourteenth Day: JFK and the Aftermath of the Cuban Missile Crisis.* W.W. Norton & Company, 2012.

Cooke, Jacob E. *The Federalist.* Edited, with Introduction and Notes. Wesleyan University Press, 1961.

Coolidge, Calvin. *The Autobiography of Calvin Coolidge.* Academy Books, 1984.

Cooper, John Milton, Jr. *Woodrow Wilson: A Biography.* Knopf, 2009.

Corsi, Jerome R. *The Obama Nation: Leftist Politics and the Cult of Personality.* Threshold Editions, 2008.

Cresson, W.P. *James Monroe.* Archon Books, 1971.

Crowley, Monica. *Nixon in Winter.* Random House, 1998.

Crowley, Monica. *Nixon Off the Record.* Random House, 1996.

Crown, James Tracy. *The Kennedy Literature: A Bibliographical Essay on John F. Kennedy.* University Press of New York, 1968.

Cunningham, Noble E., Jr. *In the Pursuit of Reason: The Life of Thomas Jefferson.* Louisiana State University Press, 1987.

Dallek, Robert. *Flawed Giant: Lyndon Johnson and His Times.* Oxford University Press, 1998.

Dallek, Robert. *An Unfinished Life: John F. Kennedy, 1917-1963.* Little, Brown and Company, 2003.

D'Antonio, Michael. *Never Enough: Donald Trump and the Pursuit of Success.* Thomas Dunne, 2015.

Davidson, John Wells. *A Crossroads of Freedom: The 1912 Campaign Speeches of Woodrow Wilson.* Yale University Press, 1956.

Dean, John W. *Warren G. Harding.* Times Books, 2004.

DeRose, Chris. *Congressman Lincoln: The Making of America's Greatest President.* Threshold Editions, 2013.

Dinunzio, Mario R. *Woodrow Wilson: Essential Writings & Speeches of the Scholar-President.* New York University Press, 2006.

Draper, Robert. *Dead Certain: The Presidency of George W. Bush.* Free Press, 2007.

Dyer, Brainerd. *Zachary Taylor.* Louisiana State University Press, 1946.

Eisenhower, David, with Julie Eisenhower. *Going Home to Glory: A Memoir of Life with Dwight D. Eisenhower, 1961-1969.* Simon & Schuster, 2010.

Eisenhower, Dwight D. *At Ease: Stories I Tell to Friends.* Doubleday & Company, 1967.

Eisenhower, Dwight D. *Crusade in Europe.* Doubleday & Company, 1948.

Eisenhower, Dwight D. *In Review: Pictures I've Kept.* Doubleday & Company, 1969.

Eisenhower, Dwight D. *Mandate for Change: 1953-1956.* Doubleday & Company, 1963.

Eisenhower, Dwight D. *Peace with Justice: Selected Addresses.* Columbia University Press, 1961.

Eisenhower, Dwight D. *Waging Peace: 1956-1961.* Doubleday & Company, 1965.

Eisenhower, Dwight D. Ed. Robert H. Ferrell. *The Eisenhower Diaries.* W.W. Norton & Company, 1981.

Eisenhower, John S.D. *Strictly Personal: A Memoir.* Doubleday & Company, 1974.

Eliot, Marc. *Reagan: The Hollywood Years.* Harmony Books, 2008.

Ellis, Ian C. *Book Finds: How to Find, Buy, and Sell Used and Rare Books.* Perigree, 2006.

Ellis, Joseph J. *American Sphinx: The Character of Thomas Jefferson.* Alfred A. Knopf, 1997.

Felsenthal, Carol. *Clinton in Exile: A President Out of the White House.* William Morrow, 2008.

Firstbrook, Peter. *The Obamas: The Untold Story of an African Family.* Crown, 2011.

Fitzpatrick, John C. *The Diaries of George Washington 1748-1799: Vol. I. 1748-1770.* Houghton Mifflin Company, 1925.

Flexner, James Thomas. *George Washington: Anguish and Farewell (1793-1799).* Little, Brown, 1972.

Ford, Betty, with Chris Chase. *The Times of My Life.* Harper & Row, 1978.

Ford, Gerald, and the Warren Commission, *A*

Presidential Legacy and the Warren Commission. Flatsigned Press, 2007.
Ford, Gerald R. *Humor and the Presidency*. Arbor House, 1987.
Ford, Gerald R. *A Time to Heal*. Harper & Row, 1979.
Ford, Gerald R., and John Corriveau. *Grand Rapids: The City That Works*. Towery Publishing Company, 1998.
Ford, Gerald R., and John R. Stiles. *Portrait of the Assassin*. Simon & Schuster, 1965.
Frank, Justin, A. *Bush on the Couch: Inside the Mind of the President*. ReganBooks, 2004
Frank, Justin A. *Obama on the Couch: Inside the Mind of the President*. Free Press, 2011.
Freeman, Douglas Southhall. *George Washington: A Biography. Volumes I & II: Young Washington*. Charles Scribner's Sons, 1948.
Freidel, Frank. *Franklin D. Roosevelt: Launching the New Deal*. Little, Brown and Company, 1973.
Frick, Daniel. *Reinventing Richard Nixon: A Cultural History of an American Obsession*. University Press of Kansas, 2008.
Frum, David. *The Right Man: The Surprise Presidency of George W. Bush*. Random House, 2003.
Giangreco, D.M. *The Soldier from Independence: A Military Biography of Harry Truman*. Zenith Press, 2009.
Glad, Betty. *Jimmy Carter: In Search of the Great White House*. W.W. Norton, 1980.
Godbold. E. Stanley, Jr. *Jimmy & Rosalynn Carter: The Georgia Years, 1924–1974*. Oxford University Press, 2010.
Goldhurst, Richard. *Many Are the Hearts: The Agony and the Triumph of Ulysses S. Grant*. Reader's Digest Press, 1975.
Goldman, Eric F. *The Tragedy of Lyndon Johnson*. Alfred A. Knopf, 1969.
Gould, Lewis L. *The William Howard Taft Presidency*. University Press of Kansas, 2009.
Graff, Henry F. *Grover Cleveland*. Times Books, 2002.
Graham, Katharine. *Personal History*. Alfred A. Knopf, 1997.
Grant, Julia Dent. Ed. John Y. Simon. *The Personal Memoirs of Julia Dent Grant*. Southern Illinois University Press, 1975.
Grant, Ulysses S. *Personal Memoirs of U.S. Grant*. Charles L. Webster & Company, 1894.
Grant, Ulysses S., III. *Ulysses S. Grant: Warrior and Statesman*. William Morrow & Company, 1969.
Gunther, John. *Roosevelt in Retrospect: A Profile in History*. Harper & Brothers, 1950.
Hagan, William T. *Theodore Roosevelt & Six Friends of the Indians*. University of Oklahoma Press, 1997.
Hamilton, Holman. *Zachary Taylor: Soldier of the Republic*. Archon Books, 1966.
Hamilton, Nigel. *Bill Clinton: An American Journey*. Random House, 2003.
Hamilton, Nigel. *JFK: Reckless Youth*. Random House, 1992.
Hayes, Rutherford B. Ed. T. Harry Williams. *Hayes: The Diary of a President, 1875–1881*. David McKay Company, 1964.
Hecht, Marie B. *John Quincy Adams: A Personal History of an Independent Man*. The Macmillan Company, 1972.
Heckscher, August. *Woodrow Wilson*. Charles Scribner's Sons, 1991.
Hoff, Joan. *Nixon Reconsidered*. Basic Books, 1994.
Hohenberg, John. *The Pulitzer Diaries: Inside America's Greatest Prize*. Syracuse University Press, 1997.
Holzer, Harold. *Lincoln at Cooper Union: The Speech That Made Abraham Lincoln President*. Simon & Schuster, 2004.
Hoover, Herbert. *The Challenge to Liberty*. Charles Scribner's Sons, 1934.
Hoover, Herbert. *The Memoirs of Herbert Hoover: The Cabinet and the Presidency, 1920–1933*. The Macmillan Company, 1952.
Hoover, Herbert. *The Memoirs of Herbert Hoover: The Great Depression, 1929–1941*. The Macmillan Company, 1952.
Hoover, Herbert. *The Memoirs of Herbert Hoover: Years of Adventure, 1874–1920*. The Macmillan Company, 1951.
Hoover, Herbert. *On Growing Up: Letters to American Boys & Girls Including "The Uncommon Man" and Other Selections*. William Morrow & Company, 1962.
Hoover, Herbert. *The Ordeal of Woodrow Wilson*. McGraw-Hill, 1958.
Hoover, Herbert, and Hugh Gibson. *The Problems of Lasting Peace*. Doubleday, Doran and Company, 1943.
Howe, George Frederick. *Chester A. Arthur: A Quarter-Century of Machine Politics*. Frederick Ungar Publishing Co., 1957.
Hurt, Henry. *Reasonable Doubt: An Investigation into the Assassination of John F. Kennedy*.
Hurt, Harry, III. *Lost Tycoon: The Many Lives of Donald J. Trump*. W.W. Norton & Co. 1993.
Jeffers, H. Paul. *Roosevelt the Explorer*. Taylor Trade, 2003.
Jefferson, Thomas. *Notes on the State of Virginia*. Holt, Rinehart and Winston, 1985.
Johnson, Andrew. Ed. Paul H. Bergeron. *The Papers of Andrew Johnson: Vol. XVI, May*

1869–July 1875. The University of Tennessee Press, 2000.
Johnson, Lyndon Baines. *This America*. Random House, 1966.
Johnson, Lyndon Baines. *The Vantage Point: Perspectives of the Presidency, 1963–1969*. Holt, Rinehart and Winston, 1971.
Kearns, Doris. *Lyndon Johnson and the American Dream*. Harper & Row, 1976.
Kennedy, Jacqueline. *Historic Conversations on Life with John F. Kennedy: Interviews with Arthur M. Schlesinger, Jr., 1964*. Hyperion, 2011.
Kennedy, John F. *The Burden and the Glory*. Harper & Row, 1964.
Kennedy, John F. *A Nation of Immigrants*. Harper & Row, 1964.
Kennedy, John F. *Profiles in Courage*. Harper & Brothers, 1956.
Kennedy, John F. *The Strategy of Peace*. Harper & Row, 1960.
Kennedy, John F. *Why England Slept*. Wilfred Funk, 1961.
Kennedy, Joseph P. Ed. Amanda Smith. *Hostage of Fortune: The Letters of Joseph P. Kennedy*. Viking, 2001.
Kennedy, Rose F. *Times to Remember*. Doubleday & Company, 1974.
Kessler, Ronald. *A Matter of Character: Inside the White House of George W. Bush*. Sentinel, 2004.
Klebanoff, Arthur. *The Agent: Personalities, Publishing, and Politics*. Texere, 2001.
Klein, Aaron, with Brenda J. Elliot. *The Manchurian President: Barack Obama's Ties to Communists, Socialists And Other Anti-American Extremists*. WND Books, 2010.
Klein, Philip Shriver. *President James Buchanan*. Pennsylvania State University Press, 1962.
Knock, Thomas J. *To End All Wars: Woodrow Wilson and the Quest for a New World Order*. Oxford University Press, 1992.
Koch, Adrienne, and William Peden. *The Life and Selected Writings of Thomas Jefferson*. The Modern Library, Random House, 1944.
Korda, Michael. *Ike: An American Hero*. HarperCollins, 2007
Kranish, Michael, and Marc Fisher. *Trump Revealed: An American Journey of Ambition, Ego, Money, and Power*. Scribner's, 2016.
Krock, Arthur. *Memoirs: Sixty Years on the Firing Line*. Funk & Wagnalls, 1968.
Kurtz, Michael L. *The JFK Assassination Debates: Long Gunman Versus Conspiracy*. University Press of Kansas, 2006.
Kurz, Kenneth F. *Nixon's Enemies*. Lowell House, 1998.
Lamb, Brian. *Booknotes: America's Finest Authors on Reading, Writing, and the Power of Ideas*. Times Books, 1997.
Leaming, Barbara. *Jack Kennedy: The Education of a Statesman*. W.W. Norton & Co. 2006
Leech, Margaret. *In the Days of McKinley*. Harper, 1960.
Leech, Margaret, and Harry J. Brown. *The Garfield Orbit*. Harper & Row, 1978.
Lengel, Edward G. *General George Washington: A Military Life*. Random House, 2005.
Levin, Phyllis Lee. *Edith and Woodrow: The Wilson White House*. Scribner's, 2001.
Lincoln, Abraham. Ed. David D. Anderson. *The Literary Works of Abraham Lincoln*. Charles E. Merrill Publishing Company, 1970.
Lincoln, Abraham. Ed. Roy P. Basler. *The Collected Works of Abraham Lincoln: Vol. III*. Rutgers University Press, 1953.
Lincoln, Abraham. Ed. Roy P. Basler. *Lincoln: His Speeches and Writings*. De Capo Press, 1946.
Lincoln, Evelyn. *My Twelve Years with John F. Kennedy*. David McKay Company, 1965.
Link, Arthur S. *The Papers of Woodrow Wilson: Vol. IV (1885)* Princeton University Press, 1968.
Lucier, James P. *The Political Writings of James Monroe*. Regnery Publishing, 2001
Lukas, J. Anthony. *Nightmare. the Underside of the Nixon Years*. Viking Press, 1976.
Lurie, Jonathan. *William Howard Taft: The Travails of a Progressive Conservative*. Cambridge University Press, 2012.
Lyon, Peter. *Eisenhower: Portrait of the Hero*. Little, Brown and Company, 1974.
Lyons, Eugene. *Herbert Hoover: A Biography*. Doubleday & Company, 1964.
Malone, Dumas. *Jefferson and the Ordeal of Liberty*. Little, Brown and Company, 1962.
Malone, Dumas. *Jefferson and the Rights of Man*. Little, Brown and Company, 1951.
Malone, Dumas. *Jefferson the Virginian*. Little, Brown and Company, 1948.
Malone, Dumas. *The Sage of Monticello*. Little, Brown and Company, 1981.
Mansfield, Stephen. *The Faith of George W. Bush*. Penguin, 2003.
Maraniss, David. *Barack Obama: The Story*. Simon & Schuster, 2012.
Mason, Alpheus Thomas. *William Howard Taft: Chief Justice*. Simon & Schuster, 1965.
Mazlish, Bruce. *In Search of Nixon: A Psychohistorical Inquiry*. Basic Books, 1972.
Mazlish, Bruce, and Edwin Diamond. *Jimmy Carter: An Interpretive Biography*. Simon & Schuster, 1979.
McCullough, David. *John Adams*. Simon & Schuster, 2001.

McCullough, David. *Mornings on Horseback*. Simon & Schuster, 1981.
McCullough, David. *Truman*. Simon & Schuster, 1992.
McFeely, William S. *Grant: A Biography*. W.W. Norton & Company, 1981.
McKinley, William. *Bits of Wisdom*. H.M. Caldwell, 1901.
McKnight, Gerald D. *Breach of Trust: How the Warren Commission Failed the Nation and Why*. University Press of Kansas, 2005.
Meacham, Jon. *American Lion: Andrew Jackson in the White House*. Random House, 2008.
Meachen, Jon. *Destiny and Power: The American Odyssey of George Herbert Walker Bush*. Random House, 2015.
Miller, Merle. *Plain Speaking: An Oral Biography of Harry S. Truman*. G.P. Putnam's Sons, 1974.
Miller, Nathan. *FDR: An Intimate History*. Doubleday & Company, 1983.
Miller, William Lee. *Yankee from Georgia: The Emergence of Jimmy Carter*. Times Books, 1978.
Mills, Judie. *John F. Kennedy*. Franklin Watts, 1988.
Morison, Elting E. *The Letters of Theodore Roosevelt: Vol. I-II*. Harvard University Press, 1951.
Morris, Edmund. *Colonel Roosevelt*. Random House, 2010.
Morris, Edmund. *Dutch: A Memoir of Ronald Reagan*. Random House, 1999.
Morris, Edmund. *The Rise of Theodore Roosevelt*. Ballantine Books, 1979.
Morris, Edmund. *Theodore Rex*. Random House, 2001.
Nagel, Paul C. *John Quincy Adams: A Public Life, a Private Life*. Alfred A. Knopf, 1997.
Nevins, Allan. *Grover Cleveland: A Study in Courage*. Dodd, Mead & Company, 1966.
Nichols, Roy Franklin. *Franklin Pierce: Young Hickory of the Granite Hills*. University of Pennsylvania Press, 1958.
Niven, John. *Martin Van Buren: The Romantic Age of American Politics*. Oxford University Press, 1983.
Nixon, Richard M. *Beyond Peace*. Random House, 1994.
Nixon, Richard M. *In the Arena: A Memoir of Victory, Defeat and Renewal*. Simon & Schuster, 1990.
Nixon, Richard M. *Leaders*. Warner Books, 1982.
Nixon, Richard M. *1999: Victory Without War*. Simon & Schuster, 1988.
Nixon, Richard M. *No More Vietnams*. Arbor House, 1985.
Nixon, Richard M. *The Real War*. Warner Books, 1980.
Nixon, Richard M. *RN: The Memoirs of Richard Nixon*. Grosset & Dunlap, 1978.
Nixon, Richard M. *Seize the Moment*. Simon & Schuster, 1992.
Nixon, Richard M. *Six Crises*. Doubleday, 1962.
Noonan, Peggy. *When Character Was King: A Story of Ronald Reagan*. Viking, 2001.
Obama, Barack. *The Audacity of Hope: Thoughts on Reclaiming the American Dream*. Crown, 2006.
Obama, Barack. *Dreams from My Father: A Story of Race and Inheritance*. Three Rivers Press, 2004.
Obama, Barack. *Of Thee I Sing: A Letter to My Daughters*. Knopf, 2010.
O'Brien, Michael. *John F. Kennedy: A Biography*. Thomas Dunne Books, 2005.
O'Donnell, John R., with James Rutherford. *Trumped! The Inside Story of the Real Donald Trump and His Cunning Rise and Spectacular Fall*. Simon & Schuster, 1991.
O'Donnell, Kenneth P., with David F. Powers and Joe McCarthy. *Johnny, We Hardly Knew Ye*. Little, Brown and Company, 1972.
Onuf, Peter S. *Jeffersonian Legacies*. University Press of Virginia, 1993.
O'Toole, Patricia. *When Trumpets Call*. Simon & Schuster, 2005.
Parmet, Herbert S. *George Bush: The Life of a Lone Star Yankee*. Scribner's, 1997.
Parmet, Herbert S. *Jack: The Struggles of John F. Kennedy*. The Dial Press, 1980.
Perlstein, Rick. *Nixonland: The Rise of a President and the Fracturing of America*. Scribner's, 2008.
Perret, Geoffrey. *Ulysses S. Grant: Soldier & President*. Random House, 1997.
Perry, Mark. *Grant and Twain: The Story of a Friendship That Changed America*. Random House, 2004.
Polk, James Knox. Ed. Allan Nevins. *Polk: The Diary of a President, 1845-1849*. Longmans, Green and Co., 1929.
Posner, Gerald. *Case Closed: Lee Harvey Oswald and the Assassination of JFK*. Random House, 1993.
Pringle, Henry F. *The Life and Times of William Howard Taft: A Biography Vol. I-II*. Archon Books, 1964.
Punke, Michael. *Last Stand: George Bird Grinnell, the Battle to Save the Buffalo, and the Birth of the New West*. Smithsonian Books, 2007.
Rayback, Robert J. *Milliard Fillmore: Biography of a President*. American Political Biography Press, 1959.
Reagan, Ronald. *An American Life: The Autobiography*. Simon & Schuster, 1990.

Reagan, Ronald, with Richard C. Hubler. *Where's the Rest of Me? The Ronald Reagan Story.* Duell, Sloan and Pearce, 1965.

Reedy, George. *Lyndon B. Johnson: A Memoir.* Andrews and McMeel, 1982.

Reeves, Richard. *President Nixon: Alone in the White House.* Simon & Schuster, 2001.

Reeves, Thomas C. *A Question of Character: A Life of John F. Kennedy.* The Free Press, 1991.

Remnick, David. *The Bridge: The Life and Rise of Barack Obama.* Knopf, 2010.

Rich, Frank. *The Greatest Story Ever Sold: The Decline and Fall of Truth in Bush's America.* Penguin, 2006.

Richardson, Don. *Conversations with Carter.* Lynne Rienner Publishers, 1998.

Rogak, Lisa. *Haunted Heart: The Life and Times of Stephen King.* St. Martin's Press, 2008.

Roosevelt, Franklin D. *On Our Way.* Da Capo Press, 1973.

Roosevelt, Theodore. *Gouverneur Morris.* Arlington House.

Roosevelt, Theodore. *Letters and Speeches.* Library of America, 2004.

Roosevelt, Theodore. *Letters to His Children.* Charles Scribner's Sons, 1949.

Roosevelt, Theodore. *The Naval War of 1812.* The Modern Library, 1999.

Roosevelt, Theodore. *Ranch Life and the Hunting-Trail.* St. Martin's Press, 1985.

Roosevelt, Theodore. *The Rough Riders: An Autobiography.* The Library of America, 2004.

Roosevelt, Theodore. *The Winning of the West.* University of Nebraska Press, 1995.

Rulon, Philip Reed. *The Compassionate Samaritan: The Life of Lyndon Baines Johnson.* Nelson Hall, 1981.

Russell, Francis. *The Shadow of Blooming Grove: Warren G. Harding in His Times.* McGraw-Hill Book Company, 1968.

Salinger, Pierre. *With Kennedy.* Doubleday & Company, 1966.

Sandler, Martin W. *The Letters of John F. Kennedy.* Bloomsbury Press, 2013.

Schlesinger, Andrew, and Stephen Schlesinger. *The Letters of Arthur Schlesinger, Jr.* Random House, 2013.

Schlesinger, Robert. *White House Ghosts: Presidents and Their Speechwriters.* Simon & Schuster, 2008.

Schwarz, Ted. *Joseph P. Kennedy: The Mogul, the Mob, the Statesman, and the Making of an American Myth.* John Wiley & Sons, 2003.

Searls, Hank. *The Lost Prince: Young Joe, the Forgotten Kennedy.* World Publishing, 1969.

Sellers, Charles. *James K. Polk, Jacksonian: 1795–1843.* Princeton University Press, 1957.

Shenk, Joshua Wolf. *Lincoln's Melancholy: How Depression Challenged a President and Fueled His Greatness.* Houghton Mifflin Company, 2005.

Sievers, Harry J. *Benjamin Harrison: Hoosier President.* Vol. III. Bobbs-Merrill Company, 1968.

Singer, Mark. *Trump and Me.* Tim Duggan Books, 2016.

Skinner, Kiron K., with Annelise and Martin Anderson. *Reagan: A Life in Letters.* The Free Press, 2003.

Skinner, Kiron K., with Annelise and Martin Anderson. *Reagan in His Own Hand: The Writings of Ronald Reagan That Reveal His Revolutionary Vision for America.* The Free Press, 2001.

Slater, Robert. *No Such Thing as Over-Exposure: Inside the Life and Celebrity of Donald Trump.* Pearson, 2005.

Smith, Gene. *When the Cheering Stopped: The Last Years of Woodrow Wilson.* William Morrow and Company, 1964.

Smith, Jean Edward. *Grant.* Simon & Schuster, 2001.

Smith, Page. *John Adams: Volumes I & II.* Greenwood Press, 1963.

Smith, Richard Norton. *An Uncommon Man: The Triumph of Herbert Hoover.* Simon & Schuster, 1984.

Sorensen, Theodore C. *Kennedy.* Harper & Row, 1965.

Steel, Shelby. *A Bound Man: Why We Are Excited About Obama and Why He Can't Win.* Free Press, 2008.

Stroud, Kandy. *How Jimmy Won: The Victory Campaign from Plains to the White House.* William Morrow & Company, 1977.

Takiff, Michael. *A Complicated Man: The Life of Bill Clinton as Told by Those Who Know Him.* Yale University Press, 2010.

Tebbel, John. *A History of Book Publishing in the United States: Vol. I. the Creation of an Industry, 1630–1865.* R.R. Bowker, 1972.

Tebbel, John. *A History of Book Publishing in the United States: Vol. II. the Expansion of an Industry, 1865–1919.* R.R. Bowker, 1975.

Tebbel, John. *A History of Book Publishing in the United States: Vol. IV. the Great Change, 1940–1980.* R.R. Bowker, 1981.

terHorst, Jerald F. *Gerald Ford and the Future of the Presidency.* The Third Press, 1974.

Truman, Harry S. *Memoirs: Year of Decisions: Vol. I.* Doubleday & Company, 1955.

Truman, Harry S. *Memoirs: Years of Trial and Hope: Vol. II.* Doubleday & Company, 1956.

Truman, Harry S. *Mr. Citizen.* Bernard Geis Associates, 1960.

Truman, Harry S. *Public Papers of the Presidents of the United States: Harry S. Truman 1952-53, Containing the Public Messages, Speeches and Statements of the President.* United States Government Printing Office, 1966.

Truman, Harry S. *Truman Speaks.* Columbia University Press, 1960.

Truman, Harry S., and Dean Acheson. *Affection and Trust: The Personal Correspondence of Harry S. Truman and Dean Acheson, 1953-1971.* Alfred A. Knopf, 2010.

Truman, Harry S. Ed. David Gellen. *The Quotable Truman.* Carroll & Graf, 1994.

Truman, Harry S. Ed. Margaret Truman. *Where the Buck Stops: The Personal and Private Writings of Harry S. Truman.* Warner Books, 1989.

Truman, Harry S. Ed. Monte M. Poen. *Letters Home.* G.P. Putnam's Sons, 1984.

Truman, Harry S. Ed. Monte M. Poen. *Strictly Personal and Confidential: The Letters Harry Truman Never Mailed.* Little, Brown and Company, 1982.

Truman Harry S. Ed. Robert H. Ferrell. *Off the Record: The Private Papers of Harry S. Truman.* Harper & Row, 1980.

Trump, Donald J. *The Best Golf Advice I Ever Received.* Crown, 2005.

Trump, Donald J. *The Best Real Estate Advice I Ever Received.* Thomas Nelson, 2006.

Trump, Donald J. *Crippled America: How to Make America Great Again.* Threshold Editions, 2015.

Trump, Donald J. *Time to Get Tough: Making America #1 Again.* Regnery, 2011.

Trump, Donald J. *Trump 101. The Way to Success.* John Wiley, 2007.

Trump, Donald J. *The Way to the Top: The Best Business Advice I Ever Received.* Crown, 2004.

Trump, Donald J., and Bill Zanker. *Think Big and Kick Ass in Business and Life.* Collins, 2007.

Trump, Donald J., and Robert T. Kiyosaki. *Midas Touch. Why Some Entrepreneurs Get Rich—And Why Most Don't.* Plata Publishing, 2011.

Trump, Donald J., and Robert T Kiyosaki. *Why We Want You to Be Rich: Two Men, One Message.* Rich Press, 2006

Trump, Donald J., with Charles Leerhsen. *Surviving at the Top.* Random House1990.

Trump, Donald J., with Dave Shiflett. *The America We Deserve.* Renaissance Books, 2000.

Trump, Donald J., with Kate Bohner. *Trump: The Art of the Comeback.* Random House, 1997.

Trump, Donald J., with Meredith McIver. *Trump: How to Get Rich.* Random House, 2004.

Trump, Donald J. with Meredith McIver. *Trump: Never Give Up.* John Wiley & Sons, 2008.

Trump, Donald J., with Meredith McIver. *Trump: Think Like a Billionaire.* Random House, 2004.

Trump, Donald J., with Tony Schwartz. *The Art of the Deal.* Random House, 1987.

Trump, Donald J. Ed. Hart Seely. *Bard of the Deal.* Harper, 2015.

Trump, Donald J. Ed. Richard Carlton London. *Trump: The Art of the Tweet.* London Calling, 2017.

Twain, Mark. Ed. Hamlin Hill. *Mark Twain's Letters to His Publishers.* University of California Press, 1967.

Twain, Mark. Ed. Harriet Elinor Smith. *Autobiography of Mark Twain: Volume I.* University of California Press, 2010.

Twain, Mark. Ed. Lin Salamo and Harriet Elinor Smith. *Mark Twain's Letters: Volume 5: 1872-1873.* University of California Press, 1997.

Tyrrell, R. Emmett, Jr. *The Clinton Crack-Up: The Boy President's Life After the White House.* Thomas Nelson, 2007.

Unger, Craig. *The Fall of the House of Bush.* Scribner's, 2007.

Unger, Harlow Giles. *The Last Founding Father: James Monroe and a Nation's Call to Greatness.* Da Capo Press, 2009.

Van Buren, Martin. *The Autobiography of Martin Van Buren.* Augustus M. Kelley, 1969.

Vestal, Bud. *Jerry Ford, Up Close: An Investigative Biography.* Coward, McCann & Geoghegan, 1974.

Wagenknecht, Edward. *The Seven Worlds of Theodore Roosevelt.* Longmans, Green & Co., 1958.

Walworth, Arthur. *Woodrow Wilson.* W.W. Norton, 1978.

Ward, Geoffrey C. *Before the Trumpet: Young Franklin Roosevelt 1882-1905.* Konecky & Konecky, 1985.

The Warren Commission (Earl Warren, Richard B. Russell, John S. Cooper, Hale Boggs, Gerald R. Ford, Allen W. Dulles, John J. McCloy). *The Warren Commission Report: The President's Commission on the Assassination of President Kennedy.* Barnes & Noble, 1992.

Washington, George. *The Diaries of George Washington: Vol. I-IV.* Houghton Mifflin Company, 1925.

Washington, George. *George Washington's Diaries: An Abridgement.* The University Press of Virginia, 1999.

Washington, George. *The Journal of Major George Washington.* Xerox, 1966.

Weinstein, Edwin A. *Woodrow Wilson: A Med-*

ical and Psychological Biography. Princeton University Press, 1981.
Weisberg, Jacob. *The Bush Tragedy*. Random House, 2008.
White, Ronald C., Jr. *The Eloquent President: A Portrait of Lincoln Through His Words*. Random House, 2005.
White, William Allen. *A Puritan in Babylon: The Story of Calvin Coolidge*. The Macmillan Company, 1938.
Wicker, Tom. *One of Us: Richard Nixon and the American Dream*. Random House, 1991.
Widmer, Ted. *Martin Van Buren*. Times Books, 2005.
Willens, Howard P. *History Will Prove Us Right: Inside the Warren Commission Report on the Assassination of John F. Kennedy*. Overlook Press, 2013.
Wills, Garry. *James Madison*. Times Books, 2002.
Wills, Garry. *Reagan's America: Innocents at Home*. Doubleday & Company, 1987.
Wilson, R.L. *Theodore Roosevelt: Outdoorsman*. Winchester Press, 1971.
Wilson, Woodrow. *The New Freedom*. Doubleday & Company, 1913.
Wolff, Michael. *Fire and Fury: Inside the Trump White House*. Henry Holt, 2018.
Woods, Randall B. *LBJ: Architect of American Ambition*. Free Press, 2006.
Woodward, W.E. *Meet General Grant*. Liveright Publishing Corp., 1965.
Zelizer, Julian E. *Jimmy Carter*. Times Books, 2010.

Index

ABC Television 115, 126
Abraham Lincoln Association 47
Acheson, Dean 102–103, 104, 106
Adams, Abigail 12
Adams, Charles 30
Adams, Charles Francis 31–32
Adams, Henry 30
Adams, John 3, 5, 141–14, 18, 23, 25, 27, 30, 167
Adams, John Quincy 4, 9, 13, 24, 25–32, 33, 39, 63, 69, 99, 142, 149, 152, 167, 185, 186
Adams, Louisa 27, 30
Adams, Thomas 27
Addresses Upon the American Road 97, 98
African Game Animals 80
African Game Trails 70, 78
Agar, Herbert 114
The Agent: Personalities, Politics and Publishing 188–189, 194
Agnew, Spiro 139, 155
Agricola, Georgius 94, 95, 191–192
Aitken, Jonathan 125–126, 129
Albert Frost & Sons 192
Alder, Bill (Books) 178
Algase, Gertrude 111
All the Best: My Life in Letters 155–156
Alter, Jonathan 161
Always a Reckoning and Other Poems 142
Ambrose, Stephen 108, 125, 128–129
America and the World War 79, 80
The America We Deserve 177–178, 181
American Big Game 76
An American Epic 98
American Historical Association 78
American Ideals 75
American Individualism 96
An American Life: The Autobiography 151–152
American Problems 78
Ammon, Harry 23–24
Anas 19
Anderson, Annelise 152
Anderson, Christopher 172
Anderson, David D. 44, 48
Anderson, Martin 152

Anthony, Carl S. 82
The Anti-Trust Act and the Supreme Court 83
Applewood, John 43
Applewood Books 47
The Apprentice 178, 181
Arbor House 128, 135
Arthur, Chester Alan 50, 65
As We Remember Joe 113
At Ease: Stories I Tell to Friends 110
Atlanta Constitution 100
Atlantic Monthly 47, 65, 67, 90
The Audacity of Hope 172–173, 174
Audiobook 147
Audubon, John James 76
An Autobiography 71, 78, 79
The Autobiography of Calvin Coolidge 91–92, 195
Autobiography of James Monroe 24–25
Autobiography of Mark Twain 53, 55, 56
Autobiography of Martin Van Buren 34–35
Autopen 104–105
Away from Home: Letters to My Family 147
Ayers, Bill 172

Back to Work 163–164
Badeau, Adam 51, 58–59
Bagehot, Walter 84, 85, 86
Baker, Jean H. 44
Baker, Russ 155, 156, 165
Bantam 139, 148–149
Barnett, Robert 159
Basler, Roy P. 47
Bauer, Geor *see* Agricola, Georgius
Belknap Press 13, 31
Benton, Thomas Hart 35, 72, 73
Bergeron, Paul 48, 50
Bernstein, Carl 126
The Best Business Advice I Ever Received see *Trump, the Way to the Top*
The Best Golf Advice I Ever Received 178
The Best Real Estate Advice I Ever Received 179
Between Hope and History 158
Beyond Peace 130

Beyond the White House 146
Bishop, Joseph 80
Black, Conrad 129
Black, Douglas M. 108
Black, Jeremiah S. 42–43
Blair, Clay 113–114
Blair, Joan 113–114
The Blood of Abraham 140, 146
Boggs, Hale 131
Bohner, Kate 177
Bonaparte, Napoleon 33, 53
A Book-Lover's Holiday in the Open 81
Book of Logick 21–22
Booknotes 130, 142, 189
Bowker, R.R. 183
Branch, Taylor 160–161, 162
Brandeis, Louis 84
Brands, H.W. 69, 71, 79
Branner, John 95
Brant, Irving 21–22
Brinkley, David 82, 152–153
Broadman Press 138–139
Brookings Institute Press 135
Brown, Stuart Gerry 24–25
Buchanan, James 42–44, 48, 68, 185
The Burden and the Glory 117
Burner, David 93
Burnstein, Andrew 33
Bush, Barbara 164
Bush, George H.W. 4, 130, 154–158, 167–168, 193
Bush, George W. 135, 163, 164–168, 173, 180
Bush, Millie 164
Business International Corporation 169
Business International Money Report 169
Butterfield, L.H. 3, 14

C-Span 130, 159, 189
Calhoun, John 28
A Call to Action 149
Cannon, Lou 150, 151
Carrell Publishing Company 67
Carter, Amy 144
Carter, Gloria 137
Carter, Jimmy 2, 4, 62, 106, 135, 137–149, 152, 163, 164, 165, 178, 188, 194, 196
Carter, Lillian 143, 147
Carter, Rosalynn 140, 143–144, 147, 149
Carter Presidential Library 140, 146–147
Cashill, Jack 171–172
CBS Television 123, 126
Celi, Lou 169
Century Company 57, 67
Century Magazine 51–53, 55, 56, 61, 67
Cerf, Bennett 100, 101
The Challenge to Liberty 96, 151

The Challenges We Face 124
Change We Can Believe In 174
A Charge to Keep 164–166
Charles Webster Company 54, 57
Chernow, Ron 5, 7
Chicago Daily News 45
Chicago Historical Society 39
Chicago Press & Tribune 45
The Chief Magistrate and His Powers 83
Childs, George 50
China Diary 157
Christ, Jesus 88
Christmas in Plains: Memories 144
Churchill, Winston 74, 111, 112, 128, 168
The Churchill Lecture 196
Clay, Henry 39
Clements, Kendrick A. 87
Cleveland, Grover 2, 66–69, 98, 178, 186
Clifford, Clark 115
Clinton, Hillary 159, 161, 163, 177, 188
Clinton, Bill 158–164, 189
cocaine 57–58, 62–63
Coleman, David C. 117
Collected Works of Abraham Lincoln 47
College Star 119
Collier's 67
Columbia University Press 106, 109
Complete Works of Abraham Lincoln 47
Complete Writings of Theodore Roosevelt, Elkhorn Edition 81
Congressional Government 86, 87
The Conservation of Womanhood and Childhood 78
Coolidge, Calvin 91–92, 96, 195
Cooper, John Milton 74, 88
Cooper, John Sherman 131
Coran, George H. 90
Corriveau, John 135
Cosmopolitan Magazine & Book Corporation 91
Creel, George 90
Cresson, W.P. 22–23
The Crimson 100
Crippled America 178, 181
Cromwell, Oliver 77
Cronkite, Walter 122
A Crossroads of Freedom 89
Crowley, Monica 130
Crown, James Tracy 117–118
Crown Business 178
Crown Publishers 174
Crusade in Europe 105, 108, 124
Culter, Lloyd N. 135, 145
Cuomo, Mario 130
Custer, George 76

Daily Advertiser 20
Dallek, Robert 116, 122
D'Antonio, Michael 175
Dark Masquerade 101
Darwin, Charles 78
Davidson, John Wells 89
De Natura Fossiliarum 95
De Re Metallica 94, 141, 191–192
Decision Points 166–167
Decline and Fall of the Roman Empire 8, 39
The Deer Family 78
Defense of the Constitution of the Government of the United States of America 12–13
De Gaulle, Charles 126, 128
Dennie, Joseph 27
Dermot MacMorrogh 31
DeRose, Chris 45
Diaries of George Washington 3, 9–11
Diary and Autobiography of John Adams 3, 13–14
Diary & Letters of Rutherford Birchard Hayes 63–64
Diary of James K. Polk 39–40
Diary of John Quincy Adams 31
Dickens, Charles 31, 52
Dinunzio, Mario R. 86, 87, 89
Dinwiddie, Robert 6, 7
Division and Reunion, 1829–1889, 88
Doubleday & Company 104, 108, 109, 110, 124, 125, 192
Douglas, Dr. John Hancock 57, 60
Douglas, Michael 176
Douglas, Stephen 45–46
Dreams from My Father 170–172, 173, 174
Drew, Elizabeth 138
Drexel, Joseph 58
Duell, Pearce 150
Duell, Sloan 150
Dulles, Allen 131
Dunlap, John 11
Duplicate Letters, the Fisheries and the Mississippi 29–30
Dystel, Jane 171

Easton Press 189, 193, 194, 195, 196
Eisenhower, Dwight D. 105, 106, 107–110, 123, 124, 125, 128, 160, 180, 195
Eisenhower, John S.D. 109, 189
Eisenhower, Mamie 124
The Eisenhower Diaries 110
Eliot, Marc 152
Ellis, Joseph 15
Ely, Richard 87
Engel, Jeffery A. 157
Engineer and Mining Journal 93, 94
Enlai, Zhou 125, 128

Essential Writings and Speeches of Woodrow Wilson 86
Everything to Gain 140, 141, 143

Faith: A Journey for All 149
Farrar & Rinehart 101, 192
Faust, A.B. 27
Feast 169
The Federalist 20–22, 68, 86
Feinman, Barbara 188
Felsenthal, Carol 159
Ferrell, Robert H. 105, 106, 110
Ferris, Henry 171
Fillmore, Millard 37–38
Financing Foreign Operations 169
Fischer, John 116
Fishing and Shooting Sketches 67, 99, 186
Fishing for Fun and to Wash Your Soul 99, 141
Fitzpatrick, John C. 36–37
Flatsigned Press 137, 195–196
Follett, Foster & Company 46
Foote, Shelby 62
Ford, Betty 131
Ford, Gerald R. 131–137, 139, 145, 152, 156, 188, 193, 194, 196
Ford Presidential Library 135
Forest and Stream 76
41: A Portrait of My Father, 167–168
Fowler, Joseph S. 49
Franklin Library 193–194, 195
Freedom Betrayed 99
Frick, Daniel 129
Frost, Albert & Sons 192
Frum, David 165
A Full Life, a Reflection at Ninety 149
Funk, Wilfred 112

Gable, John Allen 71
Gaddis, Lewis 168
Gandhi, Mahatma 126
Gardner, John W. 117
Garfield, James 50, 64, 65
Gekko, Gordon 176
Gentz, Frederick Von 27
George W. Bush Presidential Library 166–167, 168
George Washington 88
George Washington's Expense Account 11
Gibson, Hugh 97
Gideon, John 21
Gilder, Richard W. 53–54
Gilmore, James R. 74
Giving 163–164
Global Stability 196
Gold, Victor 154–155
Goldhurst, Richard 52–53, 55, 185

Goldwater, Barry 155
Good Hunting 78
Goodwin, Doris Kearns 120–122, 122, 123
Gorbachev, Mikhail 155
Gore, Al 158
Gottlieb, Robert 162
Gouvenuer Morris 77
Gouvernuer, Samuel L. 24
A Government as Good as Its People 139
G.P. Putnam's & Sons 70, 71, 72, 73, 78, 186–187, 191
Graham, Billy 165
Graham, Catharine M. 8
Graham, Katherine 159, 162
Grammy Awards 173–174
Grand Rapids: The City That Works 135
Grant, Fred 55, 59, 60
Grant, Julia 52, 53, 55, 58, 60, 62
Grant, Ulysses S 1, 34, 50–63, 67, 98, 118, 123, 127, 139, 166, 185, 195
Grant, Ulysses III 53, 56, 60
The Great Adventure 79
Great Again see *Crippled America*
Grinnell, George Bird 76, 77
Grosset & Dunlap 127
Grossman, Mahesh 188
Gunther, John 100

Halliday, Steve 149
Hamilton, Alexander 20, 21, 36
Harcourt Brace 111–112
Harding, Warren G. 83, 90–91
Harding Publishing Company 90
Harper & Row 139
Harper Brothers 88, 111–112
Harper Collins 81
Harper's Magazine 88, 114
Harrison, Benjamin 1, 65–66, 68, 186
Harrison, William H. 32–34
Harvard Educational Review 158
Harvard Law Review 170–171
Harvard University Press 113
Have Faith in Massachusetts 91
Hawthorne, Nathaniel 41
Hay, George 24
Hayes, Rutherford B. 4, 63–65
Hayes: Diary of a President 1875–1881, 63
Heaney, Seamus 159
Hecht, Marie B. 27
Heckscher, August 90
Hemingway, Ernest 71
Henry, Patrick 3, 14
Heritage Press 193
Hero Tales from American History 76
Herskowitz, Mickey 165
Hess, Stephen 125

Heymen, Ken 119
Hicks, William W. 49
Hillman, William 102, 104, 107
The History of Book Publishing in the United States 183, 193–194
A History of Political Economy in the United States 87
A History of the American People 89
History of the Rise, Progress and Termination of the American Revolution 13
History Will Make Us Right 136–137
Hitler Diaries 48
Hobart, Garret 77
Hochman, Steve 139
Holcombe, Arthur 110
Holmes, Oliver Wendell 84
Holt, Rineman & Winston 119
Holzer, Harold 45, 47
Hoover, Alan 99
Hoover, Herbert 2, 92–99, 101, 130, 141, 149, 163, 178, 191–192, 195
Hoover, Lou Henry 92, 94, 95, 97, 99, 141
Hoover Institute at Stanford University 99
Hopkins, George P. 20–21
The Hornet's Nest 145, 164
Houghton Mifflin 9, 72, 87
An Hour of Daylight 144
Houston Chronicle 165
Hubler, Richard G. 150–151
Hughes, Charles Evans 97
Hughes, Karen 165
Humor and the Presidency 135
Hunting in Many Lands 76
Hunting Trips of a Ranchman 71–72, 76, 191
Hurt, Harry 139
Hurt, Henry 176

Iacocca, Lee 175
Ihrie, George P. 58
In Review: Pictures I've Kept, 110
In the Arena: A Memoir of Victory, Defeat & Renewal 129, 189
Independent Journal 21
Ingalls, W.R. 92–93
Inquiry into the Origin and Course of Political Parties in the United States 36
International Review 86
Iron Ore 79
It Takes a Village 188

Jackson, Andrew 2, 32–34, 41, 51, 84, 157
Jameson, John Franklin 89
Jay, John 20
Jefferson, Thomas 1, 2, 5, 6, 11, 12, 13, 14–20, 21, 23, 27, 29, 32, 36, 46, 69, 81, 96, 139, 184–185, 186, 190–191, 195

Jefferys, Thomas 7
Johnson, Andrew 45, 48–50
Johnson, Lady Bird 119, 122
Johnson, Lyndon B. 118–123, 131–132, 137, 158, 167, 195
Johnson, Robert Underwood 51, 52, 56
Johnson Presidential Library 122
Jones, John Paul 100
Josephson, Marvin 139
Journal of Major George Washington 2, 6–8, 183

Kansas City Edition (Truman *Memoirs*) 192
Karger, Gus 84
Kearns, Doris *see* Goodwin, Doris Kearns
Keeping Faith: Memoir of a President 140, 148
Kendall, Amos 33
Kennedy, Eunice 113
Kennedy, Jackie 117
Kennedy, John F. 109, 110–118, 119, 124, 134, 187–188, 192, 196
Kennedy, Joseph 110, 111, 112, 113
Kennedy, Joseph, Jr. 112–113
Kennedy, Robert F. 114, 116
The Kennedy Literature: A Bibliographical Essay on John F. Kennedy 117–118
Kennedy Presidential Library 116
Khrushchev, Nikita 124, 128
King, Stephen 62–63
Kinsley, Michael 167
Kissinger, Henry 110
Kiyosaki, Robert T. 179, 180
Klebanoff, Arthur M. 188–189, 194
Klein, Philip S. 43
Knopf, Alfred A., Publishers 159, 164, 174
Krim, Arthur 119
Krock, Arthur 111
Kruz, Kenneth F. 130

Ladies Home Journal 66, 67, 89
Lansky, Harold 112
Law and Contemporary Problems 123
Lawson, Dorie McCullough 167
Leaders 128
The Learning Annex 179
Learning Annex Wealth Expo 179
Lee, Richard Henry 11
Lee, Robert E. 61
Leech, Margaret 69
Leerhen, Charles 176
Lenin, Vladimir 126
Letters of Publicola 25–26
Levin, Phyllis Lee 86
Lewinsky, Monica 162
Liberty Magazine 101
Liberty Under Law 83

Library of Congress 10, 22, 36–37, 45, 185
Library of the Presidents Series 193, 194
Life and Selected Writings of Thomas Jefferson 17
Life Magazine 102, 103, 104, 106, 130
Limited Editions Club 193, 194, 195
Lincoln, Abraham 40, 44–48, 96, 106, 144, 163, 182, 185
Lincoln Financial Association 46
Lindsey, Robert 151
Link, Arthur 88
Lipshultz, Bob 138
Literary Works of Abraham Lincoln 44
The Little Baby Snoogle Fleejar 143
Little, Brown & Company 128, 164
Living Faith 145, 146
Living History 159
Lodge, Henry Cabot 72, 73, 74, 77
Lodge, Henry Cabot, Jr. 110
Long, Loren 174
Longmans, Green and Company 39
Looking Forward (George H.W. Bush) 154–155, 156
Looking Forward (Franklin D. Roosevelt) 100
Lord John Press 135–136, 196
Luce, Henry 102, 112
Lucier, James P. 24
Lurie, Jonathan 83
Lyons, Eugene 94, 96, 97

Macon Telegraph 100
Macy, George 193
Madison, Dolley 21, 185
Madison, James 1, 5, 20–22, 185
Malone, Dumas 15, 16, 18, 139
Mandate for Change 109
Manual of Parliamentary Practice for the Senate of the United States 18
Many Are the Hearts 185
Marbois, Marquis de 16
Margolis, Jack S. 192–193
Marion Star 90
Massachusetts Historical Society 32
Mazo, Earl 124
McCloy, John 131–132
McClure, S.S. 68
McClure's magazine 68
McClurg and Company 39–40
McCormick, Ken 104, 124
McCullough, David 11, 13, 19, 73, 79, 167
McFeely, William S. 59–60, 62, 195
McGraw Hill 124
McIver, Meredith 178, 179, 180, 181
McKinley, William 69, 75, 77
McLean, A. 20
McLean, J. 20

Meacham, Jon 33, 157
Medavoy, Irena 161
Medora Edition 191
Memoirs of Harry S. Truman 101, 102, 104, 105, 106
The Memoirs of Herbert Hoover 93, 94, 95, 97, 98, 195
Memoirs of U.S. Grant 1, 47, 50, 51–63, 67, 68, 101, 108, 161, 166, 185, 195
Memorandum Books (Jefferson) 19
Mencken, H.L. 91
Mercer University Press 140
Mere Literature 88
Michel, Chris 166
Michel, Robert H. 135, 145
Midas Touch 180
Milken, Michael 176
Miller, Merle 104, 107, 122
Miller, Nathan 100
Mining Magazine 191–192
Minot, Henry Davis 81
Mr. Buchanan's Administration on the Eve of Rebellion 43–44, 48, 68
Mr. Citizen 105
Mr. Van Buren's Opinions 34–35
Modern Library 17, 71
Monroe, Eliza 23
Monroe, James 1, 17, 22–25, 28, 37
Monthly Review of London 17
Morris, Edmund 75, 140–141, 150, 151, 153–154
Morris, Gouveneur 72, 73
Morrow Publishing 148
Mount Vernon Ladies Association 9, 10
My Life 160–162, 163

Nagel, Paul 27, 29, 32, 166
Nash, Thomas 135
Nassau Literary Magazine 84
A Nation of Immigrants 116
National Strength and International Duty 79
Naval War of 1812 70–71, 73, 81, 186
NBC Television 116, 181
The Necessary Steps for Promotion of German Exports 97
Negotiation: The Alternative to Hostility 140
Nelson, Thomas 179
Nesbit, Lynn 139
Never Give Up 180
Nevins, Allan 39, 66, 67, 117
Nevins, Arthur 108
The New Day 96
The New Freedom 89
The New Nationalism 78
New York 75
New York Evening Post 86
New York Historical Society 43

New York Nation 80
New York Packet 20
New York Times 96, 109, 111, 128, 143, 146, 164, 167, 171, 175, 189
New York University Press 117
New York World 58
New Yorker Magazine 142
Newett, George A. 79
Newhouse, Si 176
Newsweek 160–161
Nichols, Roy Franklin 41
9/11 Commission Report, 137
1999: Victory without War, 129
XIX Century 49
Niven, John 35, 36
Nixon, Richard M. 44, 106, 123–131, 134, 139, 147, 156, 166, 187, 188–189, 192–193, 194, 195
No More Vietnams 128
The Nobel Peace Prize Lecture 145
Noonan, Peggy 151
Notes on the State of Virginia 2, 16–18, 29, 184–185, 190, 195
Notes on Some of the Birds of Oyster Bay 81
Notes: Ronald Reagan's Private Collection of Stories and Wisdom 153
Nothdurft, William E. 159
Nott, Charles C. 46
Noyes, David 102, 107

Obama, Barack 168–174, 180, 196
Obama, Michelle 170, 172, 174
Oberon 27
O'Brien, Michael 116
O'Brien, Tim 180
O'Donnell, John 176
Of Thee I Sing: A Letter to My Daughters 174
Off the Record: The Private Papers of Harry S. Truman 105, 106
Ohio State Archaeological and Historical Society 63
An Old Master and Other Political Writings 88
Oliver Cromwell 77
On Growing Up 98, 99
On Our Way 100, 159
The Ordeal of Woodrow Wilson 98
Origins and Principles of the American Revolution 27
Osmond, George 151
Osmond Publishers 151
Osnos, Peter 170
Oswald, Lee Harvey 131
O'Toole, Patricia 79
Our Endangered Values: America's Moral Crisis 146

Index

Oursler, Fulton 101
An Outdoor Journal 141
Outdoor Pastimes of an American Hunter 78
Outing Publishing Company 67
Outlook Editorials 78

Paine, Thomas 12, 25–26
Palestine: Peace with Apartheid 146
Panetta, Leon 161
Papers of Andrew Jonson 49
Parke-Bernet Galleries 13–114
Parker, George F. 67
Parkman, Francis 73, 74
Parmet, Herbert S. 116, 155
Patterson, James 164
Payne, J. Scott 48
Peace with Justice 109
Pearson, Drew 115
Pendleton, Edmund 18
Penguin Random House 174
Pennsylvania Gazette 7
The People the Sovereigns 23–24
Pepys, Samuel 19
The Personal Beliefs of Jimmy Carter 145
Pierce, Franklin 41, 106, 157
Plain Speaking 106
Playboy 175
Poems of Abraham Lincoln 47
Poems of Religion and Society 142
The Poetry of Richard Nixon 192–193
Political Debates between Hon. Abraham Lincoln and Hon. Stephen Douglas 46
The Political Writings of James Monroe 24
Polk, James 2, 4, 34, 38–40, 63
Port Folio 27
Portrait of an Assassin 133–134
Portraits of Courage 168
Poseidon Press 171
Powers, David F. 114
Prentice Hall 101
The Presidency, Its Duties, Its Powers, Its Opportunities, and Its Limitations 83
The President Is Missing 164
A Presidential Legacy and the Warren Commission 136
Presidential Problems 67
The President's Mystery Story 101, 192
Prichard & Hall 190
The Princetonian 86
Principles of Mining 93
Pringle, Henry F. 82, 84
The Problems of Lasting Peace 97
Profiles in Courage 2, 114, 115, 116, 124, 132, 187–188, 192, 196
Progressive Principles 79
Pulitzer Prize 115, 187

Pullman, George 50
Putnam, George Haven 74–75, 191
Putting People First 158

Quaife, Milo Milton 39

Ranch Life 72–73
Randolph, Peyton 14
Random House 100, 114, 119, 157, 158, 171, 175, 176, 177, 178
Rayback, Robert J. 38
Reagan, Nancy 151
Reagan, Patti 151
Reagan, Ronald, Jr. 151
Reagan, Ronald 4, 128, 150–154, 154–155, 168, 194–195
Reagan: A Life in Letters 152
The Reagan Diaries 152–153
Reagan in His Own Hand 152
Reagan Presidential Library 151, 153, 154
Real Peace 129
The Real War 128, 129
Realizable Goals 78
Reed, William B. 43–44
Reedy, George 118
Reeve, Richard 16
Reeves, Thomas C. 112
Regnery Publishing 181
A Remarkable Mother 147
Remington, Frederick 72
Remnick, David 170–171
Renaissance Press 177
Rendezvous with Destiny 151
Report by the Supreme Commander to the Combined Chiefs of State 107
Report of the Secretary of State Upon Weights and Measures 29
Republican Executive Congressional Committee 46
Rich Press 179
The Richard M. Nixon Library 195
Rickard, Edgar 95
Rights of Man 25–26
RN: The Memoirs of Richard Nixon 125, 126, 127–128, 129
The Road Away from Revolution 90
Roosevelt, Ellen 79, 191
Roosevelt, Franklin D. 96, 97, 100–101, 106, 164, 192
Roosevelt, Quentin 80–81
Roosevelt, Theodore 2, 4, 44, 69–82, 100, 126, 129, 141, 149, 150, 178, 186–187, 191
Roosevelt vs. Newett 79, 191
Rosenman, Sam 100, 101, 102–103
The Rough Riders 77
Rove, Karl 165–166

Rush, Benjamin 13
Russell, Jonathan 29
Russell, Richard 131–132

St. Johns, Adela Rogers 124, 125
Sandburg, Carl 47
Sanderson, Elizabeth 187
Sangamo Journal 45
Saturday Evening Post 67, 96, 106, 125
Sawyer, Diane 126–127
Schlesinger, Arthur, Jr. 114, 117, 163
Schwartz, Ted 113–114
Schwartz, Tony 175
Scowcroft, Brent 155, 167
Scribner, Charles 77
Scribner's magazine 80
Scripps, John L. 44
Searls, Hank 112
Seize the Moment: America's Challenge in a One-Superpowered World 130
Service with Fighting Men 83
Shalala, Donna 161
Sharing Good Times 145
Shenk, Joshua Wolf 163
Shiflett, Dave 177
Sievers, Harry J. 66
Simon, Richard 107–108
Simon & Schuster 107–108, 129, 145, 171, 181, 189, 194–195
Six Crises 124–125, 126, 129, 166
Skinner, Kiron K. 152
Skunk, James F. 43–44
Slater, Robert 182
Smith, Page 12, 13
Smith, Richard Norton 96
Smith, Roswell 53, 56
Social Justice and Popular Rule 79
Some American Game 76
Sorenson, Ted 114, 115, 115
Sources of Strength 143, 145, 146, 149
Sparks, Jared 185
Spaulding, Chuck 112
Stafford (Henry) Little Lectureship on Public Affairs 66–67
Stanford University Press 66, 97
The State: Elements of History and Political Politics 87
Steele, Shelby 172
Sterns, Frank 91
Stiles, John R. 132–133
Stockdale, John 17, 18, 190
Stone, Oliver 134
The Strategy of Peace 116, 117
Stratfield, Dominic 62
The Strenuous Life 77
Stroud, Kandy 137

Summary View of the Rights of British America 14–16
Summer Birds of the Adirondacks 81
Sundial 169
Syracuse University Press 24

Taft, Robert 98
Taft, William H. 80
Talking Peace: A Vision for the Next Generation 142
Taylor, John 189
Taylor, Zachary 32–34
Tebbel, John 183–184, 193
The Telegraph 164
Theodore Roosevelt's Letters to His Children 81
Think Big, Kick Ass 179
Think Like a Champion 180–181
This America 119
This Country of Ours 66, 68
Thomas Hart Benton 77
Thomson, Charles 16
Thoreau, Henry 82
Thoughts on Government 11–12
Three Rivers Press 170, 174
Through the Brazilian Wilderness 80
Through the Year with Jimmy Carter 149
Time to Get Tough 178, 181
A Time to Heal 134–135
Times Books 142, 170–171
To Assure Pride and Confidence in the Electoral Process 135, 145
To Turn the Tide 117
Trail and Campfire 76
Truman, Harry S. 100, 101–107, 109, 127, 158, 160, 187, 192, 195
Truman, Margaret 106
Truman Speaks 106
Trump, Donald J. 174–182
Trump, Donald, Jr. 179
Trump, Fred 174
Trump, Ivanka 179
Trump 101 179
Trump: Surviving at the Top 176
Trump: The Art of the Comeback 177
Trump: The Art of the Deal 175, 176, 177, 181
Trump: The Way to the Top 178
Trump: Think Like a Billionaire 178
Trump University 179–180
Tully, Grace 100
Turning Point 141, 144
Twain, Mark 53–63, 185–186
Twohig, Dorothy 10
Tyler, John 37–38

University of Arkansas Press 196
University Press of Virginia 10

Van Buren, Martin 1, 34–37, 154, 185
Van Buren, Smith 35–36
Vanderbilt, W. 58
The Vantage Point: Perspectives of the Presidency 121–122, 195
Vestal, Bud 132, 133
Views of an Ex-President 66, 186
View of the Conduct of the Executive 22–23
Virginia Historical Society Press of 9
The Virtues of Aging 143
A Vision for America 196

Wagenknecht, Edward 74
Waging Peace 109
Wallace, Mike 115
Walworth, Arthur 85, 88
Wannamaker, John 186
Ward, Henry Beecher 62
Warner Books 127, 128
Warren, Earl 131–132, 136–137
Warren, Mercy Otis 13
Warren Commission 118, 131–134, 136–137
The Warren Commission Report 131–134, 136–137, 196
Washington, George 1, 2, 3, 5–11, 12, 15, 23, 27, 33, 36, 182, 183
Washington Post 164, 175
Waste in Industry 95, 96
The Watergate Tapes 195–196
Watson, Henry S. 67
We Can Have Peace in the Holy Land 147
Webster, Charles 55, 57, 59, 186
Webster, Daniel 31, 34, 39
Webster, Noah 8, 184
Weinstein, Edwin A. 88
Weisberg, Jacob 166
West, Andrew F. 68
Where the Buck Stops 106
Where's the Rest of Me 150–151
White, Ronald 46
White, Theodore W. 125
White, William Allen 92

White House Diary 139, 147–148
Why England Slept 111, 112, 187
Why Not the Best 139, 140, 144
Why We Want You to Be Rich 179
Widmer, Ted 35, 36, 37
Wieland, Christopher Martin 27
The Wilderness Hunter 76, 82
Willens, Howard P. 136–137
Williams, Charles R. 64
Williams, T. Harry 63, 64
Williams Quarterly 65
Wills, Gary 151
Wilson, Edith 90
Wilson, Ellen 86–87, 88
Wilson, R.L. 78
Wilson, Woodrow 44, 79, 84–90, 95, 96
Winik, Jay 163
The Winning of the West 74, 75, 76, 81, 186
Wister, Owen 70, 73
Wolff, Michael 182
Woodard, William E. 58
Woods, Rosemary 119, 124
Woodward, Bob 126
Works of Theodore Roosevelt 78, 81, 191
A World Transformed 156
Write a Book without Lifting a Finger 188
Writings and Speeches of Grover Cleveland 66, 67
The Writings of Theodore Roosevelt 191
W.W. Norton & Company 110
Wythe, George 18
Wyman, Jane 151

Year of Decision 104; see also *Memoirs of Harry S. Truman*
Years of Trial and Hope 104; see also *Memoirs of Harry S. Truman*
Young Men's Central Republican Union 46

Zanker, Bill 179, 181
Zedong, Mao 125
Zondervan Publishing 149

www.ingramcontent.com/pod-product-compliance
Lightning Source LLC
Chambersburg PA
CBHW051219300426
44116CB00006B/638